IN MY OWN TIME

Richard Dobson

IN MY OWN TIME

Richard Dobson

Aspect Design

In my own Time
Richard Dobson

Published by Aspect Design 2013
Malvern, Worcestershire, United Kingdom.

Designed and Printed by Aspect Design
89 Newtown Road, Malvern, Worcs. WR14 1PD
United Kingdom
Tel: 01684 561567
E-mail: books@aspect-design.net
Website: www.aspect-design.net

A copy of this book has been deposited with the British Library Board

ISBN 978-1-9088-32-41-2

PREFACE

This book is a record of a journey I made between 2003 and 2007 on foot through Herefordshire, one of the most beautiful areas of England. It includes glimpses of the county's history, the people who made it, and the wonderful buildings they left behind. It is true that Herefordshire has for so long existed in isolation of the mainstream of English life that its inhabitants have become a race apart, a community once so totally enclosed that it was their proud boast that 'we are all cousins in Herefordshire' This is a county of hidden treasures and proud people who want it to be kept secret. Sir Roy Strong, who spent fourteen years as Director of the V&A in London but now lives in the county, once described it as 'a golden land, remote, beckoning, a place in which to hide and be hidden.' In 1891, a Birmingham author and artist Henry Thornhill Timmins broke from his European travels to take a ramble through the Herefordshire countryside, sketching en route local landmarks and some of the many beautiful old black and white houses so typical of the county. As a result, the following year his book Nooks and Corners of Herefordshire was published. Timmins was a trained architect who gave up his intended career to develop his talent for art. He travelled extensively, in particular to Italy, a country he loved, and was a regular contributor to the English Illustrated Magazine, a popular journal of his time, with illustrated articles on some of the many countries he visited. He was a stranger to Herefordshire but he found this rural backwater a delight, and his drawings of the churches, manor houses and villages that he visited have provided lasting pleasure to readers of his book. When he wrote of 'the romantic and beautiful scenery for which this rural English county is so justly admired', we can assume he wrote from the heart, so truly has he caught the spirit of Herefordshire a century ago in his charming illustrations. I make no apologies for including many of his fine sketches in my book, as well as some of the evocative descriptions of the Victorian countryside which I could not begin to imagine.

As well as the beautiful black and white villages for which the county is justifiably renowned, I had a close look at other aspects of Herefordshire's heritage, hop production and the development of the cider industry to name two. Along the way, I was privileged to meet members of some of the great families of Herefordshire; Harley, Hereford, Mynors, Croft, and Arkwright, who invited me into their homes and helped me with my research. I am indebted to them all for their hospitality.

Timmins made use of the many railway lines that then criss-crossed the county as his means of moving between bases and start points. Most of those small country lines have long gone and so, too, the stations and halts from which he would alight to begin his walks. Nevertheless, wherever I could I followed his exact route using quiet country lanes, old tracks, and footpaths, some of which have since become busy A roads! But there were other changes in the landscape. For example, I visited as many landmarks and buildings as possible which he had recorded in his bold ink illustrations, but I did not always see what he saw as some of the buildings have gone. I did discover, however, objects of great interest that he may not have seen from the confines of his railway carriage or that weren't there at all in his day. There were no way markers in Timmins's day of course but there have been footpaths and tracks across the Herefordshire landscape since ancient times and he would have had little difficulty following them. It would have been necessary then as it is now to use the main commuter routes occasionally. These narrow uneven highways were very often choked with people on the move with wagons of all shapes and sizes carrying essential materials between communities, all of which was made more difficult by the poor condition of the dirt roads. In winter, progress would have been slow and uncomfortable, if not impossible. The road network has changed dramatically since 1891, as has the mode of transport. Motor cars, vans, lorries, and buses, have replaced the horse drawn carts and coaches. Construction of tarmac dual carriageways and by-passes eats up more of the precious countryside each year and the volume, speed and noise of traffic has become part of our life. My journey inevitably required some road walking and although always inconvenient, it was never dull and always enjoyable.

Throughout his many visits to Herefordshire, Timmins was helped by Walter Pilley, a local businessman, antiquarian, and one time mayor of Hereford who introduced him to the owners of some of the many buildings he sketched. Pilley would have also encouraged a meeting with members of the Woolhope Naturalists' Field Club, a group of local enthusiasts who researched and recorded details of archaeological and historical significance in and around Herefordshire and with whom he shared at least one of his walks. The Club is still in existence today and has become the definitive reference for scholars of local history and archeology.

The weather of 2003 is now on record as being one of the driest, and I was extremely fortunate that the walking was always a pleasure. I can't remember any bad days, and there was never any problem with the ground beneath my feet which was firm almost all of the time. The most memorable experience was to be able to see one of the finest corners of Britain in all its seasonal glories, the crowning of which was the most beautiful autumn I have ever witnessed.

AUTHOR'S INTRODUCTION

The English county of Herefordshire is located south of the West Midlands, sandwiched between Worcestershire and the Malvern Hills which dominate the skyline on its eastern border and Wales to the west. By some quirk of nature, it is practically circular in shape with the north-south A49 and the east-west A438 roads crossing in the centre of the city of Hereford itself and forming four almost equal sections. To the north is Shropshire, the county border being, in part, the tumbling river Teme, and the hills of Powys. To the south east the Forest of Dean, a source of timber, iron ore and coal before even the Romans arrived, provides the backdrop and the border with Gloucestershire, while to the south west the brooding bulk of the Black Mountains separates Herefordshire from south Wales. Almost the whole surface area is covered with red sandstone, the resulting rich clay soil providing fertile red loam well suited for the county's vast hop fields and apple orchards. Four major river sytems drain the central plains. In the north west of the county, the Arrow meets up with the Lugg near Leominster. These two then merge with the Frome flowing down from Bromyard in the north east before feeding the greatest of Herefordshire's waterways, the Wye, which the Romans called Vaga,'the wanderer'. Separate from this activity are the smaller Monnow and Dore in the far south west which join near Pontrilas, and eventually merge with the Wye at Monmouth.

'Here-ford' was an ancient term which meant 'a place where an army can cross'. Roman armies did indeed cross the Wye, but settled a few miles further to the west where they built a town called Magnis in the present day parish of Kenchester. Life really began at Here-Ford in 676 when the first Bishop, Putta, built a cathedral of wattle and daub construction which he dedicated to St Mary. In 757 Offa acceded to the throne of Mercia and established a palace at Sutton Walls, four miles to the north of the city. He became the most infamous early player in Herefordshire's history when he murdered Ethelbert, the young King of Anglia, whilst the latter was a guest at his palace. When the first stone cathedral was built in Hereford in 829, the name of St Ethelbert, by then considered a martyr, was added to the dedication. Hereford Cathedral remains to this day the church of St Mary and St Ethelbert. The early people of Hereford had two saints to whom they could pray for their deliverances. In addition to Ethelbert, there was also Guthlac, a local British youth who, tired of fighting other youths in the nearby Welsh kingdom of Ergyng, pledged his life to God 'if I am spared another day' and founded a religious settlement just outside the city boundary in the eighth century. Later still, in the thirteenth century, the city produced two more saints; St Thomas Cantilupe, whose shrine remains in the present cathedral, and St John Kemp, a Roman Catholic martyr of the reformation, a relic of whom is kept in St Francis Xavier's church on Broad Street.

The city's defences in Saxon times were comprised of a ditch and wooden palisades. In the early part of the tenth century, Queen Aethelfreda, the daughter of King Alfred, strengthened the defences in time to repel an attack by the Danes, but the improvements didn't prevent the Welsh from destroying the city and cathedral in 1053. Harold Godwinson, then the Earl of Wessex, but later to succeed Edward the Confessor as King of all England, recognised Hereford as an important buffer outpost and replaced what was left of the palisades with a stone wall. A castle was probably started about this time, too. As a reward for his support against Harold, at Hastings in 1066, William the Conqueror gave land at Hereford to Walter de Lacy who built the first of Herefordshire's great houses just over the river Wye at Holme Lacy. Elsewhere, from the county's second town Leominster, Lady Godiva set out in 1057 to perform her famous naked horse ride through the streets of Coventry in protest against crippling Mercian taxation laws imposed by her own husband, Earl Leofric, after whom Leominster is named. At Wigmore Castle in the far north west of the county, the great Mortimer marcher lords built their mini-empire, held Owain Glyndwr at bay during the Welsh prince's campaigns in the late fourteenth and early fifteenth centuries, and eventually fought their way to the throne of England. Edward Mortimer's victory for the House of York at Mortimer's Cross near Kingsland in 1461 resulted in his being crowned Edward IV. Hereford's military importance has been developed throughout its history, first by the Saxons, who recognized its strategic position near the river crossing, and later by the Normans who wished to keep out the opportunist Welsh. During the Civil Wars, Hereford's military role once again came to the fore when the Parliamentarian and Royalist forces fought there vigorously in an attempt to gain a foothold. So extensive was the fighting that the city changed hands four times before it was finally occupied by the Parliamentarians and held until the restoration of the monarchy in 1660. In modern times, Hereford's location has been of continued military significance with the wartime production of ammunitions at Rotherwas, and even today the presence of a major army base at Credenhill.

Hereford has had a fair share of famous sons and daughters. Nell Gwynne was born here in 1650 before later moving to London and immortality, as did the eighteenth century actor and stage manager David Garrick who was born at The Angel Inn, close to the city centre, where his mother and father were staying during a visit. Another member of the acting profession, Sarah Siddons, who was described as the finest English tragic actress of all time also acted under the directions of Garrick. Although she was born in Brecon in 1755, her family home was in Hereford, at Church Street, within yards of the cathedral. Her father, Roger Kemble, was an actor as were her brothers John and Charles Kemble, all leading members of the London stage. Charles Kemble's daughter, Fanny, became an actress on the early American stage. The man who championed the mysterious ley lines phenomena, Alfred Watkins, was also born inHereford, in a local brewery. In 1815, David Cox, the Victorian landscape painter claimed by many to be the equal of the better known JMW Turner, came to live and work in Hereford.

In modern times, Hereford has become the cider capital of the world, with the growth of the Bulmers Cider Company, and is also where the first ready-to-eat chicken were introduced by the Sun Valley Company. Another important present day employer is the specialist metals manufacturer, Wiggins Limited, which made components for Rolls Royce's Olympus engines on the Concorde aircraft. The city has a thriving racecourse and a football team, which until relegation in 1997 was in the third division of the football league. The city's treasure though is the cathedral, with its chain library and the Mappa Mundi, which attract thousands of visitors each year.

Second only to the apple, as Herefordshire's main agricultural crop, is the hop, a prime ingredient in beer making. Hop production has declined in recent years as fewer pints of beer are consumed but it remains an important industry here as in the other hop growing counties of Kent and Sussex. In early autumn, the fields of east Herefordshire, particularly those close to the town of Bromyard, are bursting with ripe hop cones ready for harvesting. At the same time of year, cider apples are transported from the multitude of orchards to Bulmer's Plough Lane factory, and the sweet smell of apples and hops pervades the air almost everywhere. And then there is, perhaps, Herefordshire's most famous export, the white-faced red bull. There are many explanations as to the origins of this distinctive breed but it is generally agreed that it was founded on oxen descended from small red cattle of Roman Britain and a large Welsh breed once numerous along the Welsh border. William Galliers, of Wigmor, founded a herd of superior cattle in 1740 and was known to have procured a red bull with a white face and wide horns from Yorkshire in the process. In the seventeenth century the first Viscount Scudamore was said to have imported red coloured Flemish cattle in order to develop a breed of distinction and quality, and one of his descendants, the first Earl of Chesterfield, in his quest for improvement, purchased similar livestock from the Ukraine. From the early part of the eighteenth century, the objective was to breed, into one strain of animal, all the desirable traits of hardiness, early maturity, prolificacy, and a capability for the swift and efficient conversion of grass into meat. Whether it is something in the soil, water, or climate of Herefordshire that has helped create the unique qualities of this internationaly known breed has not yet been proven, but its spectacular success has meant the Hereford bull has become the cornerstone of the beef economy of cattle raising countries throughout the world. To-day, more than five million pedigree Herefords exist in over fifty countries.

Every three years Hereford is host to the Three Choirs Festival. Centred on the cathedral and its choir, music makers from every discipline come together before enthusiastic audiences drawn, not only from the two other host cities of Worcester and Gloucester but, from all over the world. To continue with the musical theme, Hereford was, for a time, the home to one of England's greatest composers, Sir Edward Elgar. Born in Worcester in 1857, he began his career in music as a violinist and played in the Three Choirs Festival in Worcester in 1878. He later exchanged the violin for a pen and in 1899 his Enigma Variations established him as the leading composer of his day. He moved to Hereford in 1904 where he composed some of his greatest works. The Festivals in the 1920s and 1930s were dominated by Elgar and his music. Remembered mostly for the first of his five Pomp and Circumstance Marches, Elgar is strongly identified with the Edwardian era and the British Empire and became a symbol of English national pride. In 1920 his wife died and his later years were lonely and mostly unproductive. Five months before his own death, Elgar performed as a conductor in Hereford for the last time.

Far to the west of the county is Hay-on-Wye, which geographically is in Wales but which the Post Office prefers to link with Hereford. In this beautiful border setting where the Black Mountains fall steeply to meet the Wye as it flows into England for the first time, the small town of Hay has developed a reputation for second-hand book shops. There are thirty-nine in all and they form the basis of an annual book and arts festival visited by 100,000 people each year from Europe and the USA. Not to be left out, another place-on-the-Wye, Ross, holds an international music festival each year in the riverside meadows below the town.

This then is the background to an area of England I have come to know and love so well. In 1891, a relatively unknown artist set out to broaden his knowledge of a part of the country few people outside of it knew much about. One hundred and twenty two years on, Herefordshire remains, to many people, an unknown quantity - during my research, I lost count of the number of incorrect references made to Hertfordshire - and I've covered Henry Thornhill Timmins's tracks to satisfy a similar ignorance. I hope that in the following pages, you may come to enjoy the resulting blend of discovery over two different centuries. There are, of course, places, events, and people worthy of mention who, due either to ignorance or lack of space, I have omitted. To them, my apologies, but the omissions might yet provide me with an excuse, if one were needed, for further exploration of this multi-faceted county.

Richard Dobson, June 2013

PART ONE

Hereford - The start of a journey

HEREFORD, FROM BROOMY HILL.

> *'The most fastidious visitor to this cathedral city will have cause to congratulate himself on his surroundings. Situated upon one of those graceful bends for which the Wye is justly famous, it is environed on every hand by gardens and cornfields, hop grounds, and orchards; the whole encompassed at no great distance by picturesquely wooded hills, around whose feet the silvery curves of devious Vaga enfold themselves beneath a sky innocent of factory smoke.'*

Thus Henry Thornhill Timmins sets the scene for his visit one hundred and twelve years ago. His introduction will serve me just as well as I begin my own tour of my favourite part of England.

The city of Hereford is the administrative and geographical centre of the county. Like the hub of a wheel, major connecting roads radiate outwards towards the county borders. In Henry's time the railways, too, connected the city to Leominster to the north, Hay to the west, Ross to the south, and Ledbury and the Malvern Hills to the east. Today, there are no lines to Hay or Ross, although there have been failed attempts during the last forty years to persuade the railway companies to re-instate the Ross line. Hereford was initially a Saxon town, with the great cathedral church of St Ethelbert and St Mary at its centre. In 1696, the remarkable Celia Fiennes visited Hereford and described it as a *'pretty little town of timber buildings with well paved streets handsome as to breadth and length'*. In the surrounding countryside, she noted *'apple and pear trees growing in abundance even in their corn fields and hedgerows'*.

Daniel Defoe was less impressed in 1720. He saw it as *'large and populous, an old mean built and very dirty city'*. He did, however, take a shine to the local brew. *'we could get no beer or ale in their public houses, only cider, and that so very good so fine and so cheap'*.

I planned to look around the beautiful old cathedral later, but for now I would take a short walk out of the shadow of that great symbol of ancient times, along narrow, cobbled, Church Street, and into the sunlight of the city's commercial centre of High Town. In Saxon days this modern central area was outside the defensive ditch which formed the city's northern limits. When the Normans arrived they extended the boundary northwards to a line marked now by the city's ring road, where they built an encircling wall around the city with seventeen towers and six gate houses. Large parts of the wall and the remains of two gatehouses can still be seen today. Back in High Town, the modern square mirrors a typical city centre shopping area. A wide carpet of concrete spreads around where once black and white town houses, separated by narrow cobbled streets, used to abound. One of the old city's crown jewels, a spectacular black and white timber framed town hall erected by Herefordshire's great timber frame builder of the seventeenth century, John Abel, supported on massive oak pillars once dominated the square but a victim of neglect it had gone by 1862. The site is marked today by coloured paving slabs over which tradesmen park their fast food wagons, and at holiday times their bouncy castles and merry-go-rounds.

The last remaining complete timber house on what was Butchers Row, built between 1570 and 1620 for a wealthy merchant, sits uneasily at the east end of the central precinct. Above the entrance to Littlewoods store is the restored black and white frontage of another merchant's house. During the area's remodeling in 1966, the remains

The Old House in High Town, Hereford, the last remaining part of Butchers Row built in 1621

of this last historic house were moved a few yards from its original position and tucked into its present slot on the first floor of a new row of retail outlets. It must have been quite a challenge. The move seems to have interrupted reported ghostly activities in the attic of the old house. The story goes that an apothecary was called out one night to attend to a sick boy in a nearby house and decided to get to his patient via the interconnecting attics. In the dim light, he gave the poor child a poison by mistake with agonizingly fatal results. The distraught apothecary paced the attics reliving the shocking experience until he finally hanged himself from one of the beams. Heavy footsteps tramping above their heads have terrified previous tenants of this house but nothing apparently has been heard since the move, presumably much to the relief of the store's workers. A few doors down is the entrance to the nineteenth century Butter Market. As the name suggests, it was once dedicated entirely to the sale of locally produced butter, cheese and other dairy products. Today, a substantially wider choice can be found on the numerous stalls, including apples and soft fruits from some of the multitude of orchards for which the county is renowned, home grown flowers and vegetables from surrounding villages; all manner of meats and poultry reared on local farms; and even seasonal salmon from the river Wye, a veritable feast of authentic flavours of Herefordshire. Beyond the eastern side of the square is the tall spire of St Peter's, the oldest surviving church in Hereford and founded in 1070 by the conquering Norman Duke William's ally, Walter de Lacy. Not long after the church was finished, De Lacy died after falling from the church's roof whilst inspecting the completed work. The tower of St Peter's is a powerful construction and dates from the later part of the thirteenth century. Inside are six very old bells. The oldest, the treble, is said to have been cast around 1450 and is one of only twenty five known to be pre-Reformation. Apart from the chancel which belongs to a twelveth century rebuild, the church has lost much of its ancient character. However, worthy of note is a rare wooden carving of the royal arms of William III on the north wall of the north aisle by the seventeenth century Dutch master craftsman, Grinling Gibbons.

Gibbons was born in Rotterdam in 1648 but moved to England in 1667 where a boom in construction work, following the great fire of London, promised an opportunity for his skills as a sculptor. Adept at working in wood or stone, he was brought to the attention of Charles II in 1671, and Sir Christopher Wren, who was in charge of rebuilding London, employed him on his new St Paul's cathedral. Later he was commissioned by William III to redecorate the state apartments at Windsor Castle and Hampton Court Palace in London. As an apprentice in the Netherlands, Gibbons was subject to influences which he subsequently introduced to England, the most important of which was the use of limewood as his prime material rather than the oak used by his English counterparts. Limewood is strong but workable, can be carved against the grain and its stability prevents warping. Gibbons had an enormous influence on interior design and decoration throughout the golden age of English country house building and on later craftsmen such as Thomas Chippendale. He is said to have invented the trophy panel, a freestanding carved tableau, which is somewhere between a painting and sculpture, an example of which is the carving here in St Peters. It is not surprising that the first Viscount Scudamore, then head of one of Herefordshire's great and ancient landowning families, should have asked Gibbons to furnish his great house at Holme Lacy on the outskirts of Hereford with his magnificent carvings. The Holme Lacy mansion still stands as a glorious reminder of the Scudamores' wealth but has been altered regularly over the centuries by subsequent owners and Gibbons's carvings were lost.

In 1833, the vicar of St Peter's was the Reverend John Venn. During his tenure, he became a one-man social reformer, creating a soup kitchen; a credit union; almshouses and schools, whilst campaigning for public baths and allotments. He built a corn mill in nearby Bath Street where the poorest people could buy cheap wheat and flour. Long before James Rankin built his Free Library in Broad Street, John Venn started St Peter's Literary Institute providing the working classes with a reading room and the opportunity to borrow books. Beyond St Peters church, at the far end of St Owens Street to the east of the city centre where one of the city's medieval gates once stood, the tiny St Gile's Chapel, was an early object of my attention. This chapel was built in 1927 to replace an earlier one erected in 1682. During the demolition of the seventeenth century chapel, the foundations of a round Templar church from the twelveth century were discovered – the Templars had founded a hospital for lepers here about that time. Preserved from that church and now displayed behind glass on the outside west wall of a row of almshouses nearby is a unique Tympanum, an elaborate stone carving said to be a typically fine example of a renowned

The Stoning of St Stephen - a woodcarving by Grinling Gibbons (V&A)

team of Norman sculptors who became known as the Herefordshire School. These highly skilled craftsmen were introduced into Britain by Oliver Merlimond who first saw their work while on a pilgrimage to Santiago de Compostella in northern Spain in 1131. In time, their fabulous carvings came to grace many church fonts and doorways, and examples still survive throughout Herefordshire.

During Hereford's recent history, the central streets have been home to a spring fair often referred to as St Ethelbert's Fair, evidence perhaps of the long attachment Herefordians have to their saints. For three days in May the area is cordoned off and becomes choked with stalls offering gentle amusements for all ages. In the evenings, prime ground goes, not unexpectedly, to those in search of greater thrills and those stomach churning, throw-u-around contraptions which defy gravity and must be a health and safety inspector's nightmare. In John Pollard's book *No County to Compare,* he describes a childhood scene from his bedroom window overlooking High Town in 1915 at the time of the May Fair: '*....on Saturday night when the whole town went wild and it was unsafe for respectable folk to be abroad. Girls screamed in mingled fear and ecstasy as swains, rendered reckless by beer and cider, stuffed bags of confetti down mock-reluctant necks. Every now and then a fight broke out and policemen pushed through the packed thong.*' So it was then and now, and presumably for ever more.

One of the oldest of Hereford's thoroughfares is Widemarsh Street, which is still one of the main exits running north from the centre. In ancient times it passed through the north gate of the city walls. One of the many commercial buildings lining this busy street in 1716, was the Angel Inn and it was here that the actor David Garrick was born when his parents were visiting Hereford from Lichfield. Because he spent his youth there, Garrick considered Lichfield and not Hereford as his home town. He eventually ended up in London where he set up a wine merchants business with his elder brother and it was the necessities of trade that brought him into contact with theatres and other places of entertainment which persuaded him to turn to the stage. He became a legend overnight following his performance as Richard III at a theatre in Goodman's Fields in London, and was thereafter in demand at the top venue, the Theatre Royal in Dury Lane. By 1747, he had become a part owner of the Theatre Royal and the most highly rated actor of his day. When he eventually gave up acting in 1776 and sold his shares, he became a very rich man, too. Unfortunately, he didn't live long enough to enjoy his retirement and died on 20th January 1779 from kidney failure. The Angel burnt down sometime in the nineteenth century and although rebuilt as The Raven, it didn't survive long as a public house. In the eighteenth century, the city authorities tried to regulate the inns and pubs of Hereford and the disorder they generated. There were constant reports of *'singing and roaring unceasingly, rangling and quarrelling, brawling, cursing and screaming, playing the fiddle and enjoying the company of young women bare in clothes.'* So, after three hundred years, no changes there then!

Almost opposite the old Angel is the Imperial Hotel, a rambling public house recently refurbished to the modern standards of the day. In the mid nineteenth century, the Imperial as well as being a hotel also housed one of the city's first breweries. It was run by Charles Watkins whose son Alfred abandoned any ideas of carrying forward the family business after developing photographic techniques, at a time when the camera was a new invention. The Watkins Imperial Brewery moved from Widemarsh Street to larger premises nearby after Charles's death in 1888 where it was renamed the Hereford Brewery. In time the Hereford Brewery was acquired by the Whitbread Company and with all that is inevitable in these days of acquisition and progress, eventually closed down, was demolished and replaced with a supermarket. Hereford's beer brewing tradition, however, has not been lost entirely. Two small local breweries, The Wye Valley Brewery and The Spinning Dog Brewery, are currently thriving and have so far remained independent.

After his father died, Alfred Watkins had no appetite for running the family brewing business. He wanted to spend more time on his photographic work and started the Watkins Meter Company, making exposure meters and photographic accessories. His success earned him the presidency of the Royal Photographic Society. It was while he was testing his equipment in the Herefordshire countryside that he developed an interest in archeology and particularly a phenomena he called ley lines. He coined this term when explaining his theory that ancient sites such as stone circles, burial mounds, and churches around Britain had actually been constructed giving alignments between and across the inhabited landscape. Watkins spent the last fourteen years of his life accumulating evidence to support this controversial view and wrote it all down in his book *The Old Straight Track* which is still in print.

One of Hereford's major industries is that of brewing cider, and Bulmers, based on the west side of the city is the largest cider maker in the world. The Bulmer's business, now owned by the giant Heineken corporation, was founded by Henry Percival Bulmer, a clergyman's son, at the age of twenty, in 1887. He was joined by his elder brother, Fred, the following year, and within three years had acquired no less than twenty thousand customers. Initially, the brother's cider was only available in bottles, but then wooden casks were introduced and bulk supply rapidly became the main method for distribution to 'own label' bottlers and pubs and inns selling on draught. The famous medium sweet Woodpecker brand was introduced in 1926 but only as a bottled version. By the early 1960s, sales of Woodpecker reached fourteen million bottles per year, and it was acclaimed the most popular cider in the world. The strong dry brand Strongbow has rapidly become as popular in recent years. Today, Bulmers make some sixty percent of all UK cider production, export all over the world, and have plants in Europe, America, the Far East, South Africa, and Australasia. Around the county, ten thousand acres of orchards grow traditional cider apples for Bulmer's Hereford cider mill resulting in over eighty thousand tonnes of apples being pressed each autumn. During October, the air around west Hereford is heavy with the sweet smell of apple pulp.

Beyond the City's north gate site, about half a mile from the centre, stands a seventeenth century almshouse museum. This well preserved building housed Thomas Coningsby's Red Coat Hospital, so named because patients wore a red uniform and it was probably the model for the Chelsea Hospital for pensioners in London.
Timmins said of it:

Upon entry, each inmate was provided with a fustian suit of ginger colour of a soldier-like fashion seemly laced, a hat with a band of white, red slip-

pers, a soldier-like jerkin with half sleeves, a square skirt with a Spanish cap, a soldier-like sword with a belt, a cloak of red cloth lined with baize of red reaching to the knee, and a seemly gown of red cloth reaching down to the ankle, lined likewise with red baize to be worn in walks and journeys.'

The Courtyard, Coningsbury's Hospital

Sir Thomas Coningsby lived at Hampton Court, near Leominster, but built his hospital here outside the city walls of Hereford in 1614 as a refuge for old worn out soldiers. He created medieval sheltered housing complete with nursing facilities. In addition, he bequeathed a sum of two hundred pounds per year to the hospital, then comprising just twelve patients. The hospital was fully restored in the nineteenth century and later modernized in order to to cater for six elderly folk. For a couple to have qualified for residency, the husband must have been local, over sixty five, and have put in at least four years military service. To the rear of the hospital are the ruined domestic quarters of a Black Friar's monastery, a Dominican house built in 1346 on land given to them by a certain Sir John Daniel. When construction was completed, the dedication ceremony was attended by Edward II, the Black Prince, and three cardinals indicating the monastery's importance. In spite of his generosity, poor old Sir John was later arrested and beheaded by the King for 'interference' during the Baronial Wars. Close by is a preaching cross erected by the Friars at the time they built their monastery. It is in remarkable condition and is a rare surviving example in Herefordshire.

Back in the city, the skyline is dominated by the great central tower of the cathedral. However, close by is the spire of another church of character, All Saints. Externally, this church which is at the western end of the central square appears a large and rugged ancient building of local sandstone. There is no churchyard, being surrounded by streets on three sides and hemmed in by shops and offices on the fourth. The tower is said to lean and the reason put forward for this, discovered during excavations in 1993-94, was that it was built on a twelveth century swamp which caused the tower to eventually sink slightly. Try as I might, I have not been able to determine any lean in the tower, so maybe after many attempts at realignment over the centuries it was finally straightened out. During his visit to All Saints in 1891, Timmins was impressed by the well-proportioned and dignified interior. His great concern however, was that alterations to the fabric of the church were pending, carrying with them the likelihood of permanent damage. He wrote,

> *'We would direct the attention of the Society for the Protection of Ancient Buildings to the impending restoration of this fine church which in its present state is unusually interesting. It is hoped that the alterations will be carried out in a conservative spirit.'*

Unfortunately his fears were justified, as in 1892 there was a characteristically Victorian restoration which included the removal of old wall plaster and with it the loss of medieval wall paintings, save one on the east wall of the chancel. Had he been here today, he might not have been prepared, nor was I, for the impact of a more recent refurbishment. Following more extensive modernization of the nave, a café has been built, using modern materials and style, inside the west end of the church, where visually it appears to intrude. What was once majestically medieval is now an amalgamation of the fourteenth century with the twenty first. At the time of my visit in 2004 priest-in-charge Andrew Mottram, who was the instigator of this transformation, told me that the intention was to bring *'what is of the world and what is of God'* to meet and interact on easy terms; and presumably to bring in badly needed funding to maintain the church. As a consequence, Holy Communion now regularly takes place at the front of the church in full view of those having lunch at the back! The only areas of the church to survive wholesale restructuring are the chancel and side chapels. In the chancel, the original canopied stalls of fourteenth century dark oak with superb carvings survive and are magnificent. The pulpit is also carved and is probably Jacobean, as is the massive communion table. The roof is said to be fifteenth century but was for some reason boarded in the late nineteenth century. There is no altar now in the south side chapel as it is used these days for small local gatherings and craft shows, another plan perhaps to bring God and commerce together. Gone too, are the 285 volumes of ancient chained books, previously in this chapel but since 1992 transferred to the cathedral and now forms part of their famous collection. Theological intentions apart, for me the changes are too radical. The two cultures look and are at odds with each other, and what has been created is a mish-mash of incompatible functions and styles, the medievalness eclipsed. I hope your innovation works, Andrew, but I wish there could have been another way.

Leaving All Saints by the south porch, a wide stretch of inner city road, appropriately called Broad Street, led me first past the elegant façade of The Green Dragon Hotel, the premier city inn and older than it looks, then the tall Doric columned portico of the catholic church of St Francis Xavier, where the composer Edward Elgar often played the organ. Within this tall un-churchlike nineteenth century building is displayed the severed hand of St John Kemble, a Catholic priest who was executed on Widemarsh common in 1679 at the age of eighty! After death, a follower succeeded in severing and secreting the martyred priest's hand, and the relic is preserved here in a casket.

17th century Grapes Tavern behind Hereford City centre. The plaque on the side wall describes how the London Letter was delivered by stagecoach each week

Beyond the high columns of St Francis Xavier is the great church of St Mary and St Ethelbert, Hereford cathedral. Previously there had been at least two other cathedrals on or near this site. King Offa built a stone church here in 829 in atonement for his involvement in the murder, at Sutton Walls, north of Hereford, of his fellow King, Ethelbert, whose remains were interred in Offa's church. Ethelbert's violent end, and claims of miracle cures by the early Saxon inhabitants ensured a special place for his shrine in the hearts of Herefordians. It became a venue for pilgrimages until the Welsh destroyed both church and shrine when they sacked the city in 1053. As a replacement for Ethelbert's tomb, a reliquary of St Thomas Becket was brought to the city and installed in a new cathedral. However, it was another shrine, that of St Thomas Cantilupe which was destined to become the miracle maker for the people, and the cathedral's saviour from 1320 onwards. Cantilupe was Bishop of Hereford from 1275 until his death in 1282. It was not a long or distinguished ministry, but he was renowned for his piety and commitment to the needs, earthly and spiritual, of the people of Herefordshire. His easy going style wasn't approved by Archbishop Peckham of Canterbury and disputes between the two were frequent and lengthy. Thomas was self assured but stubborn and in the end the Archbishop ran out of patience and excommunicated him. Thomas travelled to Rome to appeal directly to the Pope but fell ill on the way. A lifetime of fasting left him unable to resist his illness and he died on 25 August 1282. Peckham would have been bitterly disappointed to learn that the subsequent requiem mass was attended, as a mark of respect, by no less than five cardinals including the future Pope, Nicholas IV.

When Thomas's remains were returned to Britain the disgruntled Archbishop at first refused permission for them to be buried at all but, following intervention by the King, Edward I, he relented and agreed to burial at Hereford. The relics were interned in a tomb built in the north transept of the cathedral where they remain to this day. Almost immediately, miracle cures were claimed by the people of the city who in life had held him in high esteem. Between 1282 and 1317, five hundred cures were recorded. Modern medical analysis might explain away most claims as natural and some as exaggerated or misleading. But without the benefit of twenty first century learning, the populace of the thirteenth century was convinced that Thomas had indeed repaired their ailing bodies from his grave. His progress to sainthood seemed unstoppable. As far as the people of Hereford were concerned the first requirement, proof of miracles, had already been achieved. In turn, the cathedral itself was in desperate need of repair and the clergy would not readily denounce any claims of cures for fear of losing donations provided by equally desperate pilgrims. However the ensuing canonization process contained necessary lengthy procedures which were time consuming, but in due course Pope John XXII agreed that Hereford would have its saint. Thomas was sanctified following the Easter celebrations of 1320 and his feast day would be 2nd October.

Construction of the present cathedral started in 1080 and took almost five hundred years to complete. Although the fabric of the building has been altered many times, it remains basically Norman. The north transept was replaced in 1240 in a French style similar to Westminster Abbey which was being rebuilt at the same time. In contrast, the south transept, completed in 1147 has altered little and remains Norman in style and construction. The 165 foot high central tower is fourteenth century and is decorated with stone ballflowers, typically found on many Herefordshire churches. The lofty heights of the tower are still accessible for those with a stronger constitution than mine. Indeed, Timmins himself went up there and said of it:

> *'let not the visitor omit to climb the tower from whose summit a goodly prospect is commanded; the view extending away from the clustering roofs and spires of the old city, and embracing the utmost confines of the county: the whole forming a scene which will quite repay the fatigue of climbing some two hundred or more steps to attain it.'*

On Easter Monday, 1786, the cathedral's west front collapsed under the weight of a single west tower which had been added without adequate foundations. The tower was never replaced and as a consequence the cathedral today is significantly shorter than before. By the early part of the nineteenth century, more major surgery was needed and as a consequence it was the Victorians who created the marvellous character the cathedral has today. They erected a wrought iron screen across the chancel which Timmins saw there in 1891 and referred to as *'modern'*. Decorated with copper and brass, the screen housed seven

[HEREFORD CATHEDRAL.

bronze statuettes and must have been something to behold. Nevertheless, it didn't survive the tastes of the twentieth century congregation and was replaced by a huge corona resembling Christ's crown of thorns. The iron screen is now in the Victoria and Albert museum.

Famous amongst the cathedral's many treasures is the fifteenth century chained library, a collection of documents and manuscripts from monastic libraries dispersed after the dissolution. The chains were an early form of security, enabling readers to view the books but not remove them. The cathedral archives – a continuous record of accounts, court rolls, grants, leases and personal documents from the twelfth century - are also housed here. Another star exhibit is the cathedral's copy of Henry II's 1217 revised version of the Magna Carta, one of four copies still surviving (the other three are in the Bodlian Library in Oxford) and includes many reforms still in existence. The greatest treasure of the cathedral is the Mappa Mundi, a thirteenth century map of the world. The original map was drawn by Richard de Bello around 1270. The copy now on display was made by Richard de Haldingham in 1330 and since 1996 has been housed in a new building at the west end of the cloisters. Prior to that time, this priceless artefact was hung in a dark corner of the cathedral, and was almost sold to pay for urgent restoration work. Drawn on calf skin approximately 1.5 metres square, the Mappa was designed as a medieval learning tool rather than an aid to travel, and superimposed onto the continents are drawings of the history of humankind. Jerusalem is shown at the centre with four hundred and twenty known religious and other important sites radiating outwards. Hereford is represented in the far west by a drawing of the cathedral. In the thirteenth century, many parts of the world had still to be discovered and explored. Consequently, fantasy occasionally replaced reality and descriptions are made on the map of extraordinary humanoids, some with huge ears which they could wrap around themselves to keep out the cold, or one enormous foot held over the head as shade against the sun. Africa is populated by beings with heads between their shoulders. India seems to have been the medieval version of El Dorado depicted as having 5,000 cities and fabulously wealth, an accurate vision some might say of India at the time of the Raj. The Mappa Mundi is an irreplaceable time capsule to the thirteenth century.

Opposite the cathedral close is an architectural gem of the Victorian age standing in the midst of mediocre 1960s buildings. Broad Street Library was built by philanthropist James Rankin in 1874 as a free library for the *'good of the people of Hereford.'* The bold Venetian gothic style in which it was constructed was given short thrift by the much travelled writer of architectural guides, Sir Nikolaus Pevsner, who described it as 'pretentious'. Its appearance is that of a medieval Italianate palace. The architect chosen by Rankin to design the library was Frederick Robertson Kempson who Rankin had employed to complete Bryngwyn, his country mansion at Wormelow a few miles south of Hereford. Kempson was an ardent follower of Augustus Pugin, the father of gothic revivalism. An upper room was provided and is still used for meetings of the local Woolhope Naturalist Field Club, of which both Rankin and Alfred Watkins were members, and which houses its own extensive library. The Club was founded in 1850 as a society of learned people of geology, archeology, and natural history, who took part in observing the Herefordshire landscape and reporting their findings. These were then printed in a journal referred to as Transactions, first published in 1866 and annually ever since. The name of the Club was adopted from a local geological feature known as the Woolhope Dome, about which I will explain more later.

Beyond the cathedral buildings, and close to the river, is a large flat grassy area where once stood a huge motte bearing the keep of Hereford castle. The castle was one of the great landmarks of the old city but seems to have had a relatively quiet and undistinguished existence. It covered a large area but apart from the castle walls and a towered keep, building work was minimal and there was never any record of a fortified home here indicating lengthy guardianships. However, the eminent Tudor traveller, John Leland has been quoted as saying *'it is the fairest, largest and strongest castle in all England'*. By the early part of the 16th century, it was in ruins and most of the buildings in the bailey had already disappeared. The end came with the Civil Wars when the castle suffered further severe and irretrievable damage. By 1757 the castle mound had been removed and the bailey landscaped and now provides the city with a pleasant recreational area. Before either the cathedral or the castle was built, and not long after the city itself was founded, a celtic warrior, turned monk, called Guthlac founded a religious community and built a church near what eventually became the site of the castle. The exact whereabouts of Guthlac's monastery was uncertain until excavations on castle green in 1960 discovered evidence of a religious settlement pre-dating the castle. Local archaeologist, Ron Shoesmith, who supervised excavations in 1971 and discovered evidence for a Saxon cemetery, believes there may yet be more discoveries to be made beneath the green. In the twelveth century, following more attacks by the Welsh, the monks decided on a move to a safer place inside the walls and re-built their priory close to the centre of the old city. Sadly, the site of this second priory has also been lost and foundation evidence destroyed following heavy-handed building developments in 1983.

> *Repassing the cathedral, a winding lane is seen leading from the bishop's palace grounds towards the river. Here stood the cottage where 'pretty witty' Nell Gwyn was born, adjacent to the palace occupied at a later period by her grandson, Bishop Beauclerk, to whom the city is indebted for the laying out of the castle green'*

Nell was born in what was then Pipe Lane, now Gwynne Street, in 1650 but moved to London to perform as an actress in front of noblemen and royalty. A blue plaque commemorates the site of the house in which she spent her early days. In London Nell attracted many suitors from illustrious circles, not least Charles II, who took her on permanent hire as a mistress. Her second son, an issue from her liaisons with the King, became the first Duke of St Albans. By sheer coincidence, the Duke's son, Nell's grandson, became Bishop of Hereford and it was he who removed the dwellings on Pipe Lane, including his grandmother's house, and incorporated the land into the grounds of the Bishop's Palace. Apparently Nell received the equivalent of £450,000 a year for being the King's prostitute. With so much financial security, she became renowned for her generosity towards others. Following one such defining moment after being accosted in the Mall by an old soldier begging, she persuaded the King to fund the building of the Royal Chelsea Hospital for redundant and destitute soldiers, similar to Sir Thomas Coningsby's hospital on Widemarsh Street, even down to the red uniform. Thus was the beginning of the Chelsea Pensioners. Although the King had continued to have many mistresses, Nell had been his favourite. She in turn had been proud to have said of Charles, *'I may only be one lover to the King but he is my one lover'*

Nell Gwyn's birthplace in Pipe Lane, Hereford

Without doubt, the main feature in the story of Hereford is the river Wye, on which the city stands, referred to as *'devious Vaga'* by the Romans. It is one of the great sporting rivers of Britain, loved by fisherman and boating folk alike. Hereford Rowing Club was founded in 1872 and has one hundred and fifty members, seventy of whom are active rowers. In 2004, at sixty nine years of age, Nim Hodges was the elder statesman of the club, and according to his friends and members *'what he didn't know about the club and rowing in general wasn't worth knowing'*. During an early season team training session Nim and I sat down in a quiet corner of the committee room, him with a pint of his usual and me with a cup of tea, and he told me about his life on the river.

'I've been a member here since 1949, but associated with the club since I was two years old. Roundabout that time my father used to occasionally row my mother and me up and down the river. He would often row us as far as Ruckhall where the Ancient Camp Inn is. That's a seven mile round trip! The river was very popular even in those days. There were many stories of boat loads of chaps rowing as fast as they could to get to the inn before it opened, and trying to row back in the afternoon after closing time. You can imagine the scene of boats wandering all over the river and none making much progress!'

In his time, Nim has been Captain twice and served for three years as President. Now, he spends much of his time there helping to organize and assist with the regular events held at he club.

'Throughout the year there are local and invitational regattas here, but the big one is the Spring Bank Regatta when teams come from all over the UK. It's a great time for us.'

Not being familiar with the sport's great achievers, I asked him if there had been any famous Hereford rowers.

'There have been one or two on the fringe, but our proudest moment was at the Henley Regatta in 1971 when our coxed four won the Britannica Cup. Griffiths, Hanby, Lambert, and Johnson were in the boat. Nigel Causer was the cox.'

I could see he had devoted a good part of his life to the club so I asked him what other memories he cherished.

'Well, there were the icebergs in 1962! We have to cope with regular flooding here, but those came as a bit of a surprise to say the least. During

that year, the river upstream froze and when the thaw started, the ice broke up into huge chunks. There were large crowds on the old Wye Bridge watching the bergs crashing into the columns. Then there was the time we acquired an eights boat way back in 1950. It was sixty two and a half feet long and needed a re-varnish. We couldn't afford to hire the appropriate transport to deliver it to the paint shop in Hereford, so we carried it upside down over our heads through the streets. People must have wondered how to react seeing a giant centipede in their midst! When we brought it back, it wouldn't fit in the club house so we had to knock a hole in the wall. We still laugh about it but at the time it was all a matter of needs-must.' Then in a more somber tone he said *'We are planning a major refurbishment of the clubhouse but money is hard to come by so we have decided to sell the committee room table which we know could be valuable so might bring a few pounds in.'*

Our conversation was interrupted by a rapid chattering, from outside the committee room window, signalling the end of activities on the river, and I left him to his rituals and headed back to the city along the river path.

In an article in the Hereford Times on 25th February 2004 a story ran: 'The financial future of Hereford Rowing Club has been secured at a stroke. An antique table which the club put up for auction fetched £66,000 when £6,000 was expected at the most. Even experts at the Brightwells' Leominster saleroom were astonished. The table eventually went to a trade buyer from London.' I imagine Nim Hodges would have been very happy with that.

A few oars' length from the rowing club is a fifteenth century six arched stone bridge over the river, once the only way out of the city to the south west and wide enough for only a single lane of traffic. A modern replacement was built in 1966 to carry the A49 and now takes the traffic away from Hereford, to Ross, Hay-on-Wye, the Black Mountains, and beyond into the far reaches of south Wales.

PART TWO

Towards the Monmouthshire Border and Ross-on-Wye

KILPECK CHURCH.

Turning our backs upon the cathedral city, we cross the rapid flowing Wye by a mediaeval bridge, the scenery becoming evermore varied in character as we advance, the heights of Aconbury, Orcop, and Saddlebow hills showing a broken line ahead..

The walk from the centre of the Hereford along the A49 Ross-on-Wye road was a drag. Neither the Lower Bullingham nor the Red Hill district which the main road splits, are pretty. Two miles out, I was standing by a stile beside the Graftonbury Hotel on the southern outskirts of the city. The footpath sign told me I was about to start The Violette Szabo Trail, opened in August 2000 and dedicated to the memory of a heroine of the Second World War. At the end of the trail is the village of Wormelow and there I had arranged to meet Rosemary Rigby who runs a museum built by the people amongst whom Violette had lived for a short time. The trail was developed by Mike Colton, an ex 22nd Special Air Services (SAS) officer and founder of The Allied Special Forces Association. It was late April, and recent persistent rain meant the ground underfoot would be heavy and it was going to be slow progress, at least for a while. The Violette Szabo Trail crosses the busy A49 Hereford to Ross-on-Wye road twice along its six mile length, the first time almost at once, and heads due east towards high ground close to the village of Bullinghope. Once I had reached the ridgetop lane, I turned south towards Aconbury Hill. In the tiny hamlet below Aconbury stands a small and very old church dedicated to St John the Baptist. In 1255 a priory for Augustinian nuns was built here by Margery de Lacy to educate the daughters of the local gentry, but, in spite of a petition to Henry VIII, the king did not spare the priory in his dissolution programme and it was demolished in 1539. As if in consolation, the priory church was left untouched for the parishioners to worship in and now represents an unspoilt example of early English architecture. Traces of blocked entrances to the old cloisters and dormitory can still be seen on an external wall. Just yards from the church, in a hillside field, is an ancient spring surrounded by a small retaining wall. This is St Ann's Well and it is said to have healing powers, particularly for those with eyesight problems. The legend is that an effective cure could be achieved using the first water drawn from the well after midnight on twelfth night and within living memory, some local women have been known to have competed for the first bucketful.

Beyond the well, the footpath climbs the northern flanks of Aconbury Hill leading to an iron age fort of some considerable size. On the wooded summit a thousand wood anemones glistened in the bright afternoon sun, and the wild garlic smell of early shoots of ramsoms was accentuated after a short April shower. The village of Kings Thorn at the southern foot of Aconbury was named after a cutting said to have come from the Holy Thorn at Glastonbury was planted there after being gifted by Charles I on a visit to Hereford. Though knarled and fragile, it still grows by the side of a narrow track at the heart of the village, and like Holy Thorns elsewhere, it is said to blossom on twelfth night. In the cozy Castle Inn, I was told the story of Higgins's Well next to the village church. Mr Higgins owned an earlier well which used to be in a meadow above the present outlet. He became so annoyed by constant trespassers to his well that he had it filled in. Shortly afterwards, water began to rise through the floor of his house and thinking it was water spirits exacting some sort of punishment for his actions, he decided to dig a new well on the present site. This apparently was enough to molify the spirits as the waters in his house subsided and did not return. Thus there was water again for the villagers and immortality for Mr Higgins.

The Violette Szabo Trail continues in a southerly direction along quiet lanes and sunken tracks, though within earshot of the busy A49. A mile ahead of me a line of trees formed the garden boundary of The Laskett, home of Sir Roy Strong, previously a director of the Victoria & Albert Museum in London. Together with his wife, theatre set designer Julia Trevelyan Oman, he has created here the largest formal garden in the country. The story began in 1974 when he presided over an exhibition at the V&A to emphasize the plight of our great houses and gardens which had been in decline since the outbreak of the First World War and hadn't really recovered. This had an enormous effect on him and the embryo of his great garden at The Laskett was born. His intention was to evoke the golden age of the great gardens of Gertrude Jekyll or Vita Sackville West. In defiance of the times and the ideology of the age, he and his wife set about creating a truly English garden carved from a four acre field next to their home. As early as February 1974, Sir Roy had indicated how his garden would grow.

'It might be that sometime in the future, there will be a bungalow development in pea green plastic just beyond my land but I won't want to know about that and so the whole of my garden will be enclosed, private, a secret'.

What he planted was a garden of rooms behind hedges of yew and lines of pleached limes, each with a theme of personal or historical significance. The beginning didn't go well when a disastrous drought in 1976 and the severe winter of 1981/82 destroyed much of the early work, but the Strongs replanted and continued to spend all their spare time creating a dream. In 1987 Sir Roy resigned his directorship of the V&A after fourteen years, and built a small temple at *The Laskett* to celebrate his career. Inside the temple is a plaque of Queen Victoria and Prince Albert separated by his own unmistakable mustachioed and bespectacled features. In his subsequent book *The Laskett – The Story of a Garden* Sir Roy tells how he and Julia often sat under the temple arch 'with bottle and glass', surveying their secret world which had taken fifteen years to develop and reach maturity. How satisfying those moments must have been. Sadly, Julia died in 2003 after a brief illness, but Sir Roy has continued to look after their creation and now allows small parties to look around by appointment.

Now, turning west, I crossed the A49 for a second time before descending into Wormelow. The museum dedicated to Violette Szabo is in a curious, purpose-built bungalow at the bottom of Rosemary Rigby's garden at 'Cartref'. the very house where Violette spent many summer days. It is loaded with memorabilia connected to her life and times and was created with painstaking effort by Miss Rigby. Violette was the half-French daughter of a Brixton car dealer. During the Second World War she served with the Auxillery Territorial Service (ATS), and later as a first aid nurse assigned to Special Operations Executive (SOE), a war-time organization set up to assist nationals in oppressed countries. Tragically, her husband Etienne Szabo, an officer of the Free French Forces, was killed at El Alemein in October 1942 shortly after the birth of their daughter, Tania. Devastated by Etienne's death, Violette volunteered for duty as a secret agent in France. Her second drop in France followed immediately after the Normandy landings, but whilst giving covering fire to a French resistance leader, she was captured and incarcerated at Ravensbruck in Germany. In 1945, after being humiliated and tortured by the Gestapo, Violette was executed. She was posthumously awarded the George Cross the following year. She was just twenty three years old. In 1958, the film *Carve Her Name with Pride* starring Virginia McKenna, told Violette's tragic story.

Although Violette was born and lived in Brixton in London, her cousins lived in Wormelow, and here she spent many happy holidays. On the outer wall of 'Cartref' is a plaque placed there in 1988 by the villagers in appreciation of her outstanding courage and bravery. In 2000 they chose to honour her again for their Millenium project when the museum was officially opened by Virginia McKenna. One of the most memorable and moving displays is the code poem written for her by Leo Marx who was head of the codes section at the SOE. The words have become synonymous with Violette's life.

The love that I have is all that I have
And the life that I have is yours.
The love that I have of the life that I have
Is yours and yours and yours
A sleep I shall have, a rest I shall have
Yet death will be but a pause.
For the peace of my years in the long green grass
Will be yours, and yours, and yours.

Next to the tiny building at the bottom of Rosemary's garden are twenty three roses for each of Violette's short and tragic life, planted by local children. As we stood in the warm sunshine while Rosemary

Rosemary Rigby's museum to war heroine Violette Szabo

told me of her years of dedication, I noticed in a shaded spot nearby, a group of wild daffodils tall and fresh in late bloom. The village grass verges had already lost their spring show, but here beside a memorial to a very brave woman, was one final blossoming. Rosemary said *'Viollette's spirit will have something to do with that'.*

My intended route from Wormelow was in a south westerly direction over Bryngwyn Hill, but I wanted to make a short detour to visit a local school which does not follow the national curriculum. The Hereford Waldorf School at the nearby village of Much Dewchurch is part of a worldwide network of over six hundred such established to teach a system of learning favoured by Austrian philosopher and scientist, Rudolf Steiner. He started his first school in 1919 for children of the workers at the Waldorf Cigarette Factory in Stuttgart. Steiner challenged the one-sided emphasis of intellectual education and introduced an alternative for body, soul and spirit, so that children could receive a foundation for life through their schooling. The Much Dewchurch school was started by Greta Rishbrooke in 1980 with six children attending classes in one of the parent's front rooms. When the local village state school closed in 1983, the parents purchased the old buildings and an adjacent twelfth century farmhouse in a quiet cul-de-sac next to the church, enabling more pupils to join them. Today, there are two hundred pupils between the ages of three and sixteen years. Niki Nakamura – her husband is Japanese - is one of the administrators and invited me to look around the school while she explained the principles of the Steiner philosophy.

'We offer a structured but not formal learning here centered entirely on the children. We take them in at three years of age but we don't start teaching them until they are six. Until then, we allow them to develop relationships with one another at their own pace. Once into the mainstream school, they begin learning in the true sense of the word but even then never forced. The structure then becomes simply head work in the morning when the children are at their best, creative work in the afternoon when they need to relax.'

I asked her how different that is to that of state schools?

'It's the freedom. We allow the children to learn at their own pace. Nothing is forced upon them and there are no stats. When it's time for them to

move on to a sixth form school, they leave with a sense of self-worth. State schools in the UK are beginning to copy now what Steiner introduced a hundred years ago because it works. The difference is that we are a non-hierarchical fee paying school - there is no head teacher or Principal. Our parents and children work together to make their Steiner Waldorf School work for them, and there's no outside interference.'
The education of the nation's children has hardly figured in my daily life since my own children were little. Then, like many of my contemporaries, I was inclined to let the system get on with it but this short unplanned aside to my journey has had a profound effect on me. Parents here care *how* their offspring are taught and are themselves part of the system. Before I left her, Niki suggested that the Steiner organization was hoping for state funding in the future as in other countries. In the meantime and in spite of current financial demands on the parents, this school is oversubscribed.

I retraced my steps to Wormelow. The old name for the village is Wormelow Tump and it was so called because there was once a burial mound at the side of the road junction in the centre of the village. Legend has it that it was the grave of King Arthur's son Amr, or more likely Mordred, his nephew, who some claim Arthur slew at a place called Gamber Head, less than a mile from Wormelow. Unfortunately, any evidence of a body was destroyed when the mound was removed to widen the road in 1896. A straight track leads from the village crossroads climbing steadily towards woodland on Bryngwyn Hill. This is the Herefordshire Way, one of many long distance trails which have been introduced in recent years to promote access to the British countryside. Almost immediately, the track led me past a depressing site, the recently burnt out wreck of a once renowned local dance venue of the pre-disco era, and known affectionately as 'The Park'. During the sixties and seventies Park Hall ballroom was highly successful and young folk came from miles around to enjoy the dances of the day; waltz, foxtrot, quick-step, and cha-cha-cha. Famous bands of that era played here, Joe Loss, Syd Philips, Ray MacVay, Victor Sylvester jnr, and Syd Lawrence, legends all. The in-house act was the Russ Allen Band. Peter Chambers was a trumpeter with that band

and years later his son Martin would claim fame as the drummer in the 1980s rock group 'The Pretenders', recently voted to the Rock 'n Roll Hall of Fame in New York. Here at The Park there were bars and a large dance floor catering for a thousand people. The huge parking area, now accumulating a covering of mosses and weeds, bears witness to the volume of cars and coaches which would assemble here on a Saturday night, many from as far away as Cardiff, Gloucester, Bristol, and the Midlands. By the 1980s however the enthusiasm for ballroom dancing was over, and Park Hall closed its doors for the last time in 1983. A local man told me the buildings had been empty and unused for many years but the recent fire had been sad for those who still harbour fond memories of halcyon days. A very short distance from The Park the footpath passes close to a large grim looking Victorian manor house, as near to resembling an institution as you can get. This was Bryngwyn Manor, built in 1868 for Sir James Rankin after the Bodenhams, one of the county's great and ancient families, had sold the estate and moved to their new mansion at Rotherwas nearer to Hereford. The young impressionable Rankin had recently graduated from Cambridge and since his father's death, become the inheritor of great wealth. He had the means to employ the best architects of his day, and Frederick Kempson was one of those. The Victorian elite had developed an insatiable desire for all things Gothic and the young James was no exception. His father Robert, a Scotsman, had accumulated most of his fortune in the North American timber trade of Nova Scotia (New Scotland). James was born in Liverpool from where his father had set sail but came to Hereford in 1865 and took over Bryngwyn which his father had acquired as an investment but had never seen. And so, at twenty three years of age, Rankin junior became what his father would have liked to have been, the resident owner of a country estate. Three years later James built his mansion on an elevated eminence commanding extensive views across the Herefordshire countryside. At a time when there was little government help for the sick, the poor, the old or indeed the young, Rankin turned his attention to relieving their plight, particularly those of his adopted county. He became a member of parliament for North Herefordshire and argued for a Bill to provide pensions for the aged, long before

Lloyd George eventually introduced them. At home, he was chairman of the education committee and built the state school at Much Dewchurch, now the Steiner school, with his own money. He is even said to have, each year, supplied the children with clothes and footwear. He provided libraries for the people of Kington and Leominster, and also built the richly adorned library building in Broad Street opposite the cathedral in Hereford. Sir James Rankin died in 1915 when the ordered world he knew was falling apart. Bryngwyn was never really used as a home again after his death and although it was hired out for wedding receptions and dinner parties it was eventually abandoned and fell into disrepair. In 1963, the dilapidated building was purchased by a Birmingham engineer, George Ormerod, who moved his workshops into the old ballroom, providing for his workers the most surreal of surroundings and turned the upper floors into flats.

Onward once more passed fields of rape clinging to the northern slopes of Bryngwyn Hill. Emerging from a stretch of woodland a mile further on, I caught my first glimpse of 'The Mynde', another much larger and more classical mansion. The house had been given a new coat of cream paint, unusual for a private dwelling of such stature, and it shone like a jewel in the afternoon sun. Built in the late fifteenth century as a three storey hall house, extensive eighteenth century additions were given a Georgian façade and, curiously, three hundred and sixty five windows. For centuries, this old house was the ancestral home of the Pye family, one of Herefordshire's oldest, who settled in this area after the Norman conquest. They had maintained their baronial status and home at Kilpeck Castle in the valley below but when that was destroyed during the Civil War, they moved to The Mynde where it became one of the wealthiest estates in Herefordshire. The Pye family name evolved from the surname ap Hugh or son of Hugh, which eventually became ap Huee, then simplified to Pye. The first Hugh's daughter, Susan, married one Gilbert Becket and they had a son called Thomas, later to become Archbishop Thomas a Becket of Canterbury. When the estate was finally sold in 1916, it still extended to over 4,500 acres. Not so long ago, the house was an abandoned wreck until the present owners turned it once again into a family home.

Although the public right way through the estate passes close to the great house, the inquisitive walker might currently have any unwanted advances away from the line of the path checked by several over enthusiastic black dogs. I have never been much attached to dogs, nor do I feel particularly comfortable when I am harassed by one. On this occasion, I was not so much harassed as mugged and I was glad of having Meg with me (Meg being my stick, named after the TV fortune teller, Mystic Meg) which I used to good effect. With barking still echoing around the surrounding parkland, I climbed away along a dusty track, skirted Bowers Wood, and crossed open hillside before dropping down towards the site of one of Herefordshire's unrivalled treasures, the twelfth century church of St Mary and St David at Kilpeck.

The name Kilpeck derives from 'The Cell of St Pedic' and refers to a Celtic saint who settled here in the dark ages building himself a simple hut befitting his austere life. This is an ancient place, a Saxon stronghold in fact, built in the 8th century. Ground markings near the ancient church bear evidence of a settlement outside the present village. It is likely that the Saxons weren't the first to settle here: recent investigations indicate that some of the hidden footings are Roman. St Pedic himself may have been here around 640AD. Kilpeck castle was built by William Fitz Norman, first Lord of Kilpeck. This was an important site before the conquest and may have formed one of Offa's lines of defence against the Welsh. The extensive earthworks are now largely overgrown, but some stonework remains in the keep and the north east part of the moat is still wet. The continuing importance of this castle was mainly due to several visits made here by King John in the early thirteenth century and it must therefore have been fit for such royal attention. At the time, William de Cantelupe, Sheriff of Herefordshire and Steward of the Royal Household was living at the castle and may have been offering attractive holiday rates!

The church though, is the star and is architecturally stunning. Dedicated originally to St David, the name St Mary was added after the chapel in the adjacent castle was abandoned in favour of the Norman church.

> *Upon entering the church, we are at once impressed by the quiet dignity of this massive style of building; with its subdued touches of enrichment upon the carved pillars on each side of the arch which separates nave from chancel, and the bold zigzag ornament on the arch above. It is wonderful what an effect of length is obtained in so small a building by the double series of arches and the semi circular apse at the end.*

The carvings are the finest example of work by the Norman masons of the Herefordshire School whose work can still be seen in churches throughout the county. This remarkable red sandstone building, not least the world famous south doorway, has survived eight hundred years of weathering. There are many well preserved Norman doorways still in existence throughout England but few can compare with this little gem. It is simple in shape and form but sumptuously carved. Its excellent condition is maintained with regular inspection (the last repair was in 1982). A print of 1780 hanging in the lounge of the Red Lion Inn shows a porch around the south door which may have aided preservation. Around the roof line of the church are a series of grotesque beasts and at the top right corner buttress in the north wall, a piece of stone carving claimed to be from the original Saxon church. The wealth of carving continues inside, on the nave and chancel arches. The huge font is older than the present church and is mounted on slender stone columns said to have been the mullions taken from the windows of the castle.

South doorway, Kilpeck church

Beyond the churchyard across the valley to the west is the ancient Treville forest. Amongst its many fine old oak trees are the remains of what was listed in the Guinness Book of Records as the tallest in England, until it fell in the storm of 1991.

My route from Kilpeck was south west towards Garway Hill overlooking the Monnow valley and Welsh border lands. I had arranged to stay the night at Kentchurch Court, the ancient home of perhaps the greatest of the great Herefordshire families, the Scudamores, as a guest of Jan Scudamore. Many historians believe that the most charismatic of Welsh rebels, Owain Glyndwr, spent his last days at Kentchurch. As I followed one of the many streams falling from the Garway, I reflected on the historical significance of the old house at Kentchurch and the connection with Glyndwr. He was born at Sycarth near Llangollen in North Wales in 1349, and was by all accounts a well educated man who was called to the English Bar and resided at the court of Richard II. Although he claimed descent from the Kings of Powys, he maintained his allegiance at first to the English crown. Inevitably, in time his contemporaries began to mistrust him, and after being falsely accused of rebellious activities he was forced to flee to his Welsh homeland. Full of resentment at the way in which he had been framed, he proclaimed himself Prince of Wales and set out to establish independence for his people. For decades, his willing band of guerrillas harassed and cajoled the English marcher armies guarding the borders. However, this wasn't much of a concern to Henry IV who was busy consolidating his own position after usurping the English throne. Sometime after 1409, Glyndwr retired undefeated, by now too old to be a real threat. It is likely that he had become less antagonistic to the marcher lords because his five daughters had married into the great Herefordshire families of the Crofts, Monningtons and Mortimers. One daughter, Alice, married Sir John Scudamore and came to live at Kentchurch. There have been many theories concerning Glyndwr's final resting place, none of which have been proven beyond doubt. Some believe that the Welsh Prince may have been buried at Monnington Straddel near Vowchurch in Herefordshire's Golden Valley. Most hope, as I do, the mystery will never be solved!

Kentchurch Court is basically a fourteenth century fortified manor house. It has been home to the Scudamores for over a thousand years. However, it boasts a tower that can be traced to Saxon times.

Although the other Scudamore great house at Holme Lacy near Hereford is better known, Kentchurch was the first head house of the ancient family. Jan Scudamore has run the estate almost single handed for the last ten years. Apart from the Court the estate includes ten tenanted farms and a one hundred and fifty acre deer park. Although Kentchurch remains a family home, she has converted some of the thirty five rooms for guest accommodation, and the opportunity to stay in a stately home, particularly as it was on my route, was too good to resist. I had already explained to Jan that I wanted to include a paragraph or two in my book about the history of the house and the Owain Glyndwr connection, so I shouldn't have been surprised to find she had put me in the very room where Glyndwr is said to have slept. With a mischievous grin she told me it was a little atmospheric but thought the experience might add spice to my book. My accommodation was an ancient oak panelled room in the Saxon tower, the oldest part of the house. The furniture consisted of a four poster bed, a heavy oak dresser and an old drop down writing desk. A huge open fireplace dominated the room. Around the panelled walls were hung framed prints of Owain Glyndwr himself and another fourteenth century character known as Jack o'Kent who also stayed at the Court and is said to have fought off challenges from the Devil for his soul. Just two leaded lanterns gave off dim light. There were two windows, floor to ceiling, half hidden behind thick curtains, too long and too wide to be opened fully and obviously made for much larger windows in a grander part of the house. This was where Glyndwr had slept six hundred years ago. I remember my initial reaction projected an air of excitement, but that it was followed a moment later with a more realistic exclamation when the reality of the situation dawned. This darkened ancient dormitory of long dead heroes and villains whose restless sprits could still be around was where I had to sleep that night. My first thought was to search for the proverbial secret doors in the walls and I succeeded in finding three. Through one was a cleverly disguised wardrobe. Through another an empty space roughly the same size as the wardrobe with a small window overlooking a courtyard. A third, close to the bed opened onto a narrow spiral staircase leading upwards to God knows where. As I started to unpack, I felt reassured of the comfort I would have from my modern digital radio but after plugging it into the only available socket in the room, found there was no signal and therefore no music to distract me. The spacious bathroom was across a short landing in the corner of which was a suit of armour propped against the wall. Outside, the early spring sunshine was showing signs of fading so I decided to head off to the village pub in search of dinner and a comforting pint of beer or two.

When I returned later the lady of the house was in the smoking room watching TV and after kindly inviting me to share a pot of tea with her she told me more about Kentchurch and her struggle to keep this very old house alive. Her husband, John, had moved out some time

Timmins's drawing of the Glyndwr tower at Kentchurch Court

ago so it seemed an unenviable task looking after the house and the estate. It's a huge responsibility but one she said she had grown to accept as her role in the continuing history of Kentchurch. She told me there was much to be done to the fabric of the house before it would again be in good working order. The estate is in trust to her children and it is her wish that her son Joss inherits something he can be proud of and would want to pass on to his children with similar confidence. In 2002, as part of her plan to bring in much needed capital, the Channel Four series *Regency House Party* was filmed at Kentchurch and the income generated from that helped a great deal. Prior to the arrival of the TV series production team, Jan had bubble-wrapped the valuable contents of the house and sent them off to a secure warehouse at Heathrow airport. During the nine weeks of the filming she was in New Zealand visiting friends and the fee she received for use of her house enabled her to redecorate and re-carpet the ground floor rooms, which had been damaged in a devastating flood in 1959. Apparently, there was still enough money left to repair and clean the chandeliers in the private quarters and pay urgent attention to the aging sewerage system. Before the war, there were enough staff here to cater for everything the Scudamore family required both in and outside the house. Now there are just three staff, plus a gardener and a gamekeeper. There's no chef, so in the morning, Jan would be making my breakfast and I glowed at the thought of the lady of this monument to a great an ancient family having to pamper to my needs.

Following a very restless but thankfully ghost free night, I breakfasted alone in the main dining room sitting at the end of a very long table surrounded by portraits of Scudamores from previous centuries. I was astonished to see that above the fireplace, the large mirror was framed by the delicate wood carvings of birds and foliage by the Dutch master craftsman Grinling Gibbons and wondered if these were the missing examples which once adorned the walls at the Scudamore's great house at Holme Lacy. Jan confirmed that it was indeed his work and later showed me more carvings on display in the terrace room and hallway, all transferred to Kentchurch when Home Lacy was sold off and therefore not lost as some devotees of Gibbons might have originally thought. After serving me with breakfast she left the house to attend to her daily business leaving me free to look around the library for more research on the Scudamores. I browsed through a portfolio of newspaper cuttings and magazine articles covering the last one hundred years. The old house has had many metamorphoses over the centuries, including a contribution from the great Regency architect John Nash in 1795. However, there is much remaining from the medieval period, and several Norman revival arches in the Library provide an interesting touch. After an hour or two, I turned my attention to the many hundreds of books but decided the task would be too much of a challenge and instead donned my walking boots and took up Jan's parting invitation to stroll round the deer park. This unexpected extension to her hospitality was exciting enough, more so that she should put her staff at my disposal, but I took full advantage of a rare opportunity of being Lord of the Manor, albeit only for a few hours. On my way across the garden terrace I met Jan's gardener, busy with the Flymo, on the front lawn. He asked if I'd had a visitation while staying in the Glyndwr room. I felt a gradual slide into shock as he explained that a blonde lady had been seen many times in the past looking out of the window from the landing just outside the Glyndwr room. No-one knows who she is apparently but he told me he'd seen her himself once watching him cutting the grass by the east wing. As the family were away at the time there should have been no-one else in the house. I shivered at the realization that I had crossed that landing to the bathroom at least twice during the night. I searched for any sign of a twinkle in his eye but his expression remained sincere. I told him nonchalantly that I hadn't seen or heard anything, and headed quickly for a gate by the terrace which opened into the deer park. As I climbed away from the house, I caste a nervous glance in the direction of the aforementioned window in the tower but saw nothing.

> *We now wend our way through the spacious and finely wooded park, some four miles round, which climbs the steep shoulder of Garway Hill. Beneath the great oaks the deer are sheltering in group; and here we observe that although the foliage of the yew tree is generally injurious to animals, the dead leaves of that tree are eaten without causing any ill effect.*

The Kentchurch estate consists of 5,000 acres of farmland and the ancient deer park into which I now strode. Most of it lies on the north-west facing flanks of Garway Hill with exceptional views up the Monnow valley towards Hay-on-Wye. As I climbed the wooded hillside, fallow deer scurried ahead of me darting in and out of the fern covering. After a while, I found myself in an area of ancient oaks which included one known as 'Jack o' Kent's Oak', reputed to be almost a thousand years old. A study of this knarled and stunted specimen by English Nature a few years back decided it was already old in the year 1300, even before Jack was a lad!

Jack o'Kent was a local monk employed as chaplain at Kentchurch Court in medieval times. There are many legends about Jack and the Devil who seemed to be always challenging him in order to gain his soul. On one such occasion as Jack went to buy pigs at the market, the Devil told him that if he returned with curly tailed pigs, he would claim Jack's soul as his prize. On the way home, Jack housed the pigs for the night in a damp and cold sty which caused the tails to straighten. The following morning the Devil saw that the tails were straight and changed the rule that if the tails were still straight on his return, Jack would be the loser. That night, Jack put the pigs in a warm and dry sty so that the next morning the tails had become curly and again the Devil went away empty handed. On another occasion, the Devil offered to build a bridge over the river Monnow in Kentchurch village. The payment would be Jack's body when he died, whether buried inside or outside the church. However, even in death, Jack outwitted him by being buried in one of the walls of the church thus being neither inside nor out.

Returning from my tour of the park, I took my leave of everybody at the court and set off down the long drive towards the village. A mile or so south of Kentchurch, beyond the Devil's bridge, a footpath leaves the lane and climbs steadily towards the summit of Garway Hill, a thousand feet above the Monnow valley. I have walked up here many times since my first visit to Herefordshire ten years ago and the magnificent views across these marcher lands will no doubt draw me back time and time again. I've been told that on the clearest of days you can see eleven counties from the top of Garway. That may be so and there's no disputing the feel good factor here. I saw an episode of Michael Palin's acclaimed travelogue *Himalaya* not so long ago, and recall the emotion he expressed at his first sight of Everest and the Anapurna range. As silly as it sounds, I would argue that comparisons between the view from Everest and Garway Hill are not so far fetched. Those able bodied folk who rarely venture much beyond their armchairs should, even just once, chance a bit of limb power to see what the world is like from this height. I guarantee they won't be disappointed. From the summit, I began a gradual descent towards the distant ridge road crossing the Herefordshire landscape on its way to Monmouth. On the skyline, the church tower of St Weonards was my guide.

> *'Turning down a steep lane, we now make for Treago, the venerable home of the Mynors, catching picturesque glimpses of the mansion through the embowering trees as we approach. The noble old fortified dwelling-house remains, in its intrinsic features, as originally built, with massive stone walls some seven feet in thickness, having a circular tower at each angle; enclosing a courtyard which has been built over to meet modern requirements.'*

The name Treago originates from the Welsh Tre-Iago, the house of James. Treago is more a fortified house than a castle, nevertheless it is architecturally striking. It was probably built by Richard Mynors, a prominent administrator for South Wales, between 1466 and 1484, but has been altered and restored many times since, the last occasion being in 1990. Timmins states that the castle was built two hundred years earlier but this may have been fuelled by a discovery that some walls on the site may be older than the building itself. In 1765, Treago passed to a Mr Peter Rickards who adopted the Mynors name and the family have remained in residence ever since. Rickards wife Meliora Powell was herself descended from another ancient Herefordshire family, the Baskervilles. Not long after he took up residence Rickards Mynors became bankrupt and had to give up the castle to tenants. However, in 1840 he succeeded in reclaiming the estate and saved the castle and adjoining buildings from neglect.

Treago cannot be said to be a grand building. The large windows built into the walls and low ceilings added in the seventeenth century were to provide extra living space and the result is more in-keeping with a modern home. The present owners are Sir Richard and Lady Fiona Mynors who took over the guardianship of the estate in 1989 and have since undertaken much needed repairs and renovations. To ensure the future of the castle and the estate, eleven hundred acres of farming land has been let, the stable and servants block converted into holiday accommodation and they have allowed the castle to be open by appointment to visiting groups and for charity fund raising events. In addition, Sir Richard planted a vineyard in 1991 in the walled garden which sits on elevated ground behind the house and because of its position creates its own Mediterranean climate. He now grows, picks, and bottles each year fifteen hundred bottles of white and champagne style wines, and unusually for this part of the world, red wines from Cabernet Sauvignon and Syrah grape varieties. A fortuitous effect of a garden re-design by his predecessor in 1840 adding terraces facing the house created a natural arena, and this has been used for summer theatres. The Mynors have spent a lot of their spare time, not just preserving an ancient family home, but creating an environment to ensure Treago's future. Sir Richard is a former music teacher and still finds time to conduct the Hereford Youth Orchestra. Lady Fiona is the daughter of a former Bishop of Salisbury, and

Treago Castle, built by Sir Richard Mynors in the 15th century and still occupied by a knight of the same name.

when she's not welcoming guests at open-air events at her home, she is fulfilling her role as a reporting inspector for independent schools, as well as being Vice-Chair of the Board of Governors of Cheltenham College. Together, the Mynors have a refreshing outlook on life at Treago insisting it's about the people who go there and not just the house itself.

Garway Hill from Kentchurch

Joining the lane beside the castle, I climbed westward once again to the pretty hamlet of Garway with its pub and common overlooking the Monnow Valley. Here is a piece of history, or several pieces to be precise. The church of St Michael is thirteenth century and interesting enough in that it is joined to a substantial tower by a passageway added in the seventeenth century. However, excavations carried out in 1927 uncovered the foundations of a circular Knight's Templar church beneath the present building — they built round churches to replicate the Temple of King Soloman in Jerusalem. Traces can be seen in the ground in and outside the nave. Here in Garway the Templars also built a splendid dovecot nearby, which interestingly has six hundred and sixty six pigeon holes, a strange number to choose in view of that number's association with the Devil. From ancient times to the end of the eighteenth century, dovecotes, or pigeon houses, provided the lords of the manor with a constant supply of fresh meat. They alone were allowed to build them. The poor peasants would have felt very much aggrieved as the pigeons fed on their grain whilst they were forbidden to kill them. The young chicks, or squabs, were recognized as a delicacy but although older birds were eaten occasionally, their value was in producing eggs. In the Middle Ages, pigeon droppings were used as fertilizer and for saltpeter, an essential ingredient of gunpowder. The bird's feathers were used for stuffing bedding. Nothing was wasted, it seems. Use of dovecotes in Britain probably began in Roman times. However, the earliest known examples of dove-keeping in Britain occur in Norman castles of the twelfth century. The decline of the dovecote has been linked with the introduction of the turnip in the eighteenth century, which was discovered to be an attractive food supplement for farm animals, enabling more of them to be kept and thus ensuring a larger source of food. Built in 1326, the pigeon house at Garway is one of the finest remaining medieval examples in England. It is also one of the largest, and has a rare water trough and projecting string course to protect the birds from rats. This well preserved Templar site is in a very tranquil spot, difficult to locate. and was certainly well chosen. It became the sect's largest possession in Herefordshire.

A winding narrow lane beside the old Templar church descends for a further mile and a half before reaching the river Monnow at Skenfrith, on the Welsh side of the border with England. The name Skenfrith is derived from Ynys Cynfraeth, meaning the island of Cynfraeth, a sixth century chieftain. It is a pretty place, and in accordance with the best village traditions, has an old pub, an ancient church, attractive stone cottages, and a castle. The castle was built in the early part of the thirteenth century to guard a ford over the Monnow and the important highway passing from Wales into England. The ruin we see today is a well preserved stone replacement of an earlier Norman earth and timber structure, and occupies an idyllic position on the banks of the river. It is probably in much the same state now as it was in 1538 when the travelling Tudor antiquarian, John Leland, noted briefly that Skenfrith *'yet standith'*. St Bridget's church is early thirteenth century, about the same age as the castle, and is one of the most picturesque anywhere in the British Isles. St Bridget was a fifth century Irish Abbess of Kildare who is said to have sailed over to the isle of Angelsey off North Wales on a grass sod which on landing instantly became a hillock and the origin of the town of Holyhead. It is just as likely that there was an earlier church on or near this site as there most certainly was an earlier castle built by the invading Normans around 1075. The present church with its three foot thick walls was built to withstand Welsh invaders and would have been a refuge as well as a place of worship. It is further characterized by its massive tower and wooden belfry and the inevitable dovecote built onto the tower for storing food supplies in times of conflict. Inside the church, displayed in a glass case in the north aisle is the Skenfrith Cope, a garment embroided in the fifteenth century which appears to be in excellent condition. Also in the north aisle on the wall above a handsome box pew are two panels containing the ten commandments. They are both modern copies of sixteenth century originals which used to hang in the sanctuary either side of the east window. The original stone altar has been restored to its position after once becoming part of the floor following the Reformation.

On the opposite bank of the river, The Bell Inn completes a perfect picture of peace and serenity, and was my stop for the night.

In contrast to the good weather experienced thus far on my journey the next morning was dull and misty, and there was rain in the air, as I set off from Skenfrith across the flat river meadow. The footpath followed the English bank of the Monnow which now ran quiet and slow, seemingly recharging its batteries following early spring surges. After two miles, I turned away from the river to visit an interesting old church that I'd heard of. Scattered buildings covering a small area of raised ground above the river plain are all that remains of the once vibrant village of Llanrothal devastated by the Black Death in the fourteenth century. At that time, the little isolated church of St John the Baptist would have been surrounded by cottages and farmsteads, but now stands alone in a field some way off the present road.

Inside the church, the sparse furnishings that remain include a massive medieval altar stone and a Jacobean pulpit. In the churchyard, a long disused entrance gate in an old stone wall, perhaps dividing the churchyard from a long ploughed up ancient village street, now leads nowhere. There are no longer any services here, but the thirteenth century building has been restored and is now looked after by the Redundant Churches Fund. Following recent floods, the river here remained choked in places with uprooted trees. Tons of driftwood lay scattered along the river bank, some wedged twenty feet up in the branches of trees standing closest to the river. Walking as I was in a flat meadow a yard or two from the waters edge, I estimated that my head would have been several feet below the surface just weeks before. Now that the river had lost its power and was back to a meander, the still verdant meadow, sandwiched between rising land beyond each bank was once again a silent and pleasant place. At Tregate Bridge, I turned north east along a narrow lane which would take me out of the Monnow valley for the last time. Nestling in a hollow between Llanrothal and the village of Welsh Newton, which despite it's name is in England, is a collection of old buildings called 'The Cwm'. The old walls of The Cwm hide the remains of a once secluded college of a catholic missionary of Jesuit priests set up in 1625. This remote and isolated community became known as the College of St Francis Xavier. The area is densely wooded and many of the lanes are still mere stony tracks, familiar even now only to those who live here. It was then an ideal place for persecuted catholics on either side of the border to meet in secret.

The true name for Jesuits, is the 'Society of Jesus'. They were formed in Rome in 1540 to preach the teachings of the catholic faith throughout the world. In the mid seventeenth century, anti-catholic feeling was running high in England and Wales and growing hatred and suspicion eventually came to a head in 1678. Titus Oates, himself a disgruntled catholic, was thrown out of a college and as a result developed a hatred of Jesuits. He collected evidence against his former colleagues which was pure fiction and set out to persuade the government to defend the protestant nation against a papist overthrowing. Oates kick-started a period of plots and sub plots in an attempt to persecute priests, in particular Jesuit priests, out of existence. The Monnow valley had been an area known as a catholic stronghold since the days of Elizabeth I, and the Somersets of Raglan castle in Gwent and the Vaughans of Courtfield near Ross on Wye, were both staunch catholic families and flag bearers for their faith. The Somersets in particular sheltered priests and protected local catholics up until after the Civil War when they lost their land and did not return to Raglan. That was a blow to the catholic cause. Fuelled by Oates's revolution, the local chief protagonists against them, John Arnold of Llanvihangel Crucorney in Monmouthshire, and John Scudamore of Kentchurch Court in Herefordshire mounted their own crusade, and in December 1678 they raided The Cwm but found it deserted. The Father Superior at the time was David Lewis and anticipating an attack on the college he had ordered an evacuation. There had been seven resident priests at The Cwm up until that time but soon four of them would die as a direct result of Oates' plot. In August the following year, Father Lewis himself was captured at Llantarnum near Cwmbran as he was about to say mass and father Philip Evans was detained while on a mission at Cowbridge in Glamorgan in December. Both were eventually tried and executed. Two more priests who had evacuated The Cwm died while trying to avoid capture. Altold, throughout England and Wales, thirty five priests were killed as a result of Titus Oates' fabrications. The raid on The Cwm ended the Jesuit college there, but it did survive as a low key mission for another one hundred years.

The theme of catholic persecution continues a mile or so up the road at Welsh Newton. In the churchyard of this unpretentious little place is a simple gravestone with the message *'J.K, Dyed the 22 August Anno Do. 1679'*. This is the final resting place of Father John Kemble who was hung, drawn, and quartered at Hereford at the age of eighty merely for practicing his faith. He was the last of the Forty English Martyrs, all of whom continue to be venerated by catholics today. Kemble was a local man born near St Weonards just five miles from here in 1600, and for most of his long life exercised his office in private at nearby Pembridge castle, the home of a member of his own family. At the same time as the move on The Cwm, father Kemble was visiting the college and he, too, was arrested, surely a classic case of being in the wrong place at the wrong time. The result of his subsequent trial was a forgone conclusion. After his vicious death, a follower succeeded in secreting one of father Kemble's hands, and the relic is still preserved in a casket in St Francis Xavier's church on Broad street in Hereford. It is said that, while awaiting his execution, father Kemble asked for time to complete his prayers and smoke a last pipe of tobacco. There is even now an old Herefordshire saying of calling one last pipe (of the day), a Kemble pipe. More than a hundred years later, his illustrious actress descendant, Sarah Siddons, donated twenty pounds per annum during her lifetime towards the maintenance of his grave here at Welsh Newton. She is reported to have said of him once, *'I am prouder of his name and race than if within our veins there flowed the blood of twenty kings'.* John Kemble was beatified in December 1929 and finally canonized as a saint in October 1970.

There have been a number of documented stories of miracles connected with the Kemble relic in Hereford. In 1990, Canon William O'Connor lay dying of leukaemia and was close to death. The saint's preserved hand was laid on him in a last desperate hope of a healing. Shortly afterwards he recovered and regained sufficient strength to take a trip to Lourdes in thanksgiving for his deliverance. Although he died a year later, medical experts could not explain the causes even of the short term recovery. An article in *You* magazine in September 1995 told the story of father Christopher Jenkins who lay in a hospital bed, comatose after a massive stroke. As he hadn't been expected to recover he was given the last rites. A close friend, father Anthony Tumelty, was visiting and unbeknown to the hospital staff he carried the relic with him which he placed on his friends head. The hitherto very ill priest opened his eyes and the doctors recorded a heart and pulse rate as normal. Medical experts could only speculate on the causes of both these recoveries.

Overnight there had been a sprinkling of late spring snow, and as I climbed away from Welsh Newton through Newton Wood, the sun broke through providing me with a sparkling view back down the Monnow valley. On reaching the top of the wood I stopped to look at the tiny isolated church of St Faith looking for all the world like a concrete garage and surely one of the smallest and oddest churches anywhere. The views to the east now were of the southern Herefordshire plain and the Malvern hills beyond. The lane along which I was walking gave way to a track following the edge of Hazel Wood. Here the snowfall of the previous night had been heavier and hidden forest debris crunched under my feet. Reaching open fields, the silence that had accompanied me for most of the day since leaving Skenfrith was now rudely broken by the roar of traffic speeding towards Ross on Wye along the A40 below me. The footpath followed the field hedge downhill through the ancient hamlet of Lewstone, passing an old mill with a restored water wheel, and finally into the village of Whitchurch sitting impossibly astride the dual carriageway.

Whitchurch is about half way between Monmouth and Ross-on-Wye and is unfortunate in that it is now split in two by the busy A40. I reached the village from the west, along a narrow hill road which descends to the old crossroads, the centre of the village before the A40 dual carriageway was constructed. Next to the Crown Inn is a collection of fine Georgian buildings, which once formed an asylum. One of them is now The Portland Guest House, run by John and Jenny Jarvis and was where I would stay the night. Standing aloof by the old road is a detached clock tower constructed in 1867 by the sole surviving sister of the Panter family in memory of her brothers and sisters. The tower was erected originally in the grounds of 'Wayside', the house in the village where the Panters lived and according to a relative who still lives nearby, was there for no other reason than to commemorate family love and unity. When the house was sold in 1968 the tower was handed over to the parish council. The oldest building in the village is The Old Court across the dual carriage way in east Whitchurch, built in 1570 and now a hotel. This grade II listed manor house was originally in the black and white timber construction of the day. It was enlarged and faced in stone by the Gwillim family, the owners of the house in the seventeenth century. Whitchurch is a far cry from Canada, but nevertheless it has strong links with that country through the descendants of the Gwillims. In 1759, Thomas Gwillim, fought alongside General Wolfe at the battle for Quebec. Later, whilst he was on active duty in Germany, Thomas's wife died giving birth to their daughter and as an everlasting burden on the poor child named her Elizabeth Posthuma Gwillim. Elizabeth eventually married John Graves Simcoe who was appointed Lieutenant Governor of Upper Canada which was eventually renamed Ontario. When Elizabeth and John returned to England they settled at Wolford near Honiton in Devon. They and their children are buried there in the family chapel, now owned by the Ontario Heritage Trust and designated Canadian territory. In the churchyard of the thirteenth century chapel of St Dubricius in east Whitchurch, is the Gwillim family burial enclosure, sadly forlorn and neglected when I first saw it in 2002. On a second visit more than two years later, I discovered an attempt had been made at restoration which strangely didn't appear to have matched too well with existing stonework. Also in the churchyard is a North American tulip tree, thought to be over three hundred years old.

Beyond the church the river Wye forms many loops as it makes its torturous way through steep valleys beyond the Herefordshire border towards Monmouth and on past the picturesque ruin of Tintern Abbey to join the river Severn and the Bristol Channel. I wanted to pick up the Wye Valley Walk footpath as it entered Herefordshire from Monmouthshire and this required a challenging hike over the most significant of local hills, one called The Doward, known to have been a prehistoric sanctuary for ancient beasts and early man. There was no shortage of tracks and provided I was heading in the general direction of the river loop on the far side of hill, I knew I would not be far off target. The Doward is an area of outstanding natural beauty and is really two hills, Little Doward and Great Doward. Both are honeycombed with caves and wells, and would have been an ideal place for early settlers, as indeed it was. There is evidence that man may have been living here for thirty thousand years! One man who died here was the early British chief Vortigern who had his base at the hilltop fort on Little Doward, which is where he made his last stand against the Anglo-Saxons. At the well-visited King Arthur's Cave, excavations over several hundred years have produced relics of prehistoric occupation, although there is little evidence that King Arthur was one of them. From the middle ages until the eighteenth century, The Doward proved to be an area where iron ore could be extracted economically and a substantial iron industry was developed here. After the introduction of coke-fired furnaces to the heavy industrial areas of Britain, The Doward's iron ore lost its value and went into decline. However, quarrying and lime production remained important activities until the 1950s. Now all is quiet. The lime kilns are gradually disappearing into the undergrowth and the quarries too, are being reclaimed by nature. Man is still settling here amongst the trees and very narrow lanes. Driving a vehicle of any size on the Doward is difficult. I noticed, however, that many people who live there had (sensibly) at least one small car on their drives.

The Wye Valley Walk enters Herefordshire for the first time near a grand looking nineteenth century mansion known as Wyastone Leys on the southern flank of Little Doward. It was built in 1818 and rebuilt in 1861 for James Murray Bannerman, a lawyer of the Inner Temple, Deputy Lieutenant of Hereford and Monmouth and in 1879 appointed High Sheriff. He was related to the Bannermans of Aberdeenshire who are said to have benefited greatly from the infamous highland clearances. Wyastone Leys and the estate is now owned by The Nimbus Foundation which was established to support the Arts, and allows the use of a purpose built concert hall within the grounds for budding young musicians. Curious to learn how a classical recording company chose such a spectacular site close to the river, I called Gerald Reynolds who runs the business and asked if I could call in. After the usual introductions had been made, we retired to a delightfully furnished room in the living quarters. Though most of the buildings are used for the business, Wyastone is also home for Gerald and his family. Over coffee, he explained the origins of the company.

Nimbus was founded in the 1970s by Count Numa Labinsky, a classical singer of some renown, who thought the records of the day were poor quality and decided he would make his own. His intention was to recreate on disc the presence and sounds similar to that experienced at a live performance. The Count joined with Gerald and his brother, Michael Reynolds, and together they formed the Nimbus Classical Recording Company and produced their first LP in Birmingham in 1977.

'The first recordings were OK,' Gerald told me, *'but we thought the sound quality would be enhanced by moving away from the city noises so we decided to look for a site in the country.*

On impulse, we brought our families down here for a weekend and thought somewhere around Monmouth would be a good place. It was while we were making enquiries, that we were invited to look at Wyastone Leys, which had only recently come on the market. Not knowing what to expect, we decided to take a look. As we drove down the winding drive, our reactions were instantaneous. The position of the house at the end of a deep combe, and the south facing front across the river meadow was ideal for our needs and the rest, as they say, is history.'

I can well imagine his feelings that day as he drove through the estate. The impression I got as I walked along the winding drive descending into the combe towards the house was that this was a special place. In 1982, Nimbus changed to recording on compact disc, a bold move at the time as the technology was still in its infancy. Nevertheless, the switch was to be emphatic and in 1984 the company developed its own laser mastering system and went into full production, the first recording company to do so in the UK.

'Because of the success we had with the new recording equipment, we started a manufacturing business on the site dedicated to making laser mastering equipment, and in 1992 we sold the CD production to concentrate on making the equipment.'

'At the time, it seemed like a good idea,' he said with a smile not exactly devoid of embarrassment, *'and it was, but then we wanted to get back to making high quality recordings that we knew we were good at. So we sold the recording equipment manufacturing business to a Swiss organization who agreed to keep the operation on site here at Wyastone.'* And why not, this is a magical spot, with a natural employee friendly environment. I can't imagine why anyone who had the necessary qualifications could decline the invitation to work down here.

Gerald's willingness not only to meet me and tell me more about Nimbus but also later to show me around the recording studios and the CD processing rooms didn't really surprise me if I'm honest. I would meet many more people along the way who would agree to discuss their private lives and businesses with me. Some people might think my style presumptuous if not impudent, but if you don't ask, you don't get, and I will be forever grateful to people like Gerald Reynolds for contributions to my story.

Flowing below the south wing of the house, the river Wye has travelled the best part of forty five miles from Hereford, a journey the crow would fly in fifteen. At this point, the footpath crosses the river into Gloucestershire and follows the old track bed of the Monmouth to Ross railway, which closed in 1964. The Biblins footbridge is no ordinary well-built sturdy affair but a narrow metal structure suspended on wires which can take no more than half a dozen average size people at any one time. A warning notice claims that running, jumping, or any excessive exertions other than a gentle walking movement on this bridge are not recommended. For those with a strong constitution the experience could be an exciting one, and a swiftly running river undoubtedly adds to the drama. The river here is often in flood in winter and at such times this bridge cannot be used at all. Indeed in a particularly wet spell during October 2000, it was partially submerged. Fortunately, for the feint hearted, amongst whom I number myself, the alternative is to stay on the Herefordshire side where there is a perfectly good footpath accompanying the river as it winds through a picturesque gorge below high cliffs. Before reaching Symonds Yat, the sound of rushing water heralds the rapids at New Weir, where canoeists test their skills in white water. This is the site of a forge where iron was manufactured from the seventeenth until the early nineteenth century.

> *'Steep, wooded hills close around us as we advance, within whose leafy glades nestle quaint old mining villages, where the good people have followed the same calling as in the days when Romans first exploited the rich coal seams.'*

Not far up stream, the river bank now makes a pretty picture of inns and tearooms along the waters edge, and white washed cottages peep from wooded hillsides. It's hard to imagine that these picturesque surroundings would once have been shrouded in great volumes of smoke belching from tall chimneys, while the gorge echoed to the noise of iron hammers powered by the river as it thundered over the weir. Beyond this point, there is an ancient hand ferry which has been punting travellers across the narrow stretch of water between the two halves of Symonds Yat for several hundred years.

> *'Our shadows lengthen before us as we descend to the ferry, and in floating across the full current, we catch a charming glimpse of this beautiful spot for the moon is up, and yet not nigh, and the glow of the setting sun still lingering upon the higher summits, whose warm tints are repeated in the clear stream beneath, fretted with golden splashes of the lights from the waterside.'*

The ferry crossing would be my route later, but for the time being, I wanted to explore the west bank of this fascinating place. As I lost sight of the river momentarily, I was horrified to hear the thump thump of loud music which was emanating from a large entertainment complex ahead of me. Beyond this aberration, a smiling straw boatered Edward Hayes stood by the entrance to his Amazing Hedge Puzzle and Butterfly Zoo, and explained to me why he believes Symonds Yat is an ideal place in which to relax and have a good time. *'It's an opportunity for those who don't usually stray beyond their TV sets to visit the countryside and enjoy it in a unique fashion,'* he told me. *'There's so much choice here.'*

Do folks really need a fair ground for their entertainment when they visit the countryside? I suggested impertinently, knowing he would protect his vested interest. Wouldn't they be happy just being by the river, or walking in these wonderful surroundings?

'Not everyone likes walking you know, especially kids and the older folk. Here, it's like being at the sea-side without the sea. There's nowhere like this in the whole of Herefordshire. You have to go down to the south Wales coast to find anything similar. Now, if you will excuse me,' he growled, raising his hat to me. *'I have my paying customers to attend to.'*

There was no way he would have agreed that Symonds Yat's uniqueness was not everyone's cup of tea, that there were many who would have tried it once and may never return, so I left him to his world of OAP outings and school parties and headed back to the river. I wondered as I left him if one day Edward Hayes would open a Chamber of Horrors to celebrate the infamous activities of one, Dr Hawley Harvey Crippen, who had apparently spent a holiday here some years before murdering his wife and attempting to flee to America with another woman.

On the east side of the river is the renowned Yat Rock, where a lofty viewing platform offers a spectacular sights towards Ross and attracts multitudes of visitors throughout the year. The star here though, during the lazy summer months, is the river itself as it glides effortlessly between the rocky pinnacles of the Seven Sisters on the west bank and dense wooded slopes of the Forest of Dean on the east. There is something about a river when the sun shines that human beings find so alluring, and the Wye here has all the spellbinding attributes of any. At Symonds Yat you can sail on it, row on it, look down on it, walk next to it for miles on either bank or just sit by it. However, I found the unsympathetic commercialization of this attractive place unnecessary and more than a little tacky, so I was more than anxious to move on.

I rejoined the river path immediately below the popular Yat Rock and the high bluffs known as Coldwell Rocks, until fifty years ago the haunt of peregrine falcons. High above me, the hordes of visitors on the viewing platform would be fighting for space but down here it was particularly peaceful and I had by now grown unaware of them. In 1980, excavations of cave sites among these ancient cliffs uncovered animal paintings and tools. Although in poor state, the paintings were the first examples of Paleolithic artwork to be discovered in Britain. I was now following the old Monmouth to Ross railway track bed but still on the Gloucestershire bank. Across the river on the Herefordshire side, hidden in the undergrowth of Coldwell Wood, is a monument commemorating a personal tragedy. It was erected in memory of fifteen year old John Whitehead Warre, who in 1804 while picnicking here, was drowned attempting to swim across the river. The unfortunate boy was a member of a famous vintage port exporting family and was on holiday from his home town of Oporto in Portugal.

Leaving behind the rocks and the day trippers in their eyrie, I strode across the river meadow in pleasant mid-day sunshine. For a mile or two, I remained in Gloucestershire, the boundary with Herefordshire being the river itself which I have to re-cross. On higher ground away from the river is the village of English Bicknor. Directly opposite on the Herefordshire side is Welsh Bicknor, a clear indication that the river was also the border between England with Wales in ancient times. English Bicknor is one of the ancient villages of Dean and once the site of a Norman castle. A short stretch of King Offa's great dyke passes close to its early twelfth century church, the origins of which make it older than the famous ruins at Tintern Abbey further down the valley. Between 1982 and 1985, as part of a nationwide project carried out by the Women's Institute, the tombstones in the churchyard were surveyed and several inscriptions were uncovered. Perhaps the most interesting find was the grave of 'Charles, a black servant'. What lay behind his story? A young boy taken from the hot jungles of his native land and eventually laid to rest in a Christian plot in a beautiful corner of England? Despite its rural cloak, the Forest of Dean has been a mining area since Roman times. When Edward 1 marched north in the fourteenth century to fight his Scottish wars he took with him twelve miners from this area. These men became the first Royal Engineers of the British Army and showed their skill in undermining the border defences at Berwick-on-Tweed. As a reward, the King gave the Dean miners the right to own their own workings *'henceforth without tax or hindrance'*, a privilege which still exists today.

At Lydrook, the meadow narrows and is finally channelled behind a huge red brick factory estate that was once a thriving paper mill. Remains of the Monmouth to Ross line emerges from the factory yard and launches itself across the river along twisted supports precariously resting on rusty steel pillars. The Wye Valley footpath has been attached to the old bridge to accompany the defunct track to Welsh Bicknor on the Herefordshire bank and I had to follow. From the thirteenth century, the manor of Welsh Bicknor belonged to the Montague family. It was then in Wales and didn't become part of Herefordshire until 1845. In August 1387, the infant Henry V was entrusted here into the care of Margaret Montague at an isolated farm above the river after his birth at Monmouth castle. Clinging to a wooded hillside next to a YHA Hostel is the abandoned church of St Margaret, said to have been so named in remembrance of Margaret Montague. Throughout their time, the Montagues were a treasonable lot and several lost their heads. In 1562, Elizabeth I lost patience with them and their manor was confiscated and sold to a John Gwillym. The following year Gwillym gave the isolated farmhouse, by now called Courtfield, as a wedding present to his daughter Sybil who had married a John Vaughan, a catholic, of Llangattock, near Abergavenny, and henceforth Courtfield became the stronghold of one of the great Roman Catholic dynasties.

Throughout the Reformation, Courtfield became a haven for fleeing monks and priests, but in spite of frequent visits from local mobs, all escaped capture. At that time, Richard Vaughan was branded a papist delinquent, and suffered endless fines and land confiscations. But he was aided by his neighbours, some of whom were protestant friends, who often warned of warrants against him. Vaughan stood firm, paid his fines, and protected his property as best he could. The family motto was always at the forefront of his mind: 'Duw-a-Digon' God is sufficient. Having established Courtfield as the senior Vaughan house to that of another branch of the family at Hergest Court near Kington, their influence from the lofty manor at Welsh Bicknor was more or less regional. Until, that is, the marriage in 1830 of John Francis Vaughan and Louise Elizabeth Rolls started one of the most remarkable dynasties in the history of the catholic church. 'Eliza' Vaughan was to become the mother of a cardinal, two bishops, three priests and five nuns. In her book 'Courtfield and the Vaughans', Mary Vaughan said of her: 'As she had received everything from God, she would give everything back to God'. Eliza herself was a convert to the catholic faith but took her religion very seriously and frequently looked after local sick people, particularly children. On 24 January 1853, Eliza died giving birth to her fourteenth child, John, who was to become her second bishop. The eldest son, Herbert, founded the St Joseph's Society for Foreign Missions at Mill Hill in north London while still a priest. The Society later became known as The Mill Hill Missionary Fathers. Its purpose was to train priests and laymen to spread the Gospel among the black people of Africa and America. In 1871 Herbert left for America with the first missionaries and immediately set about teaching the indigenous population about God. On his return the following year he was elected Bishop of Salford at the age of forty. At his first public appearance Bishop Vaughan was confronted with what was a common problem in next door Manchester at that time – drunkenness. Although he hated drunkenness, he told his audience that as he was partial to the occasional tipple himself, he would not condemn those who had not yet disciplined themselves against the effects of overindulgence.

Another of his tasks as bishop was to build the school that my two brothers and I eventually attended in the 1950s, St Bede's College in the Moss Side district of Manchester. He saw the college as a place where young boys could be educated by teacher-priests with a view to priming them for future priesthood. Though the influence of my tutors and classmates to follow the path to holiness was strong, for me the call of a commercial career was stronger, and I, and indeed my brothers too, must therefore be forever cast as some of the good bishop's failures. My family's loose connection with the Vaughans had in fact started even earlier. John Spencer Vaughan, the fourteenth and last of Eliza's children became rector of St Bede's in 1912, the year my father became a pupil there. Another of the bishop's brothers, Joseph, who had joined the Benedictines and revived their order in Scotland, ended his days at a mission in Chorlton-cum-Hardy, the oft mentioned-in-jest suburb of south Manchester which was, many years later, my place of birth.

In 1892, following the death of his great friend, Cardinal Manning, Bishop Vaughan was appointed Archbishop of Westminster. It was a measure of his renowned humility that he wrote to the Pope stating his unworthiness for the job and asking that another be chosen. His words only emphasized his suitability. Unlike Manning, and others before him, Herbert Vaughan was not an intellectual. He was singularly direct and spoke his mind often. Nor was he popular with his priests who were apparently afraid of him. But he was as humble as he was haughty, and he was destined to rise further and very quickly. By the following January 1893 he was a cardinal. His next great task was to build Westminster cathedral, the premier worshipping centre for catholics in England and Wales, and on 25th January 1895 the foundation stone was laid. Eight years later the building was ready enough for the first requiem mass. that of the founder himself. For at seventy one years of age and worn out by his many accomplishments, death had come peacefully on nineteenth January 1903. He was buried according to his wishes at Mill Hill.

Vaughans still occupy the estate at Courtfield, but the great house was sold in 1950 to the Mill Hill missionary fathers as a training college for lay missionaries, the engineers and construction workers who support the preaching fathers. At the time of writing this book the house is once again on the market, surplus to requirements, an indication that missionary work, lay or otherwise, is no longer an attractive vocation.

I followed the footpath alongside the Wye for a mile or so before Courtfield, predominantly Regency in style, came into view above me. I turned away from the river bank and climbed towards it along an ancient track which no doubt has served the occupants of Courtfield for centuries. The missionary college buildings which have stood next to the main house for fifty years have been empty for some time and looked derelict and forlorn. I had telephoned Father Charles Cammack, the caretaker priest, the day before on the off chance he would be free and thankfully he had agreed to meet me. Like most priests I've met he was a pleasant, mild mannered man and appeared not in the least concerned either about my motive for being there or for his own safety should I turn out to be a rogue on the make. *'You'd think being here alone, without anybody to disturb my routine, would make life simple'* he told me *'But I've been inundated with telephone calls all day for no special reason, and it is too late now to collect my Sunday paper from the village store. So if it's the house you're here for, we have all day to talk and tour around it.'*

We sat for a while in an extraordinary large kitchen, surrounded by its modern catering facilities to suit the needs of a large group of residents, all of it now redundant.

'Apart from the room that I sleep in, this kitchen is where it all ends,' he said sadly *'a requiem for a dedicated army of God, the last supper, call it what you will. I am here to switch the lights out, plain and simple.'*

At the time of my visit the sale of the house was indeed imminent and it seemed that the current head of the Vaughan family, Patrick, living nearby in the old Dower house, was on the point of retrieving his ancestral home. Father Cammack escorted me around the main ground floor rooms which had once been the living quarters of centuries of Vaughans. The house is a mixture of many alterations and extensions but the original farmhouse in which the sickly young Henry of Monmouth was raised remains intact as part of the main block. Still hung on the walls were portraits of a religious dynasty to rival few in English history, and I felt humble and proud of my once feeble association with at least one of them. A room known as The King's Room is traditionally accepted as the infant Henry's nursery and the royal cradle remained in that room for three hundred years until a government order put it up for auction. It is now at Kensington Palace in London.

This beautiful part of the Wye valley has been and still is largely ignored. A place where a future King grew up safe and secure, and a family of catholic bishops survived against all the odds to carry the gospel to the world. Rarely has such a tiny isolated place bequeathed so much influence.

Back on the track from the river I climbed behind the deserted college buildings and turned west across the hillside towards Coppet Hill. As the way ahead stretched out before me, I reflected on the story of an air crash here in 1942. The ill-fated aircraft, a Halifax bomber came down in flames killing eleven men on board. In war time, such accidents, terrible though they were, were not uncommon. Indeed, there had been a similar tragedy just a month before when a Wellington bomber hit a tree in the churchyard at Llangrove, barely five miles from the Courtfield estate. But the destruction of the Halifax here was not just another tragic loss. This particular aircraft had been no ordinary bomber, but a flying laboratory, testing equipment vital to the war effort both against land and U-boat targets. The local rescue services who went to the scene realized they were dealing with something unusual, and although news of the crash was sent to Winston Churchill, few others were given details of the aircraft's mission. Among those who perished was Alan Dower Blumlein, a little known thirty-nine year old electrical engineer who was leading the experiment. Blumlein's work was shrouded in secrecy and following his untimely death, no obituary appeared and no tribute was given.

In 1973, a local reporter working for The Ross Gazette received a letter at the newspaper's office from a researcher in Watford requesting eyewitnesses to this long forgotten event. The resulting replies prompted the reporter to follow the story up. During the bombing campaigns over Germany in 1940 and 1941, without a practical system for locating a target, most bombs were falling literally miles from their intended targets. What was needed was a system that could locate and detect a target from the air, regardless of weather conditions, and accurate enough to allow a bomber to carry out its mission. Blumlein realised that by incorporating the basis of a binaural sound system into an aircraft sound detector, a much more accurate fix on targets could be obtained. It was this system that Blumlein was trying out when his aircraft hit the hillside at Courtfield. However, in spite of the tragic circumstances, the equipment known as H2S was a stunning success and within months was to give the Allied Air Forces complete mastery of the skies.

For many years, various people promised a biography of Blumlein, but none was forthcoming. This extraordinary engineer would have been forgotten completely, were it not for the dedication and continual hard work of those who knew him and who were determined to bring his name out of obscurity and to the forefront of public attention. For Alan Dower Blumlein's wartime work with binary sound led directly to the development of our modern stereo sound system and was destined to become one the most important advances in audio engineering of the twentieth century.

It had begun to rain hard. Deep thoughts had taken me to another time and it was the sudden sensation of dampness that brought me back to my world. I donned my waterproofs and strode on past old sand pits and ancient lime kilns. Coppett Hill rises gently northwards along a ridge to a point two hundred metres above the village of Goodrich. It is a haven for a rich variety of flora and fauna. Fallow deer roam through the dense woods and in spring, delicate grassland flowers grow in profusion. The west facing flank of Coppett is common land and people have been wandering its many footpaths for centuries enjoying stunning views across the Wye valley and beyond, as I did now. Below me, a confused river headed first northwards from Symonds Yat gorge before looping south again past a curious, single, ancient, fluted standing-stone called Queen's Stone, and on to

An overgrown corner of Goodrich Castle captured by Timmins in 1892.

Monmouth. Back in 1985, the common came up for sale and thanks to the commitment of seventy goodly Goodrich folk, The Coppett Hill Common Trust was formed to buy the land. As a result of their continuing voluntary efforts, footpaths have been re-instated and access to this wonderful place preserved for the public.

Goodrich could be described as three villages sitting astride the B4229. The first, a collection of cottages gripping the western flanks of Coppett Hill, another, on the opposite hillside surrounding St Giles's church with its conspicuous tall spire, and a third known as Cruse, the area around the village hall and public house. The whole is an attractive combination. The fourteenth century church was built by Sir Richard Talbot, who was also responsible for creating a priory at Flanesford in the same parish. Its most famous vicar was Thomas Swift who served here in 1628 and was the grandfather of Johnathan Swift, Dean of St Patrick's Cathedral in Dublin from 1713, but better known as the author of *Gulliver's Travels*. The interior of the church is relatively plain but has a few interesting features. A stone tomb decorated with arched columns but bare of any dedication is presumed to be that of the church's founder and was placed here when the chapel at Flanesford Priory was destroyed during the dissolution. There is also an enormous wooden chest with carved panels made from the remains of the pulpit of St James Church in Piccadilly in London rescued from the great fire in 1666. Oak linenfold panelling, a survivor from Goodrich Court demolished in 1950, covers the walls of the aisles and vestry. In the churchyard are the tombs of Samuel Rush Meyrick who built Goodrich Court, Joshua Cristall who established painting with watercolours as an art form in the nineteenth century, and Lt.Col. Basil Jackson, who served on the quartermaster general's staff at Waterloo. Most curious of all the churchyard monuments is the one commemorating three members of the Herbert family. Their monument is in the form of a huge boulder some twelve feet long and four feet high, which was dragged from a quarry on the Doward hill to be erected here according to the wishes of the first Herbert, a clergyman of the parish. Exactly how or why he warranted such a memorial, or the effort required to get it here, is not known.

One of the many beautiful houses in Goodrich, Granton Court, was the home for almost twenty years of Joshua Cristall. Influenced by William Cobbett's descriptions of country life in *Rural Rides*, much to the surprise of his contemporaries, Cristall moved to Herefordshire in 1823 when at the pinnacle of his career. Here he painted local scenes and portraits of peasants for his London clients. However, like David Cox in Hereford, being so far away from his market caused him to struggle to maintain his influence as a leading artist, and in 1841, following his wife's death, he returned to London. Despite its reputation for beauty, the Wye Valley has never produced any artists who recorded the landscape in a way Constable did in Suffolk. Instead the area has relied on visiting painters who fell in love with it, stayed for a short time but then moved on. Joshua Cristall was one such visitor. However, together with Cox, Joseph Murray Ince, a Cox protégé at Presteigne in the far north-west of the county, and John Scarlett Davis at Leominster, they established Herefordshire as the place where watercolour was born.

Goodrich has had at least two other residences of major significance but sadly only one survives. Goodrich Castle is a majestic, twelfth century, Norman ruin. It was for long periods home to the Talbots, Earls of Shrewsbury, and is now under the protection of English Heritage. It is typically castle shaped – square with a round tower at each corner and surrounded by a dry moat which clearly shows the bedrock on which it was built. Within its walls rises a massive Saxon keep, the most ancient part of the castle, whose grey walls are pierced by rounded arched windows overlooking the inner court. The castle survived practically untested until the Civil War when its walls were breached in 1646 by a Parliamentarian force under the command of Colonel John Birch. Timmins described the external condition of the castle as he saw it in 1891 thus:

> *Around and within the moat, a luxuriant growth of trees and shrubs veils the old walls in a mantle of delicate green foliage; while the ruined bastions which once frowned upon the drawbridge are now wreathed in masses of dark ivy*

However, it is to Goodrich Court, built in 1831 for Sir Samuel Meyrick, a leading antiquarian, that my attention was drawn. For one hundred years both castle and court stood practically side by side on rocky heights overlooking the river. The court was designed by Edward Blore, one of the great gothic revivalists of his day. This red sandstone edifice was topped with a series of pinnacles and gables culminating in a castle like keep, and was a deliberate attempt at mockery. A huge towered gatehouse formed the entrance to the estate, and happily still survives alongside the present A40. The finished article was apparently as admired for its magnificent grandeur as much as it was castigated for being a copy of Goodrich Castle itself. Sir Samuel Meyrick was recognized in his day as the most learned in matters of heraldry and weapons of warfare, and his accumulation of armoury was the largest private collection ever formed in England. Initially, Meyrick, who considered himself of Welsh descent, wanted a Welsh castle to house his collection and looked at several likely sites in Powys and in Pembrokeshire. After being refused his first choices he turned his attention to the Wye valley and was immediately attracted to the ruined castle at Goodrich perched on the rocky escarpments overlooking an ancient river crossing. The awesome scene of Meyrick's turreted eerie from the river would have provided the first 'picturesque' view of that new occupation of the Victorian rich, the 'Wye tour', and he saw his armoury collection as an additional ingredient. The fact that Goodrich was in the old Welsh kingdom of Archenfield increased Meyrick's attraction for the spot. Little wonder then that when he decided on Goodrich as a place in which to live, he first considered the old castle itself as the most likely choice. However, like his Welsh castle bids his offer to buy Goodrich Castle was summarily dismissed, so he made the decision to build his own next door. On completion, Goodrich Court became visually dominant and one wonders how it would have looked now twinned with the romantic ruin of the older castle had the court survived.

The premature demise of Goodrich Court lies in the tragic circumstances affecting family succession, which was hampered by early

Goodrich Court. This magnificent pile was demolished in 1950 and the rubble unceremoniously pushed over a nearby cliff.

deaths and childless male heirs. Sir Samuel's only son died suddenly in February 1837, and in spite of a futile attempt to prepare the unsuitable son of his cook as his heir, he eventually willed his estate to a second cousin, Augustus Meyrick, a career soldier, who as it turned out had only a minimal interest in living at Goodrich. After Samuel's death in 1848, as is often the nature of inheritors, and as soon as he moved in, Augustus set about the un-gothicing of Blore's original masterpiece. Then towards the end of the nineteenth century, the estate came into the hands of Harold Moffat, who having no reason to usurp the customary activities of change, began more alterations which were so drastic as to render the neighbouring castle unique once more. Harold's son Cecil, who would have inherited the court died, childless, in 1916 and so the estate descended to the eldest daughter, Dorothy. However, she had married into the Trafford family of Hill Court on the other side of the river some years before and presumably her husband preferred that they remain there because from then on Goodrich Court became superfluous to their requirements. Then again, in yet another tragic twist, Dorothy's eldest son was killed in a car crash in 1933, once again contributing to the never ending problem of what to do with the court. Dorothy's remaining children, Cecily, Anne, and John, none of whom ever married, considered the court too large for their needs and declined to live there. The final ironic twist in a bizarre catalogue of unforeseen circumstances and atrocious bad luck.

The last uses of Meyrick's millstone were firstly as a convalescence home for Australian soldiers after the first world war, and finally as Felsted (of Essex) School which had transferred there during the second world war and stayed until 1945. After that, the court remained unsold and neglected until Dorothy said it should come down. The sad end came in 1950 when, after furniture and fittings had been auctioned and dispersed, Goodrich Court was demolished, and the unsaleable remains pushed over the cliffs onto the river bank below.

In June 2002, I asked the then owners of a bungalow built where the court once stood and in which Cecily and Anne spent their final days, if I could look around the formal gardens which still remain and continue to bloom. The sumptuous iron gates commissioned by Harold Moffat during his ownership of the court to separate the gardens from the forecourt were removed before demolition and now form part of the railings outside the College of Arms in Queen Victoria Street in London, but a delightful stone summer house is still intact in a corner of the gardens and is now hired out for holiday occupation. Nothing at all remains of the court itself. Trees and undergrowth have reclaimed where once the turreted towers of a majestic medieval style pile rose in defiance of a genuine ruin on the opposite headland. When he finally moved into the court, Samuel Meyrick could not have known that the heraldic world he had created would be broken up within forty years, that it would be the start and the end of a fantasy. A folly it might have been then, but what a majestic treasure Goodrich Court, had it been saved, would now be for Herefordshire. As I stood on the cliff edge peering down at the overgrown mounds of broken stones, I reflected mournfully on the final ignominious act of demolition and decided to take the river path in an unscheduled detour to locate the spot below where the last of Goodrich Court had ended up. The hump of additional headland that was created by the dumping of tons of debris was unmistakable, and even fifty years of growth could not hide the occasional tell-tale fragment of red stone.

Retracing my steps to the village, I passed a hidden section of the old the ferry road, long unused but still surviving in places as a farm track. It was while crossing the river at the end of this track that Henry Bolingbroke learned of the birth of his son, the future Henry V, at Monmouth. The King was apparently so overcome with joy, he granted the income from the ferry, then under ownership of the crown, to the ferryman in perpetuity. Walking in the opposite direction, Timmins remarked about the ferry

> *Carriage folk must needs follow the road which crosses the Wye at Kerne Bridge, but the pedestrian has the alternative of a delightful approach to Goodrich by taking the lane by Walford church and striking across the meadows to a ferry. Thus the river crossed, we ascend a steep path which affords pretty views of the wooded slopes overtopped by the battlements of Goodrich Court, a noble castellated mansion where the celebrated Meyrick collection of armour was formerly deposited.*

The end of the ferry path in Goodrich is marked by a strange little house of great age, the origin of which is unknown but it could have been used as a place of rest for travellers using the ferry. This weary traveller would be staying the night at Ye Hostelrie, the curious looking village inn which Sir Samuel Meyrick bought in 1845 and to which he added Gothic turrets to mirror those of his Court down the road.

The road from Goodrich drops down to the flood-plain near the river bridge at Kerne where the remains of Richard Talbot's fourteenth century Flanesford priory continue to be chopped and changed to accommodate successive owners' whims. After the dissolution of the monasteries in 1537, the priory buildings were gradually adapted into a farm. The present owner is currently refurbishing the monk's old refrectory for holiday let. Beyond Kerne Bridge and the B4234, my path ascends the western wooded flanks of Leys Hill. Below, the flood-plain sweeps north-west following yet another loop in the Wye. The leafy footpath zigzags around the hillside before dropping off Howle Hill. A little way along a quiet lane is Cobrey Park, a Georgian country house, which in 1780 was the home of a Quaker family called Trusted. Curiously, one unfortunate son of theirs was given the name Ime Trusted. The pressure of carrying that burden must have been considerable for, in later life, the poor fellow was often in trouble for non-payment of tithes and rates!

A short distance beyond Cobrey Park an old unclassified toll road, once used by hauliers of coal and timber from the Forest of Dean to Ross and now barely more than a track in places, threads its way between Chase Wood and Penyard Hill. Geologically, the wooded hills of Chase and Penyard are actually part of the Forest of Dean but they are cut off by the deep valley which runs from the B4234 Walford road to the A40 close to the hamlet of Weston-under-Penyard. The present water course running through this valley is the tiny Castle Brook but this could hardly have cut such a large swathe through these hills. The explanation seems to be that before the Saxons settled at Ross, the great Wye had taken another route through this area and it is almost certain that this valley was created by the river as it looped from Ross to a point almost back on itself at Walford. My way ahead would now follow that original loop through Chase Wood followed by an arduous climb to an Iron Age hill fort built by the powerful ancient Silures people more than two thousand years ago, its ramparts still visible but overgrown. This ancient camp must have been an important vantage point for them as it commanded an imposing position overlooking the river and helped to protect their mining activities in the Forest of Dean.

My first close-up site of Ross came as I emerged from the tree covered hill fort which looms over the town. The path drops steeply past part half timbered sixteenth century Alton Court, now the headquarters of the PGL Group, an international business providing adventure holidays for children. Ross is an interesting little town which seems not to have capitalized on its wonderful picturesque position high above the river. The Victorian Wye Tours brought prosperity for a while, but the by-pass now connecting the M50 motorway with the A40 dual carriage way makes it a lot easier for the modern traveller from Birmingham and the midlands to continue to the resorts of south Wales without so much as a glance at the splendid view of the town across the river plain. I had already decided to drop anchor here for a couple of days to rest and discover what it had to offer.

> *'Wilton Bridge, with its massively constructed arches. Boldly projecting cutwaters, and quaint sundial, is built of the warm coloure stone of the district, which mellowed by the softening hand of time during some three centuries, forms a fascinating subject alike to artists and amateurs. Some pretty peeps, too, are obtained from hearabouts of the old town of Ross climbing steeply up the hill crowned by the tall church spire, and reflected in the clear waters of 'devious Vaga'.'*

The popular view of Ross-on-Wye, the one portrayed on every tourist brochure of the place, is of a quaintish town perched on a rocky east bank prominence overlooking the river, the tall spire of St Mary's Church and the distinctive white-washed façade of the Royal Hotel standing proud. It is the best view because the town doesn't quite live up to the promise. There are some fine buildings in its many narrow streets, but apart from the old market hall, a rare red sandstone creation of master carpenter John Abell in 1660, the centre lacks charm and can look a little drab in the wrong light. The main entry point to the town is from the river across Wilton Bridge, an impressive sixteenth century six arched gothic structure, but now partly modernised to cater for twenty first century traffic. There has probably been a river crossing here since pre-Roman times. It was protected by Wilton Castle, originally a motte and bailey built in the twelfth century, and later rebuilt in stone but by the fifteenth century it was no longer in use. A house was eventually incorporated into the remains of the structure and although much altered there is still a residence among the ruins. When I was there in June 2002, the main structure of the castle was in a poor state of repair and overgrown.

There is some argument over the origins of the name 'Ross'. One interpretation is it originates with the Welsh 'rhos' meaning a 'moor' or 'heath'. This is entirely feasible because the town grew up on the river plain and only later expansion forced it uphill to where the centre now is. As already mentioned, the Wye used to flow north of the present day town, eastward around Penyard Park, west again between Chase Wood and Howle Hill, before rejoining its present course near Walford, thus, if it had held that course, putting Ross on the west bank. The Saxons though probably settled by the crossing at Wilton. This was wild-west country, the border lands separating the outer limits of the Roman Empire from the Welsh kingdom of Ergyng, later known as Archenfield, a name which lingers on as a district of present day Ross. These names apparently meant 'The land of the hedgehog', some say due to the inhabitants being a prickly lot who didn't take kindly to strangers! It is perhaps not surprising that the hedgehog has been used down the centuries on local family crests and coats of arms, and carvings of the spiky creature can be found scattered throughout the lofty St Mary's church.

After the Normans had established themselves here in the eleventhth century, nothing much was heard of the town until the middle of eighteenth century when the Rector, John Egerton, took a boat trip down the river. He enjoyed the experience so much he told his friends that they, too, should get out more, and he was forever after held responsible for kick starting tourism in the area. A few years later, the Reverend William Gilpin, an early exponent of the 'Picturesque' ideals, began taking walking tours in the English countryside and recorded his trips with sketches. He presented the countryside in an exciting new way and the Victorian audience was captivated by his images. Encouraged by his friends, Gilpin published an account of his tour along the Wye to south Wales in 1782. Ross was at first slow or unable to capitalize on its unique position, and when the radical reformer William Cobbett arrived on his *Rural Rides*, he could give it no more praise than a 'plain country town'. Before him, Daniel Defoe on his *Tour through the Whole Island of Great Britain* had said likewise of it, and later Lord Alfred Tennyson apparently declined to say anything about it at all. In spite of its apparent lack of attraction, Ross became a favourite destination for Charles Dickens who had a regular booking at The Royal Hotel, and Nelson and Lady Hamilton are said to have stayed at Merton House allegedly while on a visit to the Forest of Dean timber hunting for his war ship building programme. Samuel Taylor Coleridge stayed for a while at the Kings Arms, which had previously been, for over seventy years, the home of the town's most famous citizen John Kyrle, and in which Alexander Pope penned his lasting memorial to Kyrle as the 'Man of Ross'. Yet it wasn't until 1931 that Ross got the suffix 'on Wye' added. Nowadays, a modern day Wye tour can no longer be taken by boat, and the A40 by-passes the town at Wilton to become the M50 Motorway to the Midlands. Isolated Ross struggles on, trying desperately to fill its hotels and guest houses, and relying once again on the name of one manto come to its aid, and whose influence on the town is graphically displayed in the upper room of the market hall.

> *'A stroll through the clean and well kept streets reveals at every turn the name of John Kyrle, the 'Man of Ross' as he is fondly termed by the inhabitants, the bright particular star of their firmament who has been immortalized of late years by the philanthropic society whose kindly work is performed under the aegis of his name.'*

John Kyrle was a local man and inherited a large timber framed house next to the old market hall in the centre of the town in 1650. Although he studied law at Oxford, he did not qualify as a lawyer. Nevertheless, he returned to Ross to act out the part on behalf of the wronged and the destitute in order to settle local disputes. He provided food for the poor, medicine for the sick, and spent most of his long life being a public spirited servant and making the place generally good to live in. Probably his major contribution to the development of the town was the introduction of a water supply which he largely financed. In his later years he took up gardening, and when not engaged with his own estate, would offer his horticultural services to his neighbours. When at rest, he could be seen in the local alehouses enjoying a pint and a pipe. He was a great supporter of the King and his loyalty to the monarchy moved him to erect a curious medallion on the market hall wall directly opposite his bedroom window commemorating his allegiance to Charles II. In 1696 he acquired a plot of land close to St Mary's church high above the river and surrounding countryside. He named it The Prospect and intended it to be used by the people of the town for recreation. When he died in 1724 at the great age of eighty-seven, the towns folk turned out en masse to pay their respects to him. Today, Kyrle's name appears throughout the town and his crest, not surprisingly a hedgehog, is the town's emblem.

The old book shop is still in business in Ross

There has never been a strong industrial presence in Ross. The town's real trade took place in the market hall and its many inns and shops, and still does. The railway came and went without making much of an impression, and in 1865 the Alton Court brewery was built in Station street. It ran into financial difficulties in the 1950s, was taken over by Stroud Brewery and then closed down. At least the wonderful old maltings building remains, albeit as a supermarket, and is perhaps the most striking modern building in the town. A rather less pleasing edifice is the strangely named Larraperz Community Centre, though it has a fascinating history of social endeavour and prolonged determination. In 1921, a group of young men banded together for no other purpose than to have a jolly good time. They worked hard, drank hard, and made music. They called themselves The Larruperz, an odd choice really as the word 'larrup' means 'thrash'. These men were not hooligans though, but a bunch of chaps who had a great sense of fun and enjoyed each others company and remained friends all their lives. After years of 'larruping' around, they decided to use their mixed musical talents to raise money for local charities. The poor children of the town were an early beneficiary when a scheme to provide them with new shoes was begun. In 1932, Ross acquired a new motor ambulance largely due to the Larruperz's enterprise and efforts. The idea to raise funds for a public hall came in 1936 to coincide with the Coronation of King George VI. A site was originally purchased overlooking the river on the west side of town which the boys had helped to clear in their after work hours but the war intervened and funds began to dry up. There was no further progress on the hall until a breakthrough came in 1985 when the Grammar School on the east side closed following a revision of Ross's educational needs and the buildings were offered for community use. The grand opening took place on 22 June 1990, fifty five years after the original plans were put forward. The Larruperz boys may have gone but the adoption of their name ensures they will never be forgotten.

I lodged for a few nights at Linden House, a three storey town house built for a Gloucester cutler in 1680 next to the church and run by Patrick O'Reilly with his wife Clare. The couple had moved in twenty years before when Ross was still on the tourist map and they were nearly always full. The business now is steady, they told me, but there are fewer tourists, rather a mixture of business people and the occasional visitor passing through. There had been just one other room booked that night.

'The problem with our little town is that it needs to smarten up a bit', Patrick told me as he stared gloomily out of the window. *'The councillors keep telling us there are no funds available for such things. I'm not sure they're trying hard enough, and that negativity seems to be washing*

off on some of us. If you visit our farmers' market for instance, you would expect to be greeted with a smile and perhaps a laugh or two. Instead some of the stall keepers just seem to stand around unenthusiastically waiting for someone to buy something. There isn't the bounce there used to be. Unlike the French who come over one day each year to set up their stalls, they really do try and it's pleasure to have them here.'

My room overlooked the churchyard and prominent in my view was a stone cross, erected to mark the burial pit of three hundred and fifteen victims of a plague in 1637.

> *'Resuming our stroll, some pretty 'bits' attract the eye as we wander through the steep narrow streets. Here overlooking the churchyard with its ancient pillar recording the time when Ross was stricken by the plague stands a row of modest almshouses built by the Rudhalls, whose monuments in the church well repay a visit.'*

The Parish Church of St Mary the Virgin stands in a commanding position on the highest point of the town. It has been the centre of Christian worship here for over seven hundred years and is one of the largest churches in Herefordshire. The tall spire, its most notable feature, can be seen from miles around and is immediately recognizable on any photograph taken to promote the town's tourism. John Kryle is buried in prime position in the chancel and there is a memorial to him on the wall close to his tomb. Fine though that is, it does not compare to the spectacular collection of alabaster monuments to the influential Rudhall family elsewhere in the church. Their fine timber framed mansion still stands in a deep valley just outside the town and I hoped to visit it later. Visitors to the church in the nineteenth century would have been surprised to find trees growing in the North transept, they were the suckers of elms planted outside which had forced their way through the stonework. They died during restoration work in 1870 but the stumps remained until they were finally removed in 1953. The most significant tombstone in the churchyard is that of a Walter Scott. In spite of its small size in the eighteenth and nineteenth century, Ross was not short of public benefactors. The Ross born Scott made a large fortune in London and eventually returned to live in Ross. With no family to leave his fortune to, he set about restoring the school where he had received his education. Scott bequeathed seven thousand pounds for a new school building, clothing and education for thirty boys and girls at the Blue Coat School on Old Gloucester Road. Founded in 1709 it unfortunately ran into trouble and closed after a short time.

Behind the church is a large cemetery in which, for centuries, the dead of Ross have been laid to rest, often on top of each other. In a quiet spot overlooking the river, two tablets lie side by side, one inscribed: 'All the way to heaven is heaven', the other: 'All of it a kiss.' These two epitaphs comprise a single quotation and were taken from *Turtle Moon*, a novel by Alice Hoffman. The novel was a favourite of Margaret Potter, wife of the playwright and novelist Dennis Potter. They, tragically, died within ten days of each other and their ashes are interred beneath the tablets.

Dennis Potter was born the son of a miner at Berry Hill in the Forest of Dean, less than ten miles away, but lived with Margaret and their three children at Morecambe Lodge, a roomy Victorian house in Ross, from 1967 until their deaths in 1994. Among Dennis's most famous plays, all shown on BBC television, were *Blue Remembered Hills, Pennies from Heaven*, and *The Singing Detective*. In spite of regular offers, he refused a biography – he always said that his plays, some set in the Forest itself, were his life story anyway. Throughout his life, Potter was plagued by ill-health and suffered years of pain and discomfort from a virulent form of psoriasis, a chronic, recurring, disease of the skin. On top of that he had severe arthritis in his hands which for someone whose career was entirely based on work with a pen, must have been damned inconvenient to say the least. Both he and Margaret were heavy smokers and the habit may have taken its toll in a savage fashion when first Margaret then Dennis was diagnosed with incurable cancers. This was the cruellest of fates, not only for Margaret and Dennis, but also for their three children who were about to lose both parents at virtually the same time. Dennis's last play, *Cold Lazarus*, written after his final illness was confirmed, was the story of his own death. Margaret died on 27 May and Dennis on 7 June, 1994. In life they had been emotionally close, in spite of Dennis being away from the family for long periods. There was talk of Dennis's affairs but in the end he always came home.

Sharing the skyline with St Mary's spire is The Royal Hotel, the creation of James Barrett in 1837 and built on the site of a twelfth century bishop's palace. During the construction of a new road into the town from the river bridge at Wilton, Barrett used some of the surplus sandstone cut away from the west facing cliffs below his hotel to build mock gothic walls and a round gazebo tower complete with arrow slits and oriels, the nearest the town ever got to having a proper castle. Even before the completion of the Royal, Barrett had been accused of encroaching on the land forming part of The Prospect, Kyrle's gift to the people and considered off limits for any developer. However, it was not known at the time that Barrett had secretly bought the lease on it. On 12 July, 1869, tired of being prevented from practicing their recreation as Kyrle had decreed, a mob entered the disputed hotel gardens and adjoining buildings and wreaked havoc. There was little sympathy for Mr Barrett from the police and in particular the town dignitaries who used The Prospect for their recreation too. The disputes continued until a local businessman, Thomas Blake, re-acquired The Prospect for one hundred pounds and presented it once again to Ross Town Commissioners in trust for the public. The hotel company was allowed to retain the portion of land on which the hotel and gardens were built.

The Prospect remains available to everyone, and as I stood by the cliff top looking down on the river plain, I caught site of the town's sports ground below and was reminded of a local story of imagination and endeavour. In an era when most of the big name soccer clubs were yet to be formed, Ross Rugby Club played a match here under floodlights. The game against Newent in 1879 was watched by fifteen hundred people under three eight thousand candle powered lights. Neither team could see the ball from beyond their own half. However, knowing the general unevenness of their own ground the home team were quick to take advantage and ran in six tries before Newent could get acclimatized. There is no record of quite how the referee and linesmen followed the play.

During a stroll around the town, I stopped to talk briefly to an old chap sat on a bench in the small cobbled square. What he told me seemed to reflect the sombre mood of the town, although he said he had lived all his life, sixty two years, in Ross and wouldn't have lived anywhere else.

'It had been a lovely town once but it's a dying town now', he told me. *'To see the shops closing down one by one with no-one willing to take them over is heartbreaking'.*

On the wall of one of those empty shops is a blue plaque indicating it had been, on one occasion, 'The King's Rest'. The building had been an inn during the nineteenthth century and the plaque commemorates a stop by George IV for an ale or two while passing through the town on his way home from Ireland. He had not planned to hang around but word got out of his imminent arrival and the subsequent traffic chaos delayed a speedy passage. He had obviously not been best pleased by the street layout, because on his return to London he sent a royal command to the people that movement through the town must be improved or it would be taken off the mailing route! As a direct result a new road was constructed which eventually became the first A40 but has now been replaced by another route which by-passes the town altogether.

My walk around the town almost done, I was beginning to agree with the general opinion that I was looking at a place heading towards its death throes. What I was looking for, indeed what Ross needs, is a modern day hero who might one day claim floor space in the market hall heritage room alongside John Kyrle, Thomas Blake and Walter Scott. Eric Rawlins might have been that man. For over forty years, Eric had been planning for the day when the Chepstow to Gloucester and Hereford via Ross railway line could be reopened. Since the day in 1960, when he first heard rumours that Dr Beeching had already decided the route from Hereford to Ross and Monmouth had no future, Eric fought vigorously, initially to try and prevent closure, and now for re-instatement. I managed to track him down to his home on the outskirts of the town where he was keen to explain what he had so far done. Eric had certainly done his work, and most of it without help. He showed me lots of photographs of the line as it was and as it is now. Over time, he had employed an experienced like minded civil engineer to do a feasibility study for reviving the line, asked a well respected firm of accountants to look at the finance of such a scheme, and invited the local MP to add his voice to the campaign. He even applied for lottery money after discovering that HRH Prince Charles had supported a successful bid for a similar rural railway project in south Wales, but Eric's bid failed. There were huge obstacles in his way, not least two major rivers, Wye and Severn, both of which had to be crossed several times. But there were also the old stations which had been sold off for private use and blocked tunnels to clear and road bridges to repair and made good. It looked an impossible task.

Eric was by then eighty years old. It had been his life's ambition but he had done all he could and unless anyone else steps forward to continue the fight it looks like the end of the line for any return of the Wye valley railway. My heart wishes someone will step forward, but my head says that is unlikely and it will remain a devoted railway man's dream.

Four miles to the east of Ross is the site of the Roman township of Ariconium. I decided to spend the next day walking out there to see what, if anything, was left of it. On the way I would walk the forest trail over Penyard Hill where I hoped to see a mysterious castle-like relic on the summit. The Territorial Army has a firing range on Penyard but on this occasion the red flags were not flying. The ascent was steep but short and the reward was fine views far to the south west of Sugar Loaf Mountain and The Skirrid, that strange broken hill, guardians both of the Welsh town of Abergavenny. On Penyard, the castle - scant remains of an ancient building mostly overgrown, lay scattered across the south facing hillside. It is likely that it was a defensive structure built here in Roman times to guard the route from Ariconium to the river crossing at Walford. Excavations in the eighteenth century discovered Saxon style columns and arches with handsome mouldings, but nothing since which might be of further historical significance. It may never have been anything more than a towered viewing platform. According to a report by the Herefordshire Historic Sites and Monuments team based in Hereford, the fine quality of some of the stonework has led to the suggestion that this site was developed more for luxury rather than military use.

A quiet corner of Rudhall Manor

Emerging from Penyard Hill I made my way along a quiet lane to the hamlet of Bollitree where a glorious folly dominates the village. Bollitree Castle is not what it appears. The walls, turrets and moat are nothing more than a mock Tudor facade enclosing a courtyard surrounded by farm buildings. This fantasy fortress was built in the eighteenth century by Thomas Merryck, apparently to impress a woman who fancied the idea of living in a castle. Unfortunately for Thomas the courtship failed and from then on he lived as a bachelor alone in his castellated manor. Beneath leaden skies, I followed an unsigned narrow track across bleak moorland towards the neighbouring village of Bromsash which sits astride an ancient highway. Below the surface of these featureless fields lie the remains of Ariconium. The Romans first built a camp here after defeating the Silures. Their camp developed as a military centre, eventually became a major district capital from around 150AD and lasted for three hundred and fifty years. Iron ore smelting was carried out here on a large scale, presumably for military use. I searched for blackened soil and any other tell tale signs of industrial activity from another time, but many hundreds of years of ploughing and planting ensured there were none. The present B4224 through Bromsash is one of a number of roads which connected Ariconium with Glevum (Gloucester), Venta Silurium (Caerwent), and their source of iron ore, the mines of the Dean Forest. Towards the end of the Roman occupation, the Anglo Saxons overran Ariconium with some ease on their journey to settle closer to the river where Ross now stands. There is some argument about the exact site of Ariconium. Excavations carried out in 1922 revealed ancient slag and broken tiles on the western facing slopes of Bury Hill nearby. The ruined walls of Roman occupation were visible here as late as the eighteenth century, before Thomas Merryck of Bollitree Castle flattened the area for agricultural use. Now there was nothing. But there is no shortage of history here. An area beside the same stretch of lane bordering the Roman site is known by the ominous name of Kill Dane Fields, where many years ago human bones were found. 13 November 2002, St Brice's day, was the one thousandth anniversary of the day when the Saxon King Ethelred ordered that every man, woman and child of the Danish race then living in England should be killed. The order went out to every town and district, so could it be that it was in these fields that that infamous activity was carried out?

In a secluded valley, a stone's throw from the windswept fields of Ariconium, an ancient manor house stands by the Rudhall brook. The manor was the home for centuries of the Rudhall family, prevalent in this area since the fourteenth century and whose monuments adorn St Mary's church in Ross. Rudhall Manor has been restored and modernized in recent years and is now a venue for classy weddings, but the multi-gabled house remains a mixture of architecture from various centuries. The core of the building is fifteenth century or earlier but additions were started by William Rudhall in 1530. However, the external splendour is the sixteenth century carved half timbered north façade of the west wing. In contrast, the south facing side of the same wing is Georgian sandstone. There are also Jacobean influences here too in the former main entrance. In the seventeenth century the Westphalings married into the Rudhalls and one of them became a Naval Officer and a close associate of Admiral Nelson. It is believed that Nelson spent some time here, not surprising if he had been visiting Ross with Lady Hamilton. It would have been discourteous not to have invited them over for tea. One curious aspect of the house is that it seems to have been built originally at the meeting point of four parishes. An old stone plinth still lies on the lawn in the garden and is reputed to be the remains of a stone cross marking that spot.

A dreary start to the day had ended in bright evening sunshine as I made my way back to Ross along the Rudhall brook. For all its lack of charm, this by-passed river crossing town on the southern edge of Herefordshire has history in abundance. The Wye was Ross's raison d'etre from the time of ancient Britains and the great river has dominated its existence ever since. But it was the Victorian followers of the picturesque movement who recognized the potential of the Wye tours and introduced tourism and prosperity. Today, Ross is more or less left with its memorials and forgotten treasures.

My stay in Ross over, I set out the following day along the riverside path below the mock Tudor walls and under the busy, modern, A40 road bridge. I was now on my way back to Hereford and soon my map told me I was on a short stretch of the old railway track out of Ross. The line once crossed the winding river at several places, and at Backney the gaunt piers of the old viaduct stand sentinel, perhaps waiting for Eric Rawlins' trains to return. The scene is repeated at two other crossings at Strangford and Carey. On the east bank of the river opposite Backney common a simple metal cross commemorates the bravery of Rev. Harry Evans, rector of nearby Brampton Abbots, who drowned near here in 1904 while attempting to save his son. The small community of Foy is a parish cut in two by the river but re-joined by an elegant iron footbridge built in 1921 to replace an earlier bridge built in 1876 and destroyed in a flood. In the silent meadows sloping down to the river, there once stood a twelfth century castle or fortified manor but today there is no trace of it. There are, though, a few very old buildings close by at the hamlet of Hole-in-the-Wall which look as if they may have been constructed from the remains of something of great age.

Further along the bank at How Caple, I left the river path and headed west, following yet another loop in the river. A small road bridge at Fawley overlooks the overgrown railway track and a filled in tunnel. The tiny station house there survives as a private house. Arriving at this spot by train from Hereford in 1891, Henry Timins began his tour of Archenfield.

'Emerging from a short tunnel, we reach the next station where we alight and walk across the open greensward to Fawley Court, a noble stone built mansion whose boldly projecting mullioned windows yet retain a few remnants

Remains of a railway crossing over the Wye along the defunct Ross to Hereford section.

of stained glass. Within, the spacious hall and handsomely panelled rooms are probably little altered since this was the home of Sir John Kyrle (a distant relative of the 'Man of Ross') who died here in 1650 at the age of eighty two.'

Sir John Kyrle's wealth came from the profits of the iron works at Symonds Yat, and the Forest of Dean. Fawley Court still survives here, little altered from Sir John's time, and now has delightful water gardens which, oddly, are on the opposite side of the road from the house. The old Strangford railway bridge over the Wye is less than half a mile from here and it was on 28 March 1947 that the centre pier of the bridge collapsed under the force of the swollen river after exceptional heavy rain. As at the other crossings, most of the old piers are still standing and appear in good condition. At King's Caple, a small millenium plaque has been erected, in the village centre, by the community to commemorate their association with the ancient Welsh kingdom of Archenfield which remained Welsh until the Mercian King Aethelbald led an English raid across the Wye in the mid-eighth century. By the mid-ninth century much of this area had become English. Archenfield and the neighbouring kingdom of Gwent shared a Welsh dialect called Gwenhwyseg, and the region retained its old Welsh customs well into the twentieth century. However, in 1911 the last of these ancient customs was finally lost when the landowner, Lord Chesterfield, successfully applied to the House of Lords for the ancient charter of free fishing rights of the Archenfield Hundred on a seven mile stretch of the Wye to be abolished. On a high point overlooking the river outside Kings Caple, the delightful thirteenth century church of St John the Baptist actually sits within the bailey of a Norman castle, the motte of which can be seen beside the passing road. In a unique ceremony dating back to medieval times, pax or peace cakes, locally made and stamped with a lamb and flag, symbol of the Paschal Lamb, are distributed amongst the parishioners after the service on Palm Sunday. They are joined by those from the little church of St Tysilio at Sellack, a mile away, who arrive in a donkey led procession. In the past, ale was also handed out until the tradition was halted in the nineteenth century. The origin of the peace cakes goes back to a Thomas More who was vicar here in 1442. He was also a wealthy man who owned the nearby manor at Pengethley and took it upon himself to be the great provider of his flock on this one day of the year. After More's death, the custom was continued by another local family of great wealth, the Scudamores of Holme Lacy.

The lane to Sellack drops down between lofty hedges and access is via another delightful pedestrian iron bridge over the river built in 1896. Here in the flood plain a church with a low tower and disproportionately lofty spire is the only church in England dedicated to St Tysilio. There are however several in Wales, notably LLANFAIRPWLLGWYNGYLLGOGERYCHWYRNDROBWLLLLANTYSILIOGOGOGOCH – 'the church of St Mary in a hollow of white hazel near to a rapid whirlpool and St Tysilio's church near to a red cave' - on Anglesey. Tysilio was born in Shrewsbury in 548AD, the son of a King of Powys. Against his father's wishes, he chose a religious life at an early age and ran away to an abbey at Meifod in Montgomeryshire. Persectued by his family, he fled to a tiny island in the Menai Straits where he became a great evangelizer on Ynys Mon (Anglesey). Later, with a group of followers, he established a monastery in Brittany where he remained out of reach of his persecutors until his death in 640AD. In the churchyard at Sellack is a stone cross on which is an embossed single hand pointing upwards and written underneath is the confident prediction 'Gone'. I searched expectantly for a similar, perhaps more humble epitaph picturing this time a pair of open hands with the question 'Whither?', but alas there was none.

From the churchyard, an old stony track rises sharply alongside Castlemead Wood, here before long I was expecting to see the sad site of a fire damaged mansion of which I had heard. The mansion is Caradoc Court, an ancient house of many re-births and now awaiting yet another. Timmins described it

> *An Elizabethan mansion of noble proportions, situated on a lofty terrace and whose quaint uneven gables overlook the river flowing far below'.*

The front section of this once magnificent house is now dominated by three Victorian built Dutch gabled bays. A disastrous fire occured in 1986 but recently a new owner has purchased what was left and vows to restore the house to its former condition. No-one knows how old the site really is. Ancient it certainly is, and there may have been a dwelling here since the twelfth century, but historians have recently been searching for an earlier, more dramatic, beginning. Excavations carried out in the floor of the west wing of the house since the fire have exposed footings of old walls at angles variant to the existing floor plan and thought to be ninth century. The British chieftain Caracticus, also known as Caradoc, lived and ruled in these parts in the first century. Although there is no evidence of occupation here earlier than the ninth century, there is no doubting its antiquity and it is maybe no coincidence that the site bears his name.

The track continues passed Caradoc, crossing the old Hereford road for yet a further mile south west over open country towards the hill top Pengethley Hotel, a splendid Georgian edifice gleaming white against a darkening sky. Regarded in the eighteenth century as one of the county's principal gentleman's seats, Pengethley was then still a medieval courtyard house. Unfortunately, that house was demolished in 1826 and replaced by the present building. A short tentative walk along the busy A49 road and then I turned north east, once again in the direction of the Wye valley. Since my last walk with the river and it's many twists and turns, I had been edging away but never too far from it and the reason for my detour would soon be in sight. Nestling at the end of a leafy meadow and almost hidden behind ancient oaks is the secluded church of St Dubricius, one of the oldest and most significant Christian sites in Herefordshire. This very old church, in the timeless village of Hentland, was named after a missionary in this part of England during the fifth century. Dubricius was born at Madeley, near Hereford, in miraculous circumstances. The legend is quite a story. His mother Eurdil, was the daughter of Peibau, a celtic chief of Archenfield. He had an unfortunate deformity of the mouth which made him dribble. One day, discovering that the unmarried Eurdil was pregnant, Peibau ordered her to be drowned in the Wye. When she survived, he had her burnt alive. Servants returning to the scene the following morning found her sitting by the ashes nursing her child whom she had named Dubricius. Sensing a miracle, Peibau was overcome by remorse and when he bent down to kiss his daughter, the child touched the king's mouth and immediately cured him. Dubricius was known to have been an enthusiastic evangelist and a major contributor to the early growth of Christianity, particularly here in Archenfield. He founded a college of priests at Llanfrother on a hillside above Hoarwithy, less than two miles from Hentland. His energetic campaigns earned him the Bishopric of Llandaff where in 518, according to the Welsh version of the Arthurian legend, he is said to have crowned Arthur at Caerleon. In later life, Dubricius retreated to a hermitage and eventual death on Bardsey Island off the south Wales coast. His remains are buried in Llandaff Cathedral.

Although much of the church at Hentland is thirteenth and fourteenth century, it is claimed that part of the north wall dates from 1050, a time when Edward the Confessor reigned. For many years, the church suffered from neglect and was in a poor state until, in 1982, a group of local benefactors agreed to begin restoration. Since then, thanks to the additional generosity of many visitors, much has been done particularly to the fabric of the church. Far more needs to be done, especially to the tower and the bell chamber, but as long as people continue to come to this ancient and most peaceful site and show their generosity, the finance will surely be available in due course to restore the church to its former glory.

I walked onwards along quiet lanes and fields high above the river before descending into the village of Hoarwithy. The gentle curves of the river here are popular with fishermen and canoeists, and, in summer, the wooded banks and hillsides are a magnet for walkers, birdwatchers and painters. Hoarwithy is a pretty place, a pleasant hotchpotch of attractive cottages and villas which in summer are partly hidden behind climbing shrubs in a blaze of colour. And of course there is a pub. The New Harp Inn has had a chequered history lately by all accounts and has changed hands several times in recent years. In 2004 it was severely damaged by fire but happily is now rebuilt and serving the community again. The jewel of the village is St Catherine's church glistening above the roof tops. Described by the architectural historian, Nikolaus Pevsner, as *southern Italian Romanesque and semi-Byzantine,* this extraordinary church was the creation of J P Seddon, a friend of the then vicar of Hentland, William Poole. Poole saw the existing brick chapel built in 1834 as *'an ugly building with no pretensions to any style of architecture'* and proceeded to transform it in a dra-

Abandoned and forlorn. St Denis's chapel in Harewood park built by the Hoskyns family in 1860

matic way. The old chapel was completely encased in red sandstone, an apse was added to the east end and an arched marbled cloister walk to the south side offering open views of the village below. The nave is the untouched old chapel but the east end is Seddon's masterpiece. Four monolithic columns in grey Devonshire marble topped with Byzantine capitals support a cupola with hanging lamps copied from those of St Mark's in Venice. Behind this is the apse covered by a gold mosaic of Christ. The altar is made of white marble inlaid with Lapis Lazuli. The choir-stalls are of oak with beautifully carved figures of local saints; Tysilio, Weonard, David and Cynog, and the end panels of a prayer desk depict scenes from the life of Dubricius. The stained glass west windows are of unknown saints. From ugly duckling into magnificent swan, vicar Poole must surely have praised the Lord many times following completion of his work. Timmins saw it as

'a modern church with an Italian campanile, curiously exotic'.

He clearly did not take a peep inside.

The following morning after consuming an 'A' class breakfast cooked by my hosts at Aspen House in Hoarworthy, I went for a walk in the park. Harewood Park is now owned by the Duchy of Cornwall and rumour is rife in the village that a newly built Harewood House could become a future home for a future King, Prince William. For the time being, a public right of way starting from Hoarworthy remains open through the park and I wanted to have a look around while I still could. A broad and straight rough track becomes a grassy bridleway through a quiet verdant valley reminiscent of an ancient river bed. Harewood was once the thriving estate of the Hoskyns family but has been deserted and abandoned for many years. In the nineteenth century, the park was renowned for its collection of both native and exotic trees, but most have now gone. Gone, too, is the main house, and close to where it used to be the partly ruined chapel of St Denis, built in 1864 to replace an earlier Templar church, looks forlorn and awaits probable demolition. The Hoskyns' family gravestones have long since been left to the brambles and nettles. There was a manor house here as early as 1215 and the last house, home to the Hoskyns's from the seventeenth century, survived well into the twentieth. Used as a hospital during the Second World War when it fell under the ownership of Guys Hospital, it was eventually sold to a building contractor who stripped the house of all saleable items including the roof. By 1959, what was left was deemed to be in a dangerous state and ordered to be taken down. The end came in dramatic style with the help of the Royal Monmouth Engineers who used it as target practice until it became a heap of rubble. The farmhouses and estate worker's cottages which still stand are boarded up and now they too, are being swallowed by rampant vegetation. It was a sad and desolate scene. However, all that is about to change. HRH Prince Charles brought the land under Duchy ownership in 2000 and has bold plans to repair all the present buildings and transform the estate into a vibrant community. With the possibility that redevelopment will even include the building of a new mansion house, it shouldn't be too long before life returns to this ghost valley.

The next day dawned unusually cold and grey but if all went well, I would be back in Hereford by nightfall. The road climbed steeply out of Hoarwithy and for the first time since I started my journey my legs felt unusually heavy. I turned onto a straight stony track and took solace in the open views down the river valley and to the high Herefordshire hills beyond. The track narrowed, enclosed between high tree hedges but then broadened again. I was walking an ancient green lane, the forerunner of the later valley road still hugging the river below me on its winding way to Hereford. The term 'green lane' has no legal meaning, and they are not all grassy, but they form an important network of once regularly used but now abandoned trade routes across the whole country. Most are now defined as rights of way, or roads used as public paths (RUPPS), but although almost all are of historical significance, there are still too many which remain unclassified and in danger of being lost. Thankfully, for the time being, Herefordshire retains a wealth of green lanes. A threat of showers had given way to bright early summer sunshine but occasional gusts of a sharp wind still persuaded me to keep a fleece jacket on. Shadows of clouds chased each other across the landscape and day old lambs in an adjoining field stared, curious as to what creature I might be.

Arriving at a junction with a narrow lane my ordnance survey map showed the name of an adjacent field as Jenny Penny Whites. I later discovered a reference to Jenny Pennywhites Cottage on a map published in the early 1900s and wondered who she was to have had her name immortalized in this way.

Once through a tiny hamlet made up of Upper and Lower Witherstone and a climb through Bolstone Wood, I was again on open ground. Before I had time to catch my breath, I had my first view of what used to be the largest country house in Herefordshire. Holme Lacy House is a magnificent red brick mansion of startling proportions. This was the grandest house of the Scudamores, and after them until 1909 the family seat of their descendents, the Earls of Chesterfield. There was once an older stone and timber house here, built by Walter de Lacy who was granted the estate by the Norman Duke William in the eleventh century in gratitude for his helping him with the conquest of Britain. Almost five hundred years later, in 1545, a brick house was started on the site by John Scudamore. The great red sandstone triple façade house I now saw before me was built in 1674 by the second Viscount Scudamore and completed in 1716 by the third. The interior decoration was, apparently, of a very high quality,

Holme Lacey House, previously home to the Earls of Chesterfield and now a holiday hotel

however, much of the delicate woodwork by the renowned carpenter Grinling Gibbons was later removed, some to the Scudamore's first house at Kentchurch Court where they had settled after the Norman conquest, and where I had earlier slept uneasily in Owain Glyndwr's bedroom. The Scudamores produced many illustrious men, of whom two are particularly renowned. Sir James Scudamore was a distinguished soldier knighted by Elizabeth I for his bravery at the siege of Cadiz in 1596. His son John, later the first Viscount Scudamore, brought the most fame for his family and county when he returned from a spell as ambassador to France with new varieties of cider apples. These included Redstreak, which he developed in his orchards at Holme Lacy and which layed the foundation for Herefordshire's flourishing cider industry. The Third Viscount was the last of the Scudamores to die without a male heir, but his daughter married Charles Fitzroy who then assumed the Scudamore name, as did Sir Edwyn Francis Stanhope when he acquired the estate shortly after 1820. Stanhope's eldest son became the ninth Earl of Chesterfield in 1883. The last family owners of the house were Mr & Mrs Noel Wills (of Wills Tobacco) before it was donated to Herefordshire County Council and converted in 1934 to a hospital for ladies. It is now a grand hotel run by Warner Holidays Limited who claim to have spent six million pounds since 1995 to provide a luxury leisure and entertainment complex.

The area around Holme Lacy near to the river has been the subject of speculation as to the whereabouts of an ancient Celtic monastic cell, claimed to be the oldest Christian site in Herefordshire. The nearby hamlet of Kilforge is one possible site although nothing remains above ground, and no evidence has yet emerged to support the theory. However, not far from the Scudamore's great house and close to a bend in the river is the church of St Cuthbert, built by the family in the seventeenth century as their monument and which now sits in splendid isolation. Why this particular site was chosen a mile or so from the house and on the flood plain too, is not known but the area appears to be dotted with unidentified earthworks, suggesting earlier occupation. The remains are perhaps of a medieval village, but could this be where the Celtic monks had their cell? The village of Holme

The Wye Invader beached during the flood of 2007 and bandoned

Lacy is also host to an agriculture college, part of the Pershore Group of colleges run in partnership with the Royal Horticultural Society. It was founded in 1896 to advise the farming community on farming techniques, livestock issues, and soil analysis. Here students take courses on beef cattle and sheep breeding, and animal care services.

Just to the west and rising six hundred feet above the river meadow is historic Dinedor Hill. Leaving the Scudamores to their mystical resting places, I set off across flat farmland bordered by Widow's Wood and Ramsden Coppice before tackling the steep eastern flank of Dinedor. On the summit is an iron age hill fort which also saw Roman occupation and was a temporary camp for Cromwell's Scottish Army during the siege of the Hereford at the time of the Civil War. Twelve thousand men spent six weeks here in the summer of 1645 waiting for the order to attack the city, but no such order came. They were poorly paid and poorly fed, and many roamed the local countryside searching for scraps of food. When news came that the Royalists were approaching with a large force, the bedraggled army retreated.

Below me at last, was the sprawl of the county's principal conurbation, Hereford. Timmins's train out of Barrs Court station on his first sojourn towards Ross passed through the district of Rotherwas at the foot of Dinedor. The line has disappeared now beneath a sewage works and one of Hereford's main industrial estates. Nestling amongst the new factories and old farmhouse remnants is a private Roman Catholic chapel built in 1583 by Sir Roger Bodenham who had converted to the faith. Bodenham lived close by at Rotherwas House, a mansion of considerable size which was still standing in 1891 and would have been visible from the old railway line. Unless he was looking the other way as his train passed by, Timmins did not pay any attention to it as there is no mention in his journal. Sadly, the house was demolished in 1925 and the land purchased by the Government who built a munitions factory and ammunitions store there. The wartime buildings themselves have now been removed and replaced by the industrial estate. Little remains of Bodenham's stately home except for a few broken lines of the old walled garden. On the river bank beside those crumbling walls is a more recent reminder of ended dreams. The final journey of the huge Dutch river barge *Wye Invader* in 1990 ended ignominiously when it failed to negotiate the shallow channels on its way to Hereford and was beached on the Rotherwas bank. It remains there still. My last two miles into Hereford should have been a pleasant stroll alongside the river, but unfortunately a section of the path had been closed off for many years, because it is unsafe, necessitating a detour through a dreary housing estate. By the time I emerged the evening sun had broken through and I was looking forward to supper and an early night.

PART THREE

Towards Ledbury and the Frome Valley

MORDIFORD.

'We join the members of the Woolhope Naturalists' Field Club and punctually at ten o'clock of a fresh May morning we are under way, shaping our course through the suburbs, and soon catching glimpses of the river on our right. Onwards past the village of Hampton Bishop, with pretty church-turret and picturesque thatched cottages modestly hiding away amidst the embowering fruit-trees, now abloom in pink and white with kindly promise for autumn, braving the driving hail-storms of a much-belated spring. Another mile brings us to Mordiford Bridge, a time-worn old structure spanning the deep water-meadows of the placid-flowing Lugg whose tide is here increased by a rapid stream coming down from the adjacent hills.'

Timmins referred to 'the pretty villas of Hampton' as he looked out of his railway carriage window when on a visit to Ross on Wye. One of these villas, Plas Gwyn, was once the home of Edward Elgar who lived there for seven years from 1904 during which time he wrote much

Old Sufton Court, the original home of the Herefords

of his best music, including the Pomp and Circumstance Marches. Today, the villas are substantial residences, half hidden behind high hedges and mature trees. No comfortable railway carriage for me, but a walk along a very busy B4224. After a mile or so a sign directed me away from the main road into open meadow towards my old friend the river Wye. Here an earthwork, a nineteenth century flood defence unflatteringly called The Stank, begins a snaking route following the course, first of the Wye and then from Mordiford, that of the river Lugg. With the inevitable demand for more housing for Hereford's commuters, the old village of Hampton Bishop with it's 'picturesque thatched cottages' has grown considerably since Timmins' day. Although the village maintains an air of quiet sophistication, not unexpectedly the old cottages have been more or less swallowed up by modern developments. However, the church and turret is still pretty. At the far end of the village I met The Stank again which had now become the river path to the ancient stone bridge at Mordiford. According to Timmins, this was the site of a legendary conflict.

'The pretty village of Mordiford, nestling under the finely-timbered slopes of Backbury Hill, was once upon a time the scene of a mighty battle between a winged dragon and a condemned malefactor, who was promised a free pardon on the sole condition of compassing the death of the formidable monster, which had inflicted serious loss on the good folks of the country-side. The man caused himself to be enclosed in a barrel and placed at a spot where the dragon was in the habit of coming down to drink at the river, whereupon the prisoner shot the monster with an arrow through the bung-hole; but at the same time the poisonous breath of the dying dragon, puffed through the aperture, proved fatal to his unlucky assailant'

The thirteenth century church, just beyond the bridge, once had a twelve foot long dragon painted on the gable end to commemorate this extraordinary story. The Victorian historian Duncombe once described it as having scales of green and gold on its body, two web-footed legs, two wings, and a long formidable tail. By all accounts a fearsome looking creature. But for all that, the effigy was removed in 1811, when the church was being restored, and nobody thought to repaint the dragon when work was completed. Close to the Moon Inn, the gentle meandering Pentaloe brook ends its short journey down from Haugh woods though it hasn't always been so gentle. On Monday 27 May 1811, this insignificant stream exploded into a violent torrent one hundred and eighty feet wide and twenty feet deep, fed by a tremendous storm over Haugh. Tons of rock and debris crashed down on the village, sweeping before it a barn, cider mill and an adjoining cottage together with its five inhabitants.

On the hillside above Mordiford are the two residences of one of the county's oldest families, the Herefords. The earliest residence, Old Sufton House, was built for Nicholas de Hereford in the fifteenth century. He was a staunch Lollard, a heretical movement of the time rebelling against the power and influence of the clergy. After a term of 'cleansing' in prison, he was surprisingly appointed chancellor of Hereford cathedral in 1391, and then treasurer in 1397. The later and more imposing New Sufton Court was built not far from the first house in 1788 by James Hereford with the help of two illustrious gentlemen of the age, the architect James Wyatt and landscape designer Humphrey Repton. When the Herefords moved into their new home, the old residence became a farmhouse and remained so until 1930 when it was again restored to a family house. The Herefords still live at New Sufton and remain one of a unique number of original families living on the same site in Herefordshire without a break.

I followed a track off the Woolhope road by the Moon Inn and climbed steadily uphill through woods onto a wide ridge. Here the ridge forms the western wall of a local phenomenon known as the Woolhope Dome. The Dome was created millions of years ago by a huge volcanic upheaval which subsequently collapsed leaving a bowl like depression that is now the Woolhope valley. For the modern walker, there is now a pleasant picnic area at Checkley Barn, high above the valley floor, from where the Dome can be traced by following the ridge in a circular fashion north then north east to the far horizon. In the foreground to the east, Haugh Woods rising from the valley floor is a remnant of the Dome after its collapse. Backbury Hill fort is the highest point along the northern ridge of the Woolhope Dome. and it was here that the young King Ethelbert is said to have spent his last night before his fatal meeting with Offa at Sutton Walls, north of Hereford. The impregnable defences of the iron age fort fall away sharply on three sides and there is only one safe access onto the tree covered ramparts. It is difficult, even now, to envisage the young king and his entourage camping out here. Most likely, he pitched his tent on the flat plateau of an adjoining hilltop. Once within the boundary of the fort, the vegetation is dense in parts, the footpaths ill defined and the remains of an old quarry, almost hidden amongst the undergrowth present another hazard. Descending from this ancient camp, I followed a narrow lane, over Tower Hill to the hamlet of Dormington, passing an area of turbulent landslip now covered by a mature wood but which Timmins was able to identify clearly.

> *'We cast a last glance around the outstretched prospect of hill and vale, and proceed on our way, clambering down by a glen where, some forty years ago (c.1850), a great landslip took place, of which striking evidences appear on every hand in the broken and honeycombed character of the ground*

In the valley below me and in the yard of a lane-side farm, the cone like tops of drying kilns were evidence of the district's hop growing activities. The introduction of hops to beer making is generally attributed to the weavers of Flanders who settled in Kent in the early sixteenth century in order to take advantage of the prosperous wool industry there. English ale had been made for centuries without hops and was strong and sweet. It wasn't until 1562 that royal consent was given by Edward VI for the use of hops in the brewing process. Hops are tall climbing plants and are related to cannabis and nettles. Flowering occurs in July and the hop cones, made up of overlapping petals, begin to form through changes within the flower. It is on the inside of the petals that sticky glands form to produce oily resinous compounds, important ingredients for creating bitterness and flavour in beer. Each year the climbing bines grow from ground level to a height of five metres and die back to ground level again after harvesting in September. The bines have to be supported so that those on which the hop cones develop can reach maturity with minimum interference. For centuries, clusters of chestnut poles were used for this purpose, taken down when the cones were ready for picking and replaced the following spring. Nowadays, harvesting is handled by modern machinery but not long ago hop picking was carried out by hand. Thousands of casual labourers were brought in from south Wales and the Midlands annually, swelling the population and putting considerable pressure on local resources. Many of these labourers eventually stayed on as improved processing operations required a permanent workforce. After harvesting, the fresh picked cones must be dried out before they are ready for the brewers so are laid out to dry in a kiln or oast house, a familiar sight in the Herefordshire landscape. Then the hops are compressed into hessian sacks or bales called pockets. They are then ready for marketing.

I had moved away from the Wye valley and was now close to that other great Herefordshire river, the Lugg. The lower Lugg valley was a favourite area of the landscape artist David Cox. He lived here from 1815 until 1827 and worked on his paintings in a modest thatched cottage overlooking the river. Like Henry Timmins, he was a Birmingham man and was considered a rival to both Turner and Constable. Cox worked for a time as an art teacher at a girls' school in

Hereford, but didn't see his employment there as anything more than temporary. He found teaching dreary and uninspiring and spent many hours wandering through the meadows beside the Wye and here by the Lugg. His watercolours were sought after and although the black and white houses of Hereford were an inspiration for many of his paintings, he began to look for ideas more often in places like Bath, in Somerset, and Devon. After twelve years he decided to move to London where most of his customers lived. David Cox eventually retired to his native Birmingham where he remained until his death in 1859. It is said that on the last day of his life, knowing that he was not long for the world, he gave one last tender look around the room that he was leaving, made a solemn reverence to the walls on which some of his choicest works were hung, exclaiming:
'Farewell, old friends, companions and solace of a long life! I shall never see you more!'

> *By the Great Western line running towards Worcester we obtain easy access to another extremely picturesque and interesting district varied by deep pastures and broken wooded heights of which Ledbury is the principal town.*

I continued my way beneath the northern boundary of the Woolhope Dome and Backbury Hill, along silent lanes, passing through hamlets isolated from the busy A438 Hereford to Ledbury road in the valley. The road shares the landscape even now with the railway and the largely forgotten Gloucester to Hereford canal, both built by a local twenty three year old engineer's clerk, Stephen Ballard. The idea for a canal from the river Severn was first proposed in 1790 primarily for the transportation of coal. Construction started at Gloucester in 1793, but by 1832 the canal had gone no further than Ledbury, a distance of less than twenty miles. By now the railway age had arrived and faced with growing apathy and lack of funds, the section of canal to Hereford was not completed until 1845. Stephen Ballard had devoted eighteen years to the project and his reputation as an engineer of note had been established. However, the canal was never going to be the success he had predicted, and in 1862, after just seventeen years of life, it was sold to the Great Western Railway Company. The railway line from Worcester had by this time reached Ledbury, and among the contractors given the job of extending the line to Hereford was none other than Stephen Ballard.

> *Approaching Stoke Edith, we get a peep at the fine mansion of the Foley family and the soaring church spire amidst the noble deer park stretching away up the slopes of the wooded hills to the rear.*

A track bordering farmland leads off behind the Foley estate towards the village of Tarrington from where the old estate grounds can be seen. Little is left now of the great mansion that was once one of the finest Restoration houses in the country containing large amounts of elegant furnishings and paintings until it was eventually destroyed in bizarre fashion. The village and surrounding land at Stoke Edith were purchased in 1620 by Thomas Foley, a wealthy ironmaster from Great Whitley in Worcestershire, and the first house was built on the estate in 1698 for his grandson, Paul who was Speaker of the House of Commons. During the eighteenth century additions and alterations were made to the house by John Nash, and Humphrey Repton added his flair and imagination to the grounds and park. Tragically, this magnificent stately mansion was gutted by fire in 1927 in extraordinary circumstances. The speed with which the fire took hold was attributed to the fact that apart from the red brick shell, the house was extensively panelled and practically the whole of the interior was made of timber. Although the estate had its own modern fire brigade, the country was in the grip of a very cold winter and the water source, the pond, was frozen at the time, as were the fire hoses, so little could be done to save the house. The toll of destruction included James Thornhill's dramatically painted hall and staircase. However an impressive needlework wall hanging was saved and is now in the Victoria and Albert Museum. The tragic loss of Stoke Edith House followed a swathe of accidental fires which destroyed many large estate houses in the early part of the twentieth century. For Christopher Hussey, a young architectural writer on Country Life magazine, the fire at Stoke Edith was a personal as well as an architectural tragedy. Writing mournfully on Christmas eve only a week later, he declared:

Stoke Edith House before fire destroyed it in 1926

The remains of Stoke Edith House. Plans for a rebuild were made as long ago as 1936 but finally abandoned in 1957

'This is the most deplorable loss that has taken place. Many are the Christmases I have spent there, and I write these notes on the very day I was to go there to spend yet another. Even now I can scarcely realise that those calm, spacious rooms, looking away to the Malvern Hills and the Black Mountains, with their store of memories and well known features, are now destroyed'.

In an ambitious attempt to rebuild their family home, the Foleys built the shell of a new house in 1936 but plans to furnish it were finally abandoned in 1957 and the shell was demolished. The Foley family, however, still live on the estate in the old rectory.

There has been a place of worship at Stoke Edith for a thousand years but the present church was built in 1740 by Thomas Foley and is very much a Foley monument. It is constructed in Palladian style but the interior is plain and uninspiring. Originally the church was dedicated to St Edith, daughter of King Edgar who became Abbess of Wilton Abbey at just fifteen years of age! Plagued by ill health Edith died, aged twenty three, on 16 September 984. She is supposed to have visited the site during the construction of an earlier church. Legend has it that the builders complained that the mortar was too dry to work, so she prayed for water. St Edith's Well at the entrance to the old rectory was the miraculous result.

I followed the old track through Stoke Edith Park to Tarrington and with a good mile or two to go before reaching my stop for the night, I had time to occupy my mind and I became aware that, in step with my marching movements, I was muttering a local saying which I had learned days before but the meaning of which I could not fathom. It ran, *'Lusty Tarrington, lively Stoke; beggars at Weston, thieves at Woolhope.'* Nor did I know it at the time but I was walking along the old Hereford to Ledbury road which Repton designed for Foley's park in 1792. He had then moved it further north and it eventually became the present A438. By the time I reached Tarrington, it was growing dark but the tall whitewashed building which was to be my accommodation was easy to find, next to the ancient crossroads in the village. The sixteenth century Swan House used to be a coaching inn and is now a Grade II listed guesthouse in delightful 'olde worlde' surroundings, run by Lizzy Parry and her husband John. In 1963, Nikolas Pevsner described the village pub, The Foley Arms, as red brick late Georgian with a Tuscan columned porch. It has since changed its name to The Tarrington Inn but externally remains the same. Although it sits astride the main Lebury road, Tarrington is a quiet little place and the residents seem to be at one with each other and the regular village events and activities are well supported. Their pride and joy is a group of brass playing musicians called 'Tarrington Brass' who for one hundred years have been performing throughout this country and abroad. They are held together by their conductor Lieutenant Colonel Trevor Sharpe who before he retired was head of The Royal Military School of Music at Kneller Hall in Twickenham.

Trevor also writes much of their music and is acclaimed as the composer of the theme tune for the BBC TV series *Dad's Army.* Recently, the whole village turned out to hear the inaugural performance of his latest work which delighted everyone with its title *Tarrington.*

Along a quiet lane in the neighbouring village of Little Tarrington is Richard Bradstock's historic farmhouse where he keeps his famous breed of Hereford cattle. Richard is the current chairman of The Hereford Cattle Society, formed originally as The Hereford Herd Book Society in 1878. There are currently over eight hundred members throughout the UK. Freetown Herefords, as the herd here has become known, have been bred on Richard's farm since 1919 and have since won countless acclamations and trophies. In a small field beside the farmhouse, shaded by a row of tall trees, one of Richard's present champions, a huge, magnificent, Hereford bull called Freetown Wellington, gazes lazily across the Frome plain.

'He won the Class Ten prize for two year olds at the Tenbury National Hereford Show this year'. Richard told me proudly as we sat down to coffee in his study, *'Its his retiring performance, and he thoroughly deserves his peace and quiet now after a busy season'.* I asked him how he had maintained such dominance with his showcase herd. *'We farm in a very fertile part of the Frome Valley and here there is no shortage of grass for them to feed on all year round. In a way, that's lucky, but it's meant we've been able to raise good beef cattle more often than farms in other parts of the county'.* It seems his luck held out in blessed fashion during the depressing period in 2001 when the outbreak of foot and mouth disease devastated farm stocks throughout the county.

'Just one field away from disaster, that's all,' he said, shaking his head, still apparently in shock at the events firmly locked in the memory.

'Farms around me suffered badly. My cousin, Margie, farms at Clyro near Hay-on-Wye and she lost her herd in the cruellest manner. Hers were free of the disease but during a cull on a neighbouring farm, a black Limousin bull broke through a boundary fence and onto Margie's land and that was it. She lost the whole herd.'

As I walked back along the long drive, I bade farewell to Freetown Wellington and pondered over Richard's final poignant words.

'The best Hereford beef is now bred in Argentina, and it's cheaper, too. These beautiful beasts have been a part of the Herefordshire landscape for over three hundred years and it would be a tragedy, not just for the county but for the whole beef industry, if the breed was lost.'
I vowed then to buy some home grown Hereford beef just as soon as I could.

Re-crossing the A438, I strode on along more narrow lanes and field paths rising towards the Marcle Hill ridge where I would be rewarded with one of the many stunning landscapes that Herefordshire would offer on my journey. As I climbed the ridge, the whole length of the west facing Malvern Hills came into view and beyond the blue shadow of the Cotswolds stretched away towards Bristol. Immediately below me lay the fertile lush valley of the stream-sized Leadon river, with long lines of fruit crops and cider apple orchards everywhere I looked. I turned along a footpath which clung to the hillside overlooking this wonderful scene and followed it for almost three miles. The Marcle ridge is the east bank of the Woolhope Dome and at times along its length it was possible, looking to my right, to see into that valley within which the village of Woolhope itself lies. But whether left or right, the picture was one of a great spread of fertile tree-covered terraces running down to lush green pastures where livestock grazed in abundant ignorance. Only the backdrops differed, and for me the more dramatic sight of the Malverns is a clear winner. Occasionally, I stopped to take it all in. Nothing beats leaning over a five barred gate listening to the sound of bleating lambs, the high twittering of skylarks, and the drone of a far away single engine aircraft, reminders all of long ago summers. Was it in such a place as this, on another day, I wondered, that W H Davies penned his immortal ode.

'What is this life if, full of care,
We have no time to stand and stare.
No time to stand beneath the boughs
And stare as long as sheep or cows
No time to see, when woods we pass
Where squirrels hide their nuts in grass

No time to see, in broad daylight
Streams full of stars, like skies at night.
A poor life this if, full of care,
We have no time to stand and stare.'

Time was getting on and Ledbury, my next stop, seemed still a continent away. I dropped off the ridge path aiming for the village of Much Marcle, passing on the way one of several major players in Herefordshire's cider industry. Cider has been made for centuries by farmers for their own use but over a hundred years ago, Henry Weston decided to supplement his income on the farm he owned in these fields. In 1880 he started making cider commercially, and the Weston Cider Company was born. Weston was aided and abetted by C W Radcliffe-Cooke who was MP for Hereford at the time. He had persistently advocated the drink's commercial development in parliament to such an extent that he became known as the 'Member for Cider'. Today, forty different types of ciders and perries are made on the same farm where Henry Weston made his first brew. The business is now run by Helen Thomas, Henry's great granddaughter. She employs eighty people making 1.4 million gallons a year, and has a turnover of seven and a half million pounds, second only to the county's other great cider maker H P Bulmer.There is also, here in Much Marcle, an unusual house of great antiquity. Essentially Jacobean but with much earlier remains attached to it, Hellens occupies an ancient site that has been inhabited for close on a thousand years, eight hundred of them by the same family. When William the Conqueror sent over monks from Corneilles in north eastern France to help educate the western English 'heathens', they found a place here below the ridge. In 1096 the manor was granted to the de Baluns who turned the monk's religious house into a castle to help guard the Welsh marches. Even Roger, the first Mortimer earl, had a spell here, but eventually guardianship was handed to Walter de Helyon who gave his name to the house which was simply Helyon's and in time became Hellens.

This is a house of many ages, but not of style. There are no classical lines here. No Wyatt, Adams or Smirke ever set foot in these dark, damp and cold surroundings. Queen Mary Tudor nearly did, and had she slept in the room especially prepared for her visit, I suspect she might have been unimpressed. Although there are glimpses of excellent carvings in the woodwork, they are not in places designed for them. This is a house for ghosts and hard living and is still occupied by descendents of the Norman de Baluns. But for all that, it is a place to wonder at, and not like any historic house that I have seen before.

Near to Hellens is St Bartholomews, a handsome church of the thirteenth and fourteenth century worthy of some attention. It was built in the usual formation of nave, chancel, north and south aisles with a chapel at the end of the north aisle. In addition, there are tall lancet windows above the nave, forming a clerestory, and unusual for Herefordshire, a central tower of substantial proportion. The church's treasures are its effigies, some of the finest in the county. In the nave is that of Walter de Helyon carved in oak and painted in the vivid colours of the day and the fourteenth century tomb of Blanch Mortimer, the daughter of Roger Mortimer. There is no mention of how old Blanche was at her death but like many medieval sculptures, she is depicted as being about thirty years of age. Above her tomb is a canopy containing the Mortimer arms. In the north aisle chapel, built at the end of the thirteenth century, lie prominent members of the Kryle-Money family and their descendants who lived at Homme House just outside the village. Pride of place on a magnificent black and white marble altar tomb goes to Sir John Kyrle, the iron man of Fawley Court and distant relative of the Man of Ross, he lies next to his wife Sybil, a Scudamore before marriage. At his feet, the ubiquitous hedgehog which, as at Ross, appears on the Kyrle crest. At Sybil's feet, bizarrely, is a paw of human appearance set in a coronet, and may be associated with the Scudamore line. Also in the chapel is the tomb of an unknown knight and his partner. It is claimed to be that of Hugh and Isolda Audley, who had an estate in Much Marcle in the late twelfth century. They would feel out of place in their position, but as they would have been placed in the church first, they might say theirs is the greater right! The tower is late fifteenth century and reputed to have been made from stones taken from the remains of Edmund Mortimer's castle situated fifty yards from the church. That Edmund was the father of the infamous Roger Mortimer, murderer of Edward II in horrible fashion at Berkley castle in Gloucestershire. Just outside the south porch is a huge ancient yew tree, claimed to be fifteen hundred years old and one of the oldest and largest surviving anywhere in the country. Inside the hollowed out trunk a semi-circular bench has been inserted where no doubt the weary traveller can sit and contemplate all that they have just seen.

This year, the Trumpet and District Annual ploughing match was being held that very day at Lower Walton in the Leadon valley, and as I had never witnessed this popular rural pursuit before, I was looking forward to the experience. The T & D event is recognized as one of the county's largest meetings. All ploughing matches are run under the rules of The Society of Ploughmen which was formed in 1972 and is a registered charity run by volunteers, and is responsible for organizing the European and World Championships as well as British Ploughing Championships. I am told matches are open to all, including women, and is not restricted to farmers. Providing you have the equipment and you can show you know what you're doing, anyone can have a go. The origins of ploughing competitions lie with Suffolk farmers of two hundred years ago who would wager an ounce of tobacco or a pint of beer on the straightness of their furrows. Over time, the wagers became competitions then, eventually, formal ploughing matches run by local associations of ploughmen. As an inducement to enter, winners were promised wage increases to reflect their achievement. Farming is the oldest industry in the world and the earliest plough would have been a crude hand held bent stick used to scratch the surface of the soil to form a tilth in which corn could be sown. That was over four thousand years ago. Now, the hydraulic reversible plough attached to the most powerful of tractors dominates, and some will be on show today. Not knowing what to expect, I was surprised to see how large the event arena was, around one hundred acres. It wasn't just about ploughing, either. There were demonstrations of rural arts and crafts with exhibits by farming communities from all over Herefordshire, and displays of vintage horticultural machinery of every kind. Probably the biggest crowd puller at theses events are the shire horses, teamed up in pairs. These magnificently turned out animals take spectators back to the days when farming was a gentler way of life. Plots of land had already been allocated to contestants for the match, which was very much a serious affair, and was well under way when I arrived. There were categories for modern, vintage and horse-drawn ploughs. The weather was perfect, dry and bright with just a slight chill in the air. As I ambled towards one of the match fields, I latched onto Elwyn Mills, a retired farmer from Kington in the far north west of the county, who patiently explained to me what was going on.

'All the competitors must be ready to start at 10.00am sharp,' he told me, *'and are expected to continue until 3.00pm. It's tough work.'* We stopped to admire one of the few contestants in the single-handed class plough which had to be pushed along.

'This is always a great day out for me,' he enthused. *'I look forward to it every year. It gives me a chance to meet up again with lots of friends. I used to have my own tractor years ago, though I was never good enough to enter matches. Mine was a 16bhp Allis Chalmers tractor with TVO,'* he recalled proudly with that hazy look in his eye of a long cherished memory. 'TVO?' I asked obligingly, knowing he would have expected that response. *'Tractor Vapourizing Oil. Many vintage models had two fuel tanks. One was for petrol which helped to start and run the engine while cold, the other for TVO. Once the engine had warmed up, you switched to the second tank.'*

We stopped again to watch an enthusiast tidying the pitch behind his tractor before starting another furrow. *'That's Keith Williams from Kings Caple. The judges take things like that into account. Keith is one of our current champions. He won the Vintage Trailing Plough Class in the British Championships at Doncaster in 2002. He usually does well some where every year.'*

'What else do the judges look for?'

'Alignment of the furrows and soil cover. Any vegetation showing on the surface once the soil has been turned is penalized.'

Suddenly, our conversation was interrupted by a marshall pulling up his Toyota off-roader at the next pitch. *'Dig deeper number thirty, you're too shallow!'*

Elwyn told me of Herefordshire's three world ploughing champions. *'Les Godwin was the first in 1958. He's a Kington man, too, and still lives there. Then there was John Gwillam from Tarrington in 1960, but*

A contestant hoping for a perfect score in the annual Trumpet and District ploughing match

he died a few years back. Vivian Samuel breeds pedigree Suffolk sheep over at St Weonards. He won in 1980. They're our heroes.'

Suitably charged with new knowledge and the constant whiff of tractor fuel, I left him with his friends and heroes and put my best foot forward again along the familiar narrow lanes.

In this county of black and white timber framed houses, Hall Court at Rushall stands out as a notable example. Built around the beginning of the seventeenth century, the facade consists of five unequal bays and a small porch. The impression is that all the parts are original but may not necessarily remain in their original place. Its most famous resident was a certain Dr John Fell, one time Bishop of Oxford, and the subject of the curious rhyme:

'I do not love thee, Dr Fell
The reason why, I cannot tell.
But this I know, and know full well.
I do not love thee, Dr Fell.'

Just below the Marcle Ridge at a spot marked on the map as *The Wonder* is the site of another landslip. However, this was no miniscule affair. According to contemporary reports, on 17 February 1571,
'The hill they call Macley did rouse itself as it were out of sleep, and for

three days together moved on its vast body with a horrible roaring noise, overturning everything in its way.'

The records indicate that trees, hedges, houses and their inhabitants were engulfed as the hillside collapsed. The old chapel serving the parish of Kynaston went, too, and it was two hundred and sixty nine years before the bell was discovered buried amidst grassy mounds formed when the hillside finally ceased moving. It was installed in the bell tower at Homme House after the Kyrle family had claimed ownership of the land on which it was found. Some of the older villagers insist they still hear the bell toll now and then and occasional strange rumblings from deep inside the hill. The great event is still celebrated each year at the local pub, not surprisingly called The Slip Tavern.

The little church at Putley seems to have been built on the site of a Roman villa, the foundations of which were discovered beneath the surface of the graveyard during restorations in 1876. Still visible above the surface in the churchyard is a rare and well preserved thirteenth century stone Calvary Cross. The lanes around Putley are surrounded by acres of fruit bearing shrubs, mainly blackcurrants, and hop laden bines, farmed mostly by the people at nearby Pixley Court. Most of the blackcurrants will end up as Ribena. Hops are now an essential ingredient which gives beer its bitterness, and hop production, mainly the Fuggles and Goldings varieties, makes a visual impact here as in much of the Herefordshire countryside.

At the hamlet of Aylton there is a trio of listed buildings. Court Farm is fourteenth century and was recently purchased by a young couple from London who have restored the farm house to its former glory. In an adjacent field is a fourteenth century barn in danger of collapse and there are plans to restore that too as soon as funds become available. In between the two is the tiny Aylton Church. Parts of it are twelfth century, which suggests there may have been a building on the site of Court Farm before the present one. The church is set on a low mound, probably for defensive reasons, and may have been stockaded to protect livestock during an attack by invading Welsh brigands while the people took refuge in the church. In the small bell turret, there are two bells, one of which is as old as the church itself and is one of only two of that age in the county. The interior is plain with a rood screen and simple furnishings. The church treasure is a seventeenth century chalice which is called by the parishioners the Restoration Chalice as it was bought to replace the original stolen by the Parliamentary commander Colonel Birch during the Civil War. In the churchyard is a gravestone indicating the last resting place of one, Emma Foulgar. The unfortunate Emma was said to have been accidentally killed by her brother who, when returning from a shooting expedition, stumbled on the steps of the house and his still loaded gun went off killing his fourteen year old sister instantly. The tragedy was prolonged when her body was stolen by grave robbers not long after her burial in 1855 and was never recovered. Her grave is still marked but remains empty.

After a mile or so along the Roman road connecting Gloucester with Wroxeter, I arrived at a crossroads by the curious, timber framed, Trumpet Inn, after which the local ploughing match is named. Previously two cottages, the Trumpet has been serving ale since 1650.

> *'Retracing our steps through deep and shady lanes, anon across meadows sweet scented with clover, where the invisible corncrake reiterates its rasping cry, we shape our course through the little hamlet of Munsley, near to the weed grown channel of the now disused canal and diverge from our course down a rough and barely distinguishable bye lane, which brings us to Fern Farm, a remote and picturesque old homestead lying on the road to nowhere whose deep browed roofs, ancient weathered stained timbers, ivy clad gables and pigeon cot improvised from a barrel, form a scene to make glad the heart of a sketcher'*

At Munsley there is another fine old church said to date from 830, dedicated to St Bartholomew. During restoration in 1863, some very ancient gravestones bearing pre-Christian crosses were discovered. An intriguing inscription found on one of theses ancient stones was deciphered as 'hamlet xheti' or Hamlet the Jute, and the date 362 AD. It was claimed to be a fragment of the sarcophagus of the original Prince of Denmark, though how it got there no one could tell me. Timmins' track to Fern Farm in *Nooks and Corners* no longer exists and appears to have been swallowed up by the march across the Herefordshire countryside of hop bines and fruit trees. However, a sign on the field gate where the track began said 'WILT PREVENTION – KEEP OUT'. The harvesting of hops takes place in mid September. Each year hundreds of gypsy hop pickers would gather for the harvest, camping in these fields some of which would be allocated to them and their horses. In October, they would gather again outside Ledbury for the annual Hop Fair. After mechanization, the few who returned as permanent employees lived in the tied houses provided by the farm owners. The remains of the old Gloucester to Hereford canal which was extended from Ledbury to Hereford in 1832 are still visible in the landscape around here, though in various degrees of dereliction and decay. Near Swinmore Farm, the canal bed has all but dried up and has now been colonized by nettles. Towards Ashperton, the canal has remained wet below very steep banks but now trees sprout from the algae coated water.

Two miles further on I arrived in Bosbury. Even now the long village street of this ancient place makes a pretty picture, with its homely gables looking out onto the centrally situated churchyard. Local tradition says Bosbury was a town long before Hereford was a city. The Bishops of Hereford built a palace here in the eighth century and the ageing Athelstan transferred his office from Hereford to Bosbury after the Welsh attack of 1055. It was a particular favourite of Thomas Cantilupe and his successor Bishop Richard de Swinfield who sought solace in these peaceful surroundings in the twelfth century. A stone arched gateway, now the entrance to a barn, is all that remains of the palace which was demolished in 1572. The church of the Holy Trinity in Bosbury was completed in the thirteenth century but there are traces of a gable and roof line on the outside west wall of an earlier Norman church. An ancient and much restored red sandstone cross is overshadowed, literally, by a huge powerfully built detached tower erected in 1230, and one of seven such towers in Herefordshire. The thick walls and narrow windows of this tower are a clear indication that it was intended as a refuge for parishioners under attack rather than a housing for just a bell! It is said that during the Civil War, the church was defaced by zealous puritan soldiers who were about to do the same to the churchyard cross when the vicar pleaded successfully for its protection. In return, he was persuaded to inscribe it with the

legend 'Honour not the cross but honour God for Christ' which is still visible. Inside the church there are two memorial slabs of some significance, each marking the burial of a Templar knight. Temple Court, formerly a possession of The Knights Templar survives as an eighteenth century farmhouse just outside the village. Holy Trinity's font, supported on five short columns is thirteenth century, but it is another font, or at least the bowl of one, which is preserved here in the church. It is the more remarkable because it is thought to be Saxon and was found beneath the floor during renovations in the eighteenth century.

In these dark days of disappearing pubs, The Bell Inn thankfully still survives here but at the opposite end of the village the once remarkable Crown Inn does not. In Elizabethan times the Crown was the home of Richard Harford, the steward of the manor. As a public house it was renowned for its magnificent 'Oak Room', containing walls of oak panelling, and a massive oak chimney piece.

Timmins also noted :

'The fireplace is surrounded by fine old blue Dutch tiles, and over it, in handsomely carved panels, appear the arms of Wrottesley, Scrope and Fox, and dated 1571. A frieze of delicate carving runs around (the walls), and at the crossing of the massive beams in the ceiling, three bosses show

respectively the bearings of Bishop Skipp, the arms of Scrope, and of Powlett, first Marquis of Westminster having the garter and coronet.'

The Inn was eventually purchased from the Whitbread brewery company in 1971 by Mr & Mrs Howe. Much of the Oak Room remains as it was with iron candleholders still in place in the panelling. Sadly though, before the Howes moved in, the blue Dutch tiles and two of the coats of arms had been removed.

Picking up the Herefordshire Trail footpath out of Bosbury, I turned towards Oyster Hill rising sharply above the village of Coddington. The spectacular view westwards from its thoughtfully placed summit bench is unbroken to the Black Hills of south Wales and the Black Mixen plateau in the Radnor Forest. Tucked away amidst tall trees on the south slopes of Oyster is Hope End House, once the home of the poetess, Elizabeth Barrett Browning. Her father, Edward Moulton-Barrett, a wealthy sugar plantation owner during the times of the slave trade, built the house in 1810 with the proceeds. The style he chose for the building was Indo-Mooresque, similar to that at the Pavilion at Brighton and Sezincote in the Cotswolds and it must have looked spectacular. It became Elizabeth's childhood home and one can imagine the pleasure she had from living in such beautiful surroundings. Her father proudly called her 'the poet-laureate of Hope End' and in 1826 arranged for her first work to be published. Two years later Edward's income came under scrutiny, his wealth dwindled, and in 1832 Hope End was sold and the family moved first to Sidmouth in Devon and later to Wimpole Street in London. Elizabeth, who never really recovered from a childhood fall from a horse, died in Florence in 1861. The Moorish house at Hope End was demolished in 1867 to make way for a conventional manor house but that too was destroyed by fire in 1910. The house visible now is the third on the site.

Ere long we see before us the spire of Ledbury's great church, soaring high above the surrounding trees that cluster in rich masses upon the steep hillside above the little town. In the centre, the road widens out and here we come upon the quaint half–timbered market house standing upon sixteen stalwart pillars of sweet chestnut wood brought from the once far famed 'chase' of Malvern, and erected by that ubiquitous Elizabethan builder, John Abell.'

Ledbury lies to the south west of the Malvern Hills and is an attractive mixture of ancient black and white half-timbered buildings and modern red bricked terrace cottages. The approach to the town from the north is dominated by an impressive thirty arched railway viaduct built in 1859 to bridge the tiny Leadon river. It took over five million bricks to complete. At Ledbury railway station, the tiny picturesque timber ticket office is privately run by John Goldrick. At one time, the station reflected its status as an important junction on the Paddington to Hereford line but in the sixties the much maligned Dr Richard Beeching changed all that and everything was swept away, leaving a neglected and unstaffed halt. Since 1988, however, Mr Goldrick's ingenuity has brought life back to the platforms by providing a rare personal service from the homely surroundings of his station hut. This small but welcome act of innovation is financed from a commission on sales of tickets. The attractive market house in the town centre was built by John Abell in 1633 and there has been a right to sell anything in the Ledbury streets since the days of King Stephen in the twelfth century. Until 1887, the livestock market took place every second Tuesday of the month when the local farmers drove their animals along the roads into the town centre and sheep and pigs were penned around the market house. Later, all livestock was removed from the high street to a new purpose built venue at the back of the town. But even today, non-livestock market stalls are permitted between the market house's ancient oak columns. At the start of the nineteenth century, a row of old houses existed in the middle of the high street but were demolished soon afterwards to provide freedom of movement through the town. One of the old houses was rebuilt as a

MARKET-PLACE, LEDBURY.

museum in the delightful cobbled Church lane. Also in the high street and resembling a church, St Katherine's hall is the original hospital founded by Bishop Hugh Foliot in 1231 in honour of St Katherine of Alexandria, whose grim death gave the name to the Catherine Wheel. Almshouses next to the hall were converted in the nineteenth century as an accommodation block for the hospital staff. Elizabeth Barrett Browning is commemorated in Ledbury by the impressive clock tower built in her name and completed in January 1896, five years after Timmins' visit (which explains the lack of a sketch in his book), and now houses the Library.

At the top of the high street is one of the grandest black and white timber framed houses anywhere in Herefordshire. This imposing edifice called Ledbury Park was built on the site of a bishop's palace in 1595 by Edward Skynner, a wealthy clothier from Lincolnshire. The house was bought in 1688 by Anthony Biddulph who had married Edward Skynner's granddaughter and from there he began a banking dynasty which in time accumulated great wealth. It later merged with that of the Cocks family of Eastnor Castle to form the Cocks Biddulph Bank. Also in Ledbury was yet another family based banking dynasty by the name of the Martins, and the bond between them and Cocks Biddulph was strengthen by marriage in 1837, eventually bringing those two businesses together in 1919. These historic local family and business unions came to an end when, in 1969, Martins Bank was swallowed up by Barclays. The Biddulphs continued to own Ledbury Park well into the twentieth century until the death of the third Earl Biddulph, and this magnificent building which has dominated the southern end of the high street for over four hundred years and been home to the creators of one of England's great banking institutions during most of that time is now an estate of private apartments.

> *'We now turn along a narrow lane bearing evident traces of great antiquity, which leads direct to the church affording a pretty glimpse of the detached tower and spire seen between overhanging gables.'*

Here Timmins is describing the much photographed cobbled pic-

CHURCH LANE, LEDBURY.

turesque street of fifteenth century early Tudor buildings leading to the imposing minster church of St Michael and All Angels. Included among the tightly packed black and white buildings in Church Lane is the Prince of Wales pub, a true gem for any beer enthusiast. The first stone built church at the lane's end was started in the twelfth century and parts of it survive today, the best and immediately obvious is the great west door of distinct Norman style. The tower and spire is one of Herefordshire's seven detached bell towers and is the focal point from miles around. Inside the church two great memorials in the south aisle reflect the power and wealth of the Skynners and the Biddulphs, while in the north chapel is the monument to Elizabeth Barrett Browning's parents. The north aisle is dominated by The Heaton Memorial Window, a modern stained glass window installed in 1991, which has aroused mixed feelings, especially amongst the traditionalists. But, as the church guidebook author preaches; 'it is a good reminder that each generation brings its own offerings to God and there is no one period or style which is correct'.

By the north entrance is St Katherine's Chapel – not a memorial to the St Katherine of the hospital in the high street but to Katherine Audley. She was born in 1272 into a wealthy family and it is claimed received a vision from God telling her to travel to a place where the bells appeared to ring of their own accord. There she was to settle and devote her life to caring for the poor and the sick. She arrived with her maid at Ledbury in 1313 to hear bells ringing, apparently she thought without human assistance, and so settled on the outskirts of the town. She built a hermitage at what is now Hazel Farm, south west of Ledbury, where she spent the rest of her life caring for those in need. Her mission lasted only ten years before she died in 1323. She was never proclaimed a saint but the people of Ledbury nevertheless gave her the title that they believed she rightly deserved. The poet John Masefield is another of Ledbury's townsfolk to achieve fame. Though he left Ledbury at the age of thirteen, childhood impressions of life in his native Herefordshire were to have a profound effect on Masefield throughout his life. In 1930, he was appointed Poet Laureate at the time when Elgar was Master of the Kings Music, creating a double top for the Malvern area. Masefield never returned to Ledbury and died near Abingdon in 1967 at the age of eighty-nine.

Ledbury still carries the scars from skirmishes during the Civil War, though none lasted long enough to be called battles, and the town escaped any serious damage. There are bullet holes in St Michael's church's doors, and elsewhere, which may be authentic and the result of some inaccurate volleying. That so many doors were shot at may also be the result of over exuberance on behalf of town planners who saw a commercial value in providing what tourists liked to see. The canal from Gloucester arrived on the outskirts of Ledbury in 1798 but for many years went no further. There were doubts that the proposed extension to Hereford would ever be built. Until, that is, the engineer in charge of the project, Stephen Ballard, gained the support of the wealthy and influential Ledbury banker, John Biddulph. Convinced of the canal's worth, Ballard continued to survey and plan the eventual route, and excavations began on 17 November 1832. Ballard was an extraordinary single minded man who lived in close proximity to the canal workings, moving as each section was completed, controlling affairs closely and working sixteen hours a day. However, almost within sight of Hereford, he became depressed at the apparent lack of enthusiasm for the canal. The support for the new transport system, railways, had continued to develop at pace and funds for Ballard's canal were drying up. Faced with growing apathy and little prospect now of the canal ever making a profit, the section to Hereford was finally completed on 22 May 1845. On that same day, Stephen Ballard left for another assignment in Lincolnshire, but before long he would return to the area to accomplish his other impressive engineering feat, that of completing the railway line to Hereford.

After a very pleasant stay at The Talbot Hotel, I took my exit from Ledbury via the great Norman west door of St Michael and All Angels church from where a short walk up through Coneygree Woods would take me out of the Herefordshire lowlands and into the spectacular region of the Malvern Hills. The Malverns are a nine mile long hog's back of igneous rocks running north to south. Three hundred and forty million years ago these dramatic hills were thrust up into their present position by shock waves caused when the continents of Asia and Europe collided and joined together somewhere around the Ural mountains of Russia. These ancient hills stand proud on one side from the edge of the flat Worcestershire plain spreading away to the foot of the distant Cotswold Hills, and on the Herefordshire side a landscape of rolling hills and valleys towards the Welsh border. They are by far the oldest and hardest rocks of the region. When you walk on the Malvern ridge, you are clearly on a divide between lowland and upland Britain.

> *'Eastnor Castle, princely seat of Lady Henry Somers, lies in a hollow in the hills to the east. The high road would lead us around beneath Rilbury Camp, but in preference we follow an ancient pathway called Capuchin or 'Cabbage' Lane, leading from Ledbury church by a shorter but steeper route over Eastnor Hill, descending close to the village. The castle, though standing in a low situation, has a fine appearance, the massive walls and towers mirrored in the waters of a broad lake surrounded by trees.'*

Early in the eighteenth century the wealthy Cocks family married into that of the Somers and lived at Castleditch House, long since demolished but the site of which is on one of the islands in the lake at Eastnor Castle beneath the southern ridges of the Malvern range. The combination of the valuable inheritance left by the Lord Chancellor Somers in the early eighteenth century and the banking wealth of the Cocks Biddulph merger in Ledbury gave the first Earl Somers the means to begin construction, in 1810, of the mock medieval castle that we see today. With revolution in France and the threat of invasion by Napoleon, the young architect, Robert Smirke, proposed a Norman style, reminiscent of an Edward 1 medieval fortress. The total cost of construction was a staggering £86,000, or roughly ten million pounds in today's money. There is no doubt that the imposing grandeur of Eastnor was intended to reflect the personality and stature of its creator and establish the family in the ruling classes for future generations. In 1870, to enhance his relative's medieval creation the third Earl Somers bought half of Samuel Meyrick's armory collection from Goodrich Court. However, the last Earl died in 1883 and by 1920 the family's fortunes were in decline. In 1939 the state rooms were abandoned due to lack of use and in the early 1970's, pressured by spiralling costs of maintenance, the present owner's mother considered demolition. Thankfully for us, and for James and Sarah Hervey-Bathurst, she decided against it and in the succeeding years the castle as been restored to its former glory.

The church at Eastnor, like that of Bosbury, has an ancient font which was also found beneath the floor of the nave during a Victorian rebuild. The age of the font bowl cannot be determined but the stone base is fourteenth century. It seems the bowl once had a cover, suggesting it was around at the time of Archbishop Edmund Rich of

Canterbury who in 1236, ordered that fonts should be locked as a safeguard against unqualified or 'hedge' priests usurping the rights of legitimate parish priests by baptizing infants at a reduced rate!

On the hillside opposite Eastnor are the remains of an older castle, Bronsil, which was little more than a fourteenth century moated fortified house. The impression is that this was a show castle - a place to enhance the importance of the owner, in this case Richard Beauchamp, the son of Sir John Beauchamp, Lord Treasurer to Henry VI. He obtained licence from the King to crenellate the existing house in 1460. There is no record of Bronsil ever being involved in conflict until the Civil War after which it was left in ruin and abandoned. At the southern end of the Malvern chain is Raggedstone Hill. Legend tells of a monk from the priory at Little Malvern who fell for a local lass and broke his vow of chastity. His penance was to crawl to the top of the hill on his hands and knees every day. Not surprisingly, the monk became extremely miffed so cursed the hill and anyone on whom its shadow should fall. Victims of the monk's vengeance have apparently included the unfortunate William Huskisson, who owned estates in the Malvern area, and was the Member of Parliament struck down by George Stephenson's famous train, The Rocket, on it's inaugural trip out of Manchester in 1830. To visitors wishing to avoid similar mishaps, with the line of hills being north to south it would seem prudent to approach Raggedstone from the east in the morning or the west in the afternoon!

> *'We turn now through a gate into the wide spreading park and recall to memory a certain moonlight stroll in late autumn, when the hollows lay wreathed in mist, and the barking of the deer sounded weirdly through the dusk.'*

The deer park on the western flanks of the Malverns belongs to the Eastnor Castle estate and as there was no right of way along my direct route onto the hills I had to obtain permission to enter in order to avoid a lengthy detour. For many years now, the estate has allowed the Land Rover company to use the park and the wooded countryside in the foothills to test, develop and demonstrate their range of four-wheel drive vehicles, and the result is an environmental disaster.

Deep rutted tracks which after heavy rain, fill up with water, are everywhere, disguising the depth and making it a hazardous journey on foot. It was after such wet weather that I found myself negotiating this difficult terrain. Knowing that being in the park at all, either on foot or in an off-roader, is by permission only deterred me from pursuing the matter with the Hervey-Bathursts.

The whole southern section of the Malvern skyline is dominated by an Obelisk - a monument built by the first Earl Somers in 1812 in memory of his eldest son who was killed in the Spanish Peninsular War. The ridge path northwards follows the Shire Ditch or Red Earl's Dyke, a defensive feature reputed to have been built by Gilbert de Clare, the red headed Earl of Gloucester, between 1287 and 1291. The Earl owned Malvern Chase on the eastern side of the hills and was in dispute with Thomas Cantilupe, Bishop of Hereford and owner of the western flanks, over the boundaries of their hunting grounds. The two negotiated a demarcation line down the centre of the ridge where the Earl agreed to build the Dyke. Unfortunately for the Bishop, his cunning opponent built it slightly downhill on his own side so that the Bishop's deer could jump onto the Earl's land adding to his stock but his own animals could not jump the other way! Today the ridge, not the ditch, remains the dividing line between Worcestershire and Herefordshire.

There are some historians who believe that the great iron-age fort of British Camp on the Herefordshire Beacon was one of the bases of the ancient Briton chieftain Caractacus, and it is logical to assume that it was – it was a major fort in his time. At over eleven hundred feet, it is also one of the highest. A jewelled crown discovered near the base of the camp hill in 1650 also supports the view, but there is no proof. Construction started on the fort in the third century BC and despite the hill's exposure a large community grew outside the ramparts. The foundations of their huts can still be traced. The highest point of the Malverns at just short of fourteen hundred feet is the Worcestershire Beacon towards the northern end of the chain. From this point the views stretch in all directions as far as the eye and the imagination can see.

'On either hand, the landscape spreads afar, the level of the Sev-

> *ern Valley contrasting with the more rugged character of the Herefordshire side, where tumbled hills range far way to the dark line of mountains which enfold the county towards the borders of Wales.'*

The spa town of Great Malvern clings to the eastern flanks - that is the Worcestershire side. Nevertheless, its importance to the area requires a mention. The town itself and its fame for the purity of its natural mineral water springs – there are over a hundred of them scattered around the area - grew rapidly from 1842 onwards following the Victorian's rush for 'the water cure'. Even today, water from the springs is freely available and residents and visitors alike return regularly to fill up their plastic containers. Water was still bottled commercially on the Herefordshire side at Colwall up to 2010, from where it was exported all over the world. Great Malvern Priory is the centrepiece around which the town was built and which started life a thousand years ago as a Benedictine monastery. Theatre goers will delight at the prospect of seeing West End plays at the Malvern Theatres where well known celebrities take leading roles. In Malvern Link the world famous Morgan cars have been made since 1909, and of course there was Edward Elgar, arguably England's greatest composer. He was born nine miles away at Lower Broadheath, near Worcester in 1857 but moved to Great Malvern in 1891 and found the fame he sought. Here he wrote the *Enigma Variations* and, inspired by the view of British Camp, his dramatic work *Caractacus*.

The Victorians loved the Malvern area, not just for the waters but also as a major centre for recreation, and it is not surprising that they would have taken steps to protect it. In 1884 an Act of Parliament was passed which led to the appointment of the Malvern Hills Conservators, their responsibility being to protect the rights of commoners on the hills and keep land free from enclosure. The Conservators continue today as the guardians of three thousand acres of hills and commons.

Among Malvern's other notable residents was Jenny Lind, the 'Swedish Nightingale', who became an internationally renowned and much adored singer in the mid nineteenth century and the first woman to be memorialized in Westminster Abbey with a plaque in Poet's

Corner. She moved here after her daughter married a Herefordshire man in 1877 and lived with her husband at Wynds Point at the foot of the British Camp fort. Some time earlier, in 1332, William Langland was born hereabouts and educated at Malvern Priory. He became famous as the author of *The Vision of Piers Ploughman* which he wrote following a dream he had as he slept by a Malvern stream. His poem depicts the greed and corruption of men in power and the oppression of the lower classes. Considering how long ago Langland's revelations were, some present day observers might say we haven't progressed very far.

The Malvern hills are visible from almost anywhere in this part of the world, and the urgency to be here increases the closer you get. The final reckoning as you climb the narrow ridges is quiet awe inspiring. Each summit seems to offer a different view east or west until, if you are travelling south to north, the Worcestershire Beacon provides a stunning look back along practically the whole length. At the foot of the Worcestershire Beacon is a road cut through into Herefordshire from the direction of Great Malvern from which the unsuspecting visitor is suddenly confronted with a magnificent view across to the Black Mountains of south Wales. The road leads to the sleepy village of Colwall where there is a pleasant mix of buildings; half-timbered cottages, large Victorian villas, and modern bungalows. Unlike most small communities these days it has retained facilities that cater for all daily requirements and life goes on here as if Great Malvern over the hill didn't exist. The train from Hereford stops here and it is possible for those of a mind, to travel on to London. There is a well kept cricket ground which hosts occasional minor county matches. Perhaps the most famous tournament held at Colwall is Women's Cricket Week. The first such event was organised by Mrs Molly Scott-Bowden in 1926 and lead to the formation of the National Women's Cricket Association. The church of St James the Great is just over a mile south west of the present village which moved away from it following the arrival of the railway in 1860. The centre is dominated by a three star Hotel with a five star feel about it. Built in 1909, its stylish Edwardian half timbered on red brick construction, large though it is, doesn't intrude.

Stephen Ballard's burial site above the railway tunnel he built through the Malvern Hills. The top of an air shaft from the tunnel can clearly be seen.

Colwall is where the talented engineer Stephen Ballard lived. Chosen for his heroic achievements with the canal to Hereford, he set about driving the railway from Worcester through the Malverns. His tunnel to Colwall was completed in July 1860 but was plagued by problems from rock falls and dislodging bricks and in 1926, the Great Western Railway Company replaced Ballard's tunnel with a new one. Ballard died in 1890 and is buried on his estate beneath a mound created from the spoils from the tunnel he built nearby. I found the place chosen as his last resting place, hidden away amongst shrubs not far from a public right of way. There was no sign indicating the site and no plaque commemorating the great man's achievements.

The closure of the spring water bottling plant at Colwall continues to dominate local feelings, even today. The original plant was built in 1892 by Joseph Schweppe, a German jeweller who had discovered, in his spare time, how to bottle mineral water. When he moved to the UK to set up his new business, the Victorians' thirst for the pure waters of the Malvern hills provided him with a ready made market. Since then, however, access to the many open springs on the Malverns has been and continues to be free. In addition, the quality of still tap water in the UK has been recognized for many years as being good enough for most people's taste, is also free and readily available. The Coca Cola company took an interest in the Colwall site initially in 1987 when they joined the then owners, Cadbury Schweppes, in a joint venture. By 1999 the factory was in the full ownership of the American giant and some say the sounds of real estate value became louder than the rattling of bottles. Though undoubtedly a blow for the people of Colwall, the demise of its bottling plant is more surprising for lasting as long as it did.

I have been a visitor to Colwall many times since 2003. The people there retain a strong community spirit and the village has a great deal of charm,. For those reasons and more, I will never tire of it and was in no hurry to move on. At the southern end of the central street is Brook House, a beautiful Grade II seventeenth century half timbered farmhouse with a mill stream running through extensive well kept gardens and here is where I stopped for the night with hosts Maggie and John Powell.

As hard as it was to drag myself away from the Malverns, there were many more miles to cover so, with a slightly sluggish gait, I set off once again on my next stage. The back lanes through Colwall are a delight to walk. A shaded track becomes a private road lined by attractive detached houses overlooking the valley where the Cradley Brook meanders its way towards its eventual meeting with the river Teme near Worcester. Near Mathon, I passed the entrance to West Malvern Cricket Club, an enchanting little ground with a pretty gable-fronted pavilion. By the entrance gate is a notice board displaying the fixtures for the season, the names of their opponents reflecting the club's intentions to play for fun; Old Whitgiftians, Tibberton Taverners, Woodpeckers, and Moles. Mathon has been designated a village of natural beauty. The villagers say it was famous locally for three things - its own variety of Mathon hops for pale ales, sand and gravel pits producing some of the finest building material in the area, and the Mathon Weed, a daisy-like flower with an unpleasant smell. Hops are no longer grown here and the pits have been flooded and turned over to nature. But as to the origins of the evil smelling weed, I could neither find it nor obtain an explanation. What was definitely not a beautiful sight was the state of the village's only pub, The Cliffe Arms, closed by the owner in 2005 he refused to reopen on the grounds that the villagers didn't support his business enough. With a population of over sixteen hundred, Cradley is the largest village in Herefordshire and currently without a pub. Although the Crown Inn has been closed for more than fifteen years, I am told it is still licensed to sell alcohol and there has been a lengthy campaign to have it re-opened, but so far, without success. Cradley is in effect two villages separated by the Cradley Brook. The lower half is the oldest part and includes the church and some fine half-timbered cottages. To avoid a particularly dangerous stretch of the A44, I took a field path from the neighbouring hamlet of Westfield, the upper half of Cradley, and a challenging climb up Fromes Hill. On the crest of the hill is yet another closed pub where the owners have been locked in a protracted dispute with the council over their application for a change of use.

With so many local pubs closing in this part of the county, I took time to consider the theoretical argument for keeping village pubs open. In recent years, they have been closing throughout the country at an alarming rate leaving whole communities dry and without a vital community facility. Many campaigners believe that some pub owners have deliberately run down their business to claim it as unviable and fit only for domestic use. In fairness, publicans, like everyone else want to earn a good living, and can only do so if customers spend money in their pubs. If this is not happening, they are entitled to wonder whether it is worth their effort. In most instances, the land on which the pub stands is worth considerably more than the business and the situation is exacerbated when the pub is also a home and the incumbent owner wants to stay where he is. The other side of the argument is that they should sell up to someone who might make a better go of the business through taking a more imaginative approach. Councils are right to support their communities' needs, but in the final analysis unless people use their locals regularly, they cannot survive.

Soon I would be dropping into the fertile valley of the river Frome to visit first Castle Frome, a tiny hamlet which takes its name from an ancient hill fort and is of great significance on two counts. Here is another church named after St Michael and All Angels, built in the early part of the twelfth century which, although it went through major restoration in 1878, retains many of the original Norman features. Its isolation indicates that there was once a larger community here which may have disappeared following the Black Death in the fourteenth century. Inside the church is one of the finest Romanesque sculptured fonts anywhere in England. The exquisite carvings on the bowl depict the baptism of Christ and St Matthew holding his Gospel. It stands on top of three crouching creatures of indeterminate form and symbolizes the power of the church over evil. This fabulous work is one of the best examples of the Herefordshire School of Sculptors whose art I saw previously at Kilpeck. Not far away is a collection of buildings making up Hill Farm. In March 1840,Wilford Woodruff, an American Mormon missionary, baptized the first convert in England in a pond close to this farmhouse. In the space of one month six hundred baptisms took place into the Mormon church here and by August a total of eighteen hundred had been welcomed into their faith. Following their conversions, many families left Herefordshire for the US state of Utah, the cultural centre of Mormon influence. The pond at Hill Farm has become a place of pilgrimage for their descendants from all over the world.

> *Further away in the same direction lies Bishop's Frome, with its fine church and curious Elizabethan mansion quaintly called 'China Court' containing some richly paneled chambers and old paintings.*

Timmins couldn't be blamed for referring to the group of buildings at Cheney as 'China' because that is what was recorded mistakenly on the 1832 OS map. Sadly, Cheney Court, built in the early part of the seventeenth century was destroyed by fire in 1888. The chapel alone survives amidst modern farm buildings which stand where the old house used to. Unlike Cradley and its surrounding satellite hamlets, the village of Bishops Frome still boasts two pubs. Not so long ago it had six, reminding us of the influx of hop pickers. At the peak of the picking season in the 1920s, the population of Bishops Frome swelled from seven hundred souls to over five thousand. The name of the village reflects its ancient role as one of many country retreats for the Bishops of Hereford, but the site of any episcopal palace has long since disappeared. There was no railway built connecting Hereford with this part of the county so Timmins left it out of his schedules. Significantly for me, Bishops Frome is the gateway to the seven mile long Frome Valley, an area of natural beauty with high rolling hills on either side of a meandering river which is no more than a large stream. At the end of it is the pleasant town of Bromyard, but that was for thye next day because that night I had arranged to stay in a cowshed at Avenbury, a hamlet a few miles short of Bromyard. I'll explain this later.

Once, these lush hillsides were rich with flowering hop bines, cider apple orchards and soft fruit trees. Much of it has now returned to farm land but David Longman continues the tradition at his home, Paunton Court, a Jacobean farmhouse nestling by the river. He bought the house in 1991 after retiring as president of the Interflora company, the internationally known florists. Previous owners of Paunton had grown hops on the estate but David and his wife Clare decided they would like to have a go at growing a few grapes after spending a holiday in Tuscany where they were surrounded by vineyards. I was grateful that he had agreed to meet me and as we sat in a corner of his wine shop with a glass each of Bacchus, a product of his own vineyard, I began by asking him why, after a long life of fulfillment, he had chosen to start all over again.

'I'm never happy doing nothing,' he told me. *'Even when I was at Interflora I found time to run a dairy farm in Leicestershire. When we came here, the layout of the estate with south and west facing slopes close to the river cried out for something to be done with it. It was my wife's idea to grow grapes, but I think she meant the project to be kept small.'*

The Bacchus tasted good and he must have seen me eying the bottle because he poured me another glass.

'We discovered the soil is rich in this part of the Frome valley and the mild climate and consistent rainfall would offer plentiful growing days for our crops. We had to learn the know-how, of course, and planting and cultivating vines took the best part of three years. Our first success came towards the end of

1995 and now we have over three thousand vines in our four acre vineyard.' He explained that the German varieties such as Riesling are best suited for the UK climate, and Bacchus is a Riesling hybrid. There are around four hundred vineyards in England producing good quality white wines renowned for their floral bouquets and high acidity. My own preference has always been for a red so I asked him why British wines are predominantly white.

'In this part of the world, white varieties need a hundred days to reach maturity and black varieties which are used to make red wine could take up to one hundred and twenty days. The growing season just isn't long enough here for a successful red. While our location means our grapes take a little longer to ripen than continental ones, the slower maturation does endow our wines with a distinctive freshness and quality which sets them apart from those from many countries in Europe and the New World.'

David was now thirteen years into his working retirement and I couldn't help asking how long he planned to continue the business without family help. *'My children are successful in their own right. I hope one of them will eventually take over here, but as long as I can still pull the starter on the grass cutter, I'll keep going.'*

Which is what I had to do if I was to reach my accommodation before dark, so with two bottles of the very good Bacchus tucked safely in my rucksack, I thanked him for his time and went on my way.

On the opposite side of the valley is a place where mystery and intrigue have brought fame to a tiny church. St James the Greater at Stanford Bishop stands in isolation on the high hillside, its circular churchyard suggesting pre-Christian religious significance. By the entrance gate, almost hidden in a hedge, is a standing stone which adds to this belief. There are several fine yew trees, one of which is said to be twelve hundred years old, although yews are notoriously difficult to age. It is likely that there was an earlier, wooden Saxon, church here when the old yew tree was a mere sapling, and there are remains of a Norman church in the present stone structure. Among the many treasures adorning the inside is an oak chair of some antiquity which stands in a corner of the chancel next to the altar. A small brass plaque on it reads: 'The traditional chair upon which St Augustine was seated at his historic conference with the British Bishops at the second Synod AD 603' It was discovered below the tower by Dr James Johnstone in 1846 who thought it rather old and perhaps worthy of investigation. Subsequently he became convinced of the chair's historical connection with St Augustine and such was his belief in its authenticity, the chair was taken to Canterbury in 1885. However, in 1943 it was re-examined by a panel of experts who declared that in spite of its appearance the chair had been made no earlier than the mid 1700s. In any case, there was no evidence that a meeting with Augustine took place at all at Stanford Bishop. At least the claims remained undisputed for a hundred years, during which time this little church could rightly have been proud of its great historical connection.

And so to Avenbury where my port of call for the night was a derelict cowshed, recently rebuilt as a home and called, almost reverently, The Old Cowshed. It is the splendid creation of Richard and Helen Combe who moved into the valley in 1992. Their first choice was the manorial Avenbury Court across the road which was empty when they first set eyes on it.

'There was just too much work which needed to be done with it, so we decided against the idea.' Helen told me over a pot of tea later that evening. *'We noticed opposite the manor a long single storey farm building used for housing cattle which was also ruinous, but immediately saw the potential so we bought that instead. It took two years of hard slog to rebuild the place as we wanted it, but it was worth every penny.'* As well as turning the old cattle shed into a spacious and comfortable home, Richard and Helen have landscaped the land around the house into pleasant gardens and have a clear panoramic view from their north facing rooms across the valley towards the hilltop town of Bromyard, and a marvellous outlook it is too.

The next morning after a splendid breakfast I returned to the riverside footpath where another ancient site awaited, this time one to challenge the imagination. The romantic ruins of St Mary's church lie partly hidden, beside the river and behind dense vegetation. Parts of the fabric of the ruin are Norman but its origins go back to Saxon times. In what was the churchyard, moss covered gravestones lean at impossible angles, some already collapsed and broken. Cracks in the tower walls indicate the building is in a dangerous state and overdue for a little TLC. Above all, it is a spooky place and there are many local tales of ghostly apparitions, in particular of a young woman apparently in some distress. An adjoining field is called Agatha's meadow, named after a third century martyr who once lived in the vicinity. Could the troubled young women be her? For those with a fertile mind, being here on a sombre day or starless night might not be recommended. In the eleventh century this church was one of nine superior churches of Herefordshire, on a par even with the cathedral and St Guthlac's ancient priory at Hereford. Following the great plague in the fourteenth century, the population here seems to have migrated up to the ridge road at Munderfield. Although St Mary's remained the spiritual centre for this part of the valley, in time a new chapel was

Atmospheric ruins of St Mary's church at Avenbury

opened at Munderfield leaving the scattered parishioners of Avenbury to their isolated riverside church. Services continued at St Mary's well into the twentieth century until finally in 1936 the church commissioners called time and left it to decay and fall apart.

Continuing along the river path, in less than a mile I reached the northern end of the Frome valley and the market town of Bromyard. Although Bromyard is the smallest of the county's market towns nevertheless it is the hub of the districts of north east Herefordshire. It was established in the twelfth century and lies on a plateau above the young river Frome surrounded by verdant wooded downland. There are still arguments about the origins of the town's name. Scholars define it as meaning 'a broom enclosure' but the popular local preference is simply 'an enclosure by the Frome'. Many of the houses in the town date from the late sixteenth century. Some were later converted and now have Georgian or Regency fronts. The town grew up around St Peter's church, formally an important Saxon minster and founded in the ninth century, soon after Hereford cathedral. Why it was so important remains a mystery. The present church dates from 1160 and has many distinctive Norman features, making it an exceptional building, but sadly nothing from the Saxon minster has survived. Like many small towns these days, there have been problems in recent years with wild youths, but I am told that controls have succeeded in curbing much of it which is a blessing as I have found Bromyard a pleasant and friendly little town and enjoyed several visits here.

When I asked a few locals in the Rose and Lion pub which of the town's characters they remember the best, the name Ada Chapman came high on their list. The story they told described how, between the two world wars, her father ran Chapman's Circus and they lived in a farmhouse two miles outside the town. After her father died and the circus no longer came to town, Ada kept most of the animals in cages at the farm. Because she didn't have enough room for all the animals, she was allowed to house a few elephants in stables at the back of the King's Head in the high street. Bob Eckley remembered as a child seeing Ada walk the elephants down to the river at Broad bridge to drink. *'She'd bring 'em down the street and they would pick up some of the fruit*

and vegetables on display outside the greengrocer's with their trunks as they plodded past'
To pay for the animals' upkeep, Ada rented them out to Chipperfield's Circus whenever it came to Herefordshire.
'In those days,' Bob continued, *'Ada used the trains to transport the animals to wherever Chipperfield's wanted them. Sometimes the train couldn't get up enough steam to move because of all the weight and they had to leave some behind to come back for later. One day, one of the elephants brought down the roof of its pen in the stable at the Kings Head and it died as a result of its injuries. The carcass was so big it had to be cut up to be removed from the yard. We all wondered at the time if the butcher might've picked up a bargain or two for his shop!'*

In 1842, Stream Hall just east of the town along the A44, was a smallholding containing a farmhouse and outbuildings. The landowner, William Finney, discovered that beneath it there were valuable beds of stone similar in quality to that of Yorkshire stone which could be worked easily to any shape and size. By 1876 he had opened up a quarry and three years later was manufacturing tiles and bricks on a huge scale. The company's phenomenal success was partly a result of the arrival of the trains from Worcester which ran past the works providing access to the industrial towns of England. In 1914, the company started supplying the Egyptian State Railways after receiving the largest contract for paving tiles ever placed in this country by a foreign organization. The great deep quarries seen today mark nearly a century of activity providing an unexpected source of wealth and employment for Bromyard.

Another, gentler industry which had its origins fifteen miles east in Worcester, was glove making. The Milore factory came to Bromyard in 1946, starting up in Sherwood Street before settling into purpose built premises in Old Road. At one time more than half the ladies of the town worked there. Young girls without any pretensions of a professional life went to work at Milore's straight from school. Although the company had strict quality controls, by all accounts the business was run with a high regard for the health and happiness of its employees, even to the extent of allowing several weeks off in September to let them go hop picking with their families on the many farms surrounding the town. When the girls married, those who were fortunate enough to have a sewing machine at home could carry on working for the company as outworkers. Glovemaking was an important industry in these parts and by the early nineteenth century there were up to one hundred master glovers in Worcester employing eight thousand workers, including many from nearby parishes in Herefordshire. The first signs of decline came in 1824 when cheaper foreign gloves began to be imported and by 1840 the number of master glovers had dropped by half. The Milore business hung on though until 1981 when both the Worcester and Bromyard factories closed.

Because Bromyard was not in Timmins's plans, he missed the most perfect of medieval manor houses anywhere in England. Deep in a secluded valley on the Brockhampton estate, the fourteenth century black and white timber framed manor with a rare matching gatehouse bridging a moat must be one of the finest of National Trust properties. Next to these is the ruin of a small Norman chapel. The manor house was built around 1380 by John Domulton, whose family the de Brockhamptons, had been living on the estate since the twelfth century, and is an excellent example of a home for a wealthy squire of that period. The building which can be seen today is L-shaped, although excavations have proven the original construction to be an H plan (the west cross wing has gone) and was constructed with massive timbers, probably from the estate's 1,680 acres of woodland. During the warm summer months, several species of bats are known to sleep amongst the rafters of the great hall. In the eighteenth century, a descendant of John Domulton, Bartholomew Barneby, built a large new house at the top of the valley, a mile to the south of the old house which had by then been abandoned. Barneby employed Thomas Pritchard to design his new home. Pritchard had previously claimed fame by designing the cast iron bridge built near Telford in Shropshire after which Ironbridge is named. A new chapel was built by George Byfield, the first Gothic revival example in Herefordshire but it became his one and only work. In the early part of the nineteenth century, a huge stone wall was constructed around the estate which runs for all of ten miles and reaches ten feet in height. This remarkable project, which still stands today, was said to have provided employment for soldiers returning from the Napoleonic wars. New Brockhampton House was to be the home of the Barneby family until 1946 when the last resident, Col. John Talbot Lutley (whose father was a Barneby but changed his name to Lutley) left the entire estate to the National Trust, ending nearly eight hundred years of ownership by the same family.

The Brockhampton estate is truly remarkable in size and structure. The original medieval manor house sits by the aptly named Paradise Brook and is about as isolated as you could want to be. Descending on foot from the Worcester road to the valley bottom is a considerable journey and a sterner challenge on the way back, but worth every step.

There is no access from the Brockhampton estate onto Bromyard Downs, which meant a tricky walk along the A44. The Downs are common land and there's quite a lot of it to explore. There are exquisite views to be had from many parts of Herefordshire, and these steep slopes are no exception. It is worth keeping to strolling pace and to take it all in if the weather is set fair. I was unfortunate to be there on a misty day with rain in the air and little hope of seeing much, if anything. Heading north off the Downs towards one of the least populated areas of the county, I took a field path which would take me between two more previously owned Barneby estates. Buckenhill Manor is part eighteenth century with Victorian additions and is rather dull. When Elizabeth Biddulph Phillips, a Barneby, died in 1852 followed by her husband Robert ten years later, the short lived Barneby occupation of Buckenhill came to an end. From then on the house had a chequered history as a school, hotel and country club, mail order books business, together with long periods of non-occupation. The remains of another Barneby residence, Saltmarsh Castle across the Bromyard road, now form the backdrop to a caravan park and has become even less pleasing to the eye. In 1840, Edmund Barneby inherited land at Saltmarsh from a William Higginson and built a magnificent crenellated Victorian castle. In decorating it in the Gothic style he was decidedly out to impress, but then despite being a member of the most influential of local families, Edmund inexplicably changed his name to Higginson. In 1856, he purchased

St Giles Saxon Church, Edvin Loach

another great house, Bredenbury Court, midway to Leominster, adding to the family collection of large estates in and around Bromyard. When Edmund died in 1871 childless Saltmarsh Castle passed to his nephew William and was once again lived in by a Barneby. By the 1950s, like many large houses throughout the length and breadth of the UK, the huge castle had become too expensive to maintain and most of it was pulled down. Today, Saltmarsh is a carefully laid out holiday centre, although remnants of the castle buildings still remain including long battlemented walls which stretch out in every direction. The stables, service quarters and a barn are still standing, too. Tantalising glimpses of the reception hall with its fireplace have been incorporated into the park's entertainments block, and the old garden walls and an occasional castellated tower now form part of the park layout. The owner, Harry Weekers, is now considering turning the barn, which still houses many of the old castle's original working features, including a huge stone cider press, into some sort of themed bar for the entertainment of his customers.

Mention is made in the Domesday Book of the area north of Bromyard as Yedefen. At the time, the land hereabouts was in the hands of two families, the Ralfs, and the de Loges, eventually leading to naming their respective ownerships Yedefen Ralf, which has become the village of Edwyn Ralph, and Yedefen de Loges, a hamlet now called Edvin Loach. It was the de Loges who built the first church at Edvin Loach in the late eleventh century dedicated to St Giles and this remained the primary place of worship for the locals until well into the nineteenth century. When a new church was eventually built next to it in 1860 in the much fancied Gothic style, the old church was abandoned and left to decay. Fortunately for us and scholars of early Norman architecture, large parts of the shell remain. The herringbone masonry on the inner side wall of the nave is particularly splendid and Saxon in nature. The site is also interesting in that it lies on isolated high ground and suggestions have been made that perhaps the old church may have been built into the bailey of an ancient Saxon castle. The Victorians dedicated their new church to St Mary, though why the change of saint is a mystery. A field close by is still called St Giles's Acre but the poor chap seems to have fallen from grace at some stage. An article from The Hereford Times on February nineteenth 2004 reads: 'Two of the three bells stolen from a Herefordshire church six years ago are discovered at an estate agents in Wiltshire.' They were stolen from their display cases in St Mary's church in December 1997. Ann Willis, a Trowbridge woman with knowledge of medieval bells, photographed them and put the pictures on a historian's website where they were recognised by David Bagley from Gloucestershire. He had photographed the Edvin Loach bells in the early 1990s.

'It's an amazing story,' said Allan Wyatt, St Mary's church secretary, who accompanied the vicar, the reverend David Howell to identify the bells. *'We had discussed the question of how to secure them just before they were stolen. Afterwards, as time went on we were advised that they had probably been stolen to order and exported, or worse still, melted down. The third bell, the sanctus bell and the smallest, is still missing but the vicar is optimistic that, too, may yet be found. And after all the publicity they will be of even greater interest to visitors to our church.'*

A mile below the hillside lies the twin village of Edwyn Ralph. Like that of its close relative, the twelfth century church of St Michael is built very close to, if not actually in, a motte and bailey complex. The centre of the village used to be around the church but since the Black Death of 1348 the present village has migrated a quarter of a mile and now lines the B4214 Tenbury road. There is a local legend which tells of a duel between two noblemen, one from each parish, Baron Ralph and Lord Edvin, who fought for the hand of a local lady. Hearing of the dispute, she ran between the men as they fought and was pierced by their swords. Maddened by grief the two Lords fought on until they both died from their wounds. The three are buried in St Michael's church.

This part of the county is mainly farmland and particularly beautiful. It is also renowned for its many iron age settlements. Wall Hills fort a mile or so north west of Edwyn Ralph, was one of the largest in Herefordshire indicating that the nearby village of Thornbury was an important centre of population before the arrival of the Romans. The thirteenth century church here is dedicated to St Anna and its tower is yet another massive structure designed as a refuge in case of attack. The high level narrow lane I was following passed close to the shallow ramparts of the fort. Below me to the north the large farm house that is now called Netherwood is modern but the old mansion that was pulled down to build it was medieval and had a distinguished history. It was reputed to be the birthplace of Roger Mortimer, later Earl of March and lover of Edward II's Queen Isabella, in 1287. In 1567, another historical celebrity, Robert Devereux second Earl of Essex, was also born at Netherwood. Following his father the first earl's death in 1576, the young Robert became the ward of William Cecil, secretary of state to Queen Elizabeth 1, who eventually presented him at Court. The Queen indulged in many flirtations with the youthful, dashing, but often brash, young earl but her affection for Robert was genuine, though at the age of fifty-four her feelings may have been more maternal than amorous. The earl on the other hand was hot headed and jealous of other young courtiers, especially William Cecil's son, also named Robert, who had by now taken over his father's duties to the Queen. Devereux's youthful energies were expressed most appropriately in warfare where he often behaved with conspicuous daring. However, his temper often resurfaced in court quarrels during which he would frequently demand a duel as the best means of resolving matters. In 1590, the Queen sent Devereux to Ireland to put down a long rebellion, but much to her annoyance, and against even the earl's usual resort to violent solutions, he was conned into a peaceful but unauthorized truce by the rebel Earl of Tyrone. He returned to London to face an angry and, this time, unforgiving monarch. Devereux was stripped of his powers and confined to house imprisonment where he brooded over what he considered to be his unfair treatment, and plotted a futile revolt. In spite of his popularity around London, Devereux received limited support and his small force fell away soon after the first skirmish near Richmond. The earl was arrested, tried again, but this time there was no leniency. The Queen reluctantly signed his death warrant and he was executed on Tower Hill in February 1601. He was thirty-four years old.

I arrived at the hilltop hamlet of Leysters, the most northerly point of my journey, in the early evening of 16 May 2005. At The Old Vicarage, Guy and Amanda Griffiths run a bed and breakfast establishment of quite superior accommodation. Their house, set in eighteen acres and previously a farmhouse, has hardly changed since 1859 when it was extended for use by the local parson and his family. In 1871, the Victorian diarist Francis Kilvert, described a game of croquet on the large lawn over which my spacious room looked out. Kilvert stayed at the house on a number of occasions and on that visit on 24 October, he was introduced to a young lady by the name of Caroline Stothert who was by all accounts a stranger to him. During their conversation he happened to mention that his father came from Kington Langley, a village near Chippenham in Wiltshire, whereupon Miss Stothert declared 'Why then, you must be Francis Kilvert, and I am your cousin!' It seems the world was just as small one hundred and fifty years ago as it sometimes feels today.

The name Leysters has no recognizable origin. Even the village itself has moved at least twice from its earliest known position around the church which is now isolated on a small back road to Tenbury.

The modern day village now straddles the A4112 and shares a parish with a neighbouring village, Middleton-on-the-Hill. Although there are only a total of one hundred and forty six homes collectively, their position scattered around the borders of three counties and the allocation to the parish of three postal codes has meant mail is delivered here from Hereford, Worcester and Ludlow, in Shropshire. At the top of Lever hill on the Tenbury road are a group of buildings known as The Lea. It was here in the sixteenth century that the Lloyd family farmed. Later, they became yet another Herefordshire originator of a major banking business that still bears their name.

Before moving on the following morning, I made a detour to visit Leyster's twelfth century church a stone's throw across a couple of fields behind the Old Vicarage. On the way, lying beside the back lane, I came across a curious large flat slab, known locally as the Poet's Stone. It is said to have been once carved with the initials WW and MW and is reputed to be where William Wordsworth and his wife Mary rested while out walking in this area. They were staying nearby at Bockelton Vicarage as guests of a parson Miller. He it was who arranged for the carvings to be made in memory of the great man's stay. However, the stone appears to have been regularly chipped by souvenir hunters and if the initials ever existed, they have long been spirited away.

I retraced my steps along the lane to Rosebury before turning off along a field path. Ahead of me rolling farmland stretched to the far horizon. Bach Camp hill fort perched on a small hilltop lay invitingly in my way. It was another glorious late spring day and God was surely in his heaven and all was definitely well down here. For a while, I shared this glorious emptiness with a buzzard, mewing as he watched me nervously while playing on the thermal up draughts. At the bottom of the field I saw tiny silent darting movements from a group of rabbits, edgy perhaps due to the buzzard's presence. I felt I was intruding but the guilt was brief such was my pleasure. This would have been an inspiring moment for any artist or poet but Henry Thornhill Timmins didn't come this way, or at least he doesn't mention it in *Nooks and Corners*. I wonder what he would have made of it. It is difficult to understand sometimes why so many of us nowadays prefer the crowded steaming beaches of the Mediterranean, or accept with increasing regularity the many hours waiting in an airport lounge for a delayed flight to such places.

'Don't tell them our secret', words expressed to me sincerely the previous night in the Duke of York pub at Leysters. *'Leave them to their foreign holidays. We don't want them here.'*
Those farmers' pleas wouldn't match Guy and Amanda's thoughts at the Old Vicarage, but in a way I endorse their protectionist sentiment.

I crossed the Whyle Brook and set a course towards Pudleston, one of many scattered rural communities north east of Leominster. Here, cow parsley had spread uncontrolled along the grass verges and overgrown hedges allowing me only occasional glimpses of the lush countryside beyond. Through tiny Rosedale, the scenery changed briefly as the lane passed below a wooded canopy and the cow parsley made way for an army of *Urtica Dioica*, tall nettles, infilling between trees in some places to a height of six feet and more. Then, ploughed fields give way to lush grass meadows carpeted in buttercup. I stopped to rest and chat to a small herd of young steers over a gate and was taken unawares by a group of passing cyclists. I acknowledged there greetings and odd looks and hurried away, hugely embarrassed.

At Pudleston crossroads, the delightful isolated church of St Peter, had once served a larger community, before the fourteenth century plague reduced the village to 'scattered' status. It stands opposite the imposing redbrick Old Rectory, until recently part of the Bulmer cider family's estate. At this point I was six hundred feet above sea level and the views were clear and once again breathtaking. Pudleston is a modern abandoned village. The shop and post office closed in 1977 followed in 1982 by the school. There is no evidence of there ever being a pub here, and the last bus left in 1983. One building, however, remains as a monument to phenomenal business wealth. Pudleston Court is a castellated Victorian pile built in 1846 for Elias Chadwick from the proceeds of his success as a cotton manufacturer in Wigan, Lancashire. Built in a similar style to that of Hampton Court, home of his friend and fellow Lancastrian John Arkwright, Pudleston was erected to replace a previous mansion owned by the Duppa family. The Duppas originated from Kent but had lived at Puddleston since the eighteenth century. Their name lives on in Duppa's Almhouses, one of the black and white treasures of Pembridge in the west of Herefordshire.

The much restored Pudleston Court was the home until recently of Dr Albert and Monique Heijn. Dr Heijn was the former head of the dutch company Ahold, the third largest supermarket business in the world, and instigator of the barcode system. Having spent most of their working lives in their native Holland, it is significant that they chose this lonely spot in English Herefordshire for their retirement years. Security was high around the Heijn's estate and for good reason. In 1987, Dr Heijn's brother was murdered in Holland at the hands of violent criminals who had kidnapped him hoping to receive a ransom for his release. The people of Hereford have been particularly grateful for the Heijn's contribution to the city's re-development over recent years. The regeneration of run down riverside warehouses and neglected dwellings by the old bridge over the river Wye, known as Left Bank, was due to their vision and money. Sadly, following Albert's death in January 2011, any further plans the Heijns had for investing in Hereford's future prosperity ended.

From Pudleston I turned north once again, this time for a four mile amble over empty hills and ridges, passing Bach Camp and following the Yolk brook to the ancient manor at Stockton Bury. As the Saxon name 'bury' might suggest, there has been a dwelling on this site for considerable time, since the year 660 in fact. The main house was granted manor status by Edward III and it later became a grange for the monks of Leominster Priory. In 1795, Thomas Harley of nearby Berrington Hall purchased Stockton Bury and pulled down all the existing buildings to build an elegant Georgian house. The Berrington estates subsequently came into the hands of seventh Lord Rodney who in 1885 gambled it all away at a casino in the south of France. During the resulting sale of the manor, the transfer of ownership was stopped when the reckless Rodney's luck suddenly changed with a substantial win on the St Ledger!

Stockton Bury is now a working organic farm run by Raymond Treasure and his helpers. His grass reared cattle and Clun Forest sheep have grazed here for over fifty years. It was from this farm in 1881 that Thomas Carwardine, a renowned breeder of Herefords, exported one of his bulls called Anxiety IV to the US where it became the source from which every Hereford in the US was bred. Flamboyant Mr Treasure is a keen gardener, too. The four acre layout is very well sheltered and is planted with many different varieties enabling a long growing season providing colour and enjoyment for the paying public all year round. Curiously, at the top of a barn gable end there is a bell loft containing three bells, one of which Ray had especially cast in his name.

It was soon time to turn south again, but before doing so I had planned to visit the National Trust's Berrington Hall, an imposing sandstone mansion once yet another house belonging to the Harley estate owning empire. Thomas Harley purchased Berrington from another of the counties great families, the Cornewalls, in 1775 after making a fortune in the City and then serving as Lord Mayor of London. He employed Capability Brown to design the park and Henry Holland, Brown's son in law, to build the house, which was completed by 1783. The resulting French Neo-classical style is severe, with two principal storeys topped with a balustrade running around the entire building. Dominating the west front, which unusually faces the park rather than the entrance drive, is a massive pedimented portico supported by four ionic columns. The garden lodge reflects the mood of severity and is in the form of a triumphal arch, perhaps a reminder of Harleys career in the city. In 1781, Harley's eldest daughter Anne married George Rodney, favourite son of Admiral Rodney, one of the most famous seamen of the age. Harley died in 1804 and because he had no son, from then until 1901 it was the Rodneys who lived at Berrington, at which point the gambling Lord Rodney was forced to sell to pay his mounting debts. The estate was then bought by Frederick Cawley, a successful cotton merchant from Manchester who owned the patent to pure black dye. His already substantial fortunes increased following Queen Victoria's death when the demand for black clothing rocketed. As was the ill fortune of many landowning families in wartime, so the Cawleys too were destined to be blighted, cruelly through two generations. The first Lord Cawley lost three of his four sons in the first conflict and the remaining son, who eventually became the second Lord Cawley, lost his youngest son in the second war, during which his eldest was severely wounded. Berrington Hall was eventually handed over to the National Trust when the second Lord Cawley died in 1954. Lady Cawley continued to live there until her death in 1978 at the age of one hundred.

Geographically speaking, my visit to Berrington just a few miles north of Leominster was the end of this section of my walk and not everything had gone according to plan. Even before I set out from Bromyard, I knew I could not cover all the ground I had in mind and make it to Leominster with just the one stop over at Leysters. So after a night's stay at the delightful Copper Hall in Leominster, run by Stuart and Christine Crick, I caught the number 482 bus the next morning back towards Bromyard to complete unfinished business.

Alighting at Grendon Green on the A44, I walked north along a quiet lane towards the old Fencote railway station where I knew I was in for a treat. When Ken Matthews left his native Swindon after a forty-eight year career as a railway signalman in search of a quiet life, he did not know, that more than twenty years later, he and his wife would be the proud owners of their own fully equipped railway station, together with a section of line, deep in the north Herefordshire countryside. The old station buildings and signal box at Fencote had been miraculously spared the final indignity of demolition after the line from Worcester to Leominster closed in 1952. A local farmer bought the land from British Rail but had no use for the station so when Ken learned that Fencote was up for sale, he jumped at the chance of a lifetime and bought it. I had telephoned ahead to check Ken would be there and arrived to see him, with paint brush in hand, adding a new coat to one of the platform's gas lamp holders. We sat in the station master's office drinking tea as he told me his story.

'I just couldn't get the railways out of my system' he began after I'd asked him why he had taken the momentous decision to buy Fencote, *'I'd been working with trains all my life and when I retired, I didn't know what else to do.'*

Like many of his fellow railway men, he was horrified at the devastation left by Doctor Richard Beeching's reshaping of Britain's railways in the 1960's. Beeching's Axe, as it was labelled, was based on

costs and efficiencies and by the end of 1966, six thousand route miles had been withdrawn from the network.
'It was first degree murder,' Ken continued *'that so many railway jobs were lost at a stroke, not to mention those of the people who worked for suppliers and services. I was luckier than many because I worked in the Swindon train sheds which kept going until 1986'* We walked down the empty platform and across the track for a view of the station layout. *'The old station house was in fairly good condition when I came here but the waiting room, signal box and parcel house required quite a lot of attention.'*

Ken also has plans to restore the two lines between the platforms if his money will stretch far enough. The Worcester-Leominster route was a single line but Fencote served as a passing place for trains going in opposite direction and Ken set about making the signalling system fully operational. Through his connections with many friends and departments within the railway industry, he has been able to trace old and unwanted equipment which he needed to complete the work. He furnished the signal box with levers rescued from the redundant signal box at Gerrard's Cross in Buckinghamshire after the line from Marylebone to Banbury was modernized in 1992. Gas lamps for the platforms came from Acton in west London, and Aberystwyth and Carmarthen in west Wales. He built three semaphore signal gantries from genuine parts and obtained track, crossings and timber sleepers from surplus stock rail yards. Finally, he managed to track down a viewing coach which was coming to the end of its life as a static holiday home at Dawlish Warren in Devon. It now stands beside platform one, newly painted in the famous LMS colours of maroon and gold. Ken has added to his small collection of rolling stock with the recent acquisition of a Henry Pooley timber tool van which had last been used in 1985 and which he intends to use as his workshop while the old parcel room is refurbished.

Sadly, his wife died in 2002, but he continues to dedicate himself to re-building and preserving at his own expense a treasure of a bygone railway age. Fencote Station is not open to the public, but occasionally Ken invites groups of enthusiasts to share his world for a short time. That day, there was just him and me.

Crossing Lockley's Heath I approached another interesting landmark. The village of Hatfield lies north of the A44 halfway between Leominster and Bromyard. In the centre is Hatfield Court, the home of the writer Jeremy Sandford from the 1980s until his death at the age of seventy-two in May 2003. Sandford was the author of *Cathy Come Home*, broadcast in 1963, and one of the most socially impacting plays ever shown on television. It is still considered a masterpiece. This late Victorian house replaced an earlier Elizabethan Hatfield Court which was pulled down in 1889. I stood by the drive entrance and noticed how drab and neglected the big house now looked. To one side in what I assumed was a courtyard there were numerous caravans of many shapes and sizes, presumably still occupied, a lingering sign of Sandford's generosity towards the homeless and his desire and life absorbing campaign for social justice.

Jeremy Sandford grew up at Eye Manor, near Leominster. His father, Christopher Sandford, founded the Golden Cockerell Press, a fine-book publishing company, and in 1947 helped launch The Folio Society. Jeremy's mother, Lattice, an engraver for her husband's book covers, later developed a fascination for corn dollies about which she wrote a book. Although he had been educated at Eton and Oxford, Jeremy considered himself a socialist and was appalled by the social injustices of the day, especially to the homeless. He developed a particular fascination for Romany gypsies which he inherited from his grandmother who herself travelled in a horse drawn caravan known as a vardo and spoke Romany. In 1957, he married Nell Dunn, a wealthy Canadian heiress, who herself eventually became a successful author and chronicled the exploitation of the working class in *Up the Junction* and *Poor Cow*. These books also became successful television productions. When 'Cathy' was first televised by the BBC in 1966, it caused uproar, caused the calling of a special Cabinet meeting, and immediately changed local authorities' policy concerning the separation of husbands from their families at a time of desperate need. It won many awards, played a major part in the creation of Shelter, the housing and homelessness charity, and in recent years was voted the most popular television play ever shown. Sandford followed 'Cathy' in 1971 with *Edna, the Inebriate Woman*, the story of a bag lady, which won him four further awards. By then his marriage to Nell was over, and she had returned to the high society of Chelsea. Left alone to brood over his own uncertain future, Sandford became influenced by New Age philosophies and opened the grounds of his home at Hatfield to travellers hosting music and dance summer camps. He travelled with them in their old buses and vans and attended solstices, ethnic music gatherings, rainbow circles and New Age cultural conventions. He began to dress like them, wore old corduroys, torn jerseys, and ethnic jewellery. At Hatfield, he slept on the floor, still embracing the basic and free spirited existence of travellers. Throughout this period, he continued to support the gypsies, whom he had always considered the real inheritors of the common lands and grass verges of the countryside. His audio cassette publication *Songs from the Roadside* celebrates contemporary gypsy songs, and one of his last works was as director of *Spirit of the Gypsies* commissioned by the Gypsy Council and starring David Essex. It was shot at a horse fair at Stow-on-the-Wold in the Cotswolds. Sadly, he fell out with the council over royalties and the row affected him to such an extent his closest friends are convinced it lead to his eventual breakdown and subsequent stroke towards the end of 2002.

Robert of Yoke was a contemporary of Jeremy Sandford and, like him, invited homeless people onto his estate at Upper Hill, four miles south west of Leominster. Although they were friends, it was Robert's guests that Jeremy had a closer affinity with and he often used to travel the ten miles from Hatfield just for a chat. Robert bought The Yoke, a thirteenth century manor house nestling below the northern wooded slopes of Westhope Hill, in 1969. Knowing him to be a friend of travellers, I telephoned him to say I was writing an article about Jeremy and he invited me to visit him. As I walked up the narrow lane to the house, I passed a traditional gypsy caravan, a vardo, parked on a small triangular grassy patch next to the entrance. It appeared to be deserted, but the ground surrounding the caravan was littered with various homely items as if the occupiers had emptied the van of all their belongings and were now living outside. I noted that the vardo was not on Robert's land and his gate was closed to them as it was to me temporarily. A few moments later I was standing outside the overgrown yard beside what seemed to be a neglected farmhouse. This was The Yoke.

Robert approached, shook my hand, and lead me along a darkened stone slabbed hallway, and through a curtain door into the living quarters. The room was lit by a single window and I strained my eyes to take in the surroundings. This was a room like I had never been in before. It was dominated by a large wooden table around which were half a dozen chairs, each one unlike the other. A dresser covered the length of one wall, and opposite this an ancient Aga filled a fireless inglenook. The window was a small bay and beneath it was a settee on which a whippet was curled up asleep, seemingly oblivious to my entrance. Stone flags appeared to extend throughout the ground floor of the house and every inch of surface with the exception of the floor was taken up by books, clothing, bric-a-brac, and every kind of flotsam and jetsam. On the table were the remains of a breakfast, an open box of cereal, a half filled teapot and several unwashed cups. We sat at the table and talked for a while. Later, Gretel Fletcher, a neighbour of Robert's joined us. She had been a close friend of Sandford's and, along with his second wife Philippa, helped him through his final days. At first she was suspicious of my motives for being there, but when I explained that I had become enthralled with Sandford's life and wanted to include a tribute in my book, she agreed to talk.

Final resting place of a misunderstood but much loved man. His ashes were buried in the churchyard at Eye Manor where he was born

'He never really recovered from the put down by the gypsy council over the Stow film', she recalled first with emotion and then with real anger. *'Jeremy had devoted much of his life to their cause and had become a loud voice in striving for reform and fairness. He was very generous with his money almost to the*

extent of being frivolous. When he died, there was hardly anything left of his possessions apart from Hatfield Court itself.'

Jeremy Sandford died peacefully in his sleep on twelfth May 2003 and his ashes were interred beneath the memorial to his mother and father in the churchyard next to his childhood home at Eye Manor. Before I left Leominster a few days later to return to Hereford, I visited the church at Eye Manor to pay my own last respects to a special person at his final resting place. There was no gravestone, no separate memorial to him, just an insignificant marker in a corner of the churchyard. When I returned a few years later, a plaque had been fixed to the wall above the spot where Jeremy's remains are buried. A small but inadequate contribution to a great life.

PART FOUR

To the Marcher Lands and the Welsh Border

A BIT OF OLD LEOMINSTER.

'Taking the train on the line running from Hereford to the North, we traverse a district of rich flat pastureland through which the river Lugg takes its leisurely way. Onward through Moreton station where, for some time after the opening of the line, the hollow trunk of an ancient oak did service as a waiting room.'

After a few weeks break back in Bristol to attend to my business affairs, I returned to Hereford and set out once again towards the north. The railway out of the city still crosses the Lugg valley on the outskirts where much of the land is common and old tracks remain, though some are overgrown and impassable in places. Here, too, once again we meet the remnants of the Gloucester to Hereford canal. Most of the canal bed has been ploughed out or filled in leaving tantalizing glimpses of crumbling locks and bridges, the only evidence now of mans' commitment to improving distribution of the essentials of life to local communities. Timmins referred to St Bartholomew's twelfth century Norman church at Holmer as a mixture of external age and beauty with internal modernity and simplicity. The most striking feature inside the church is the elaborate organ. It started off in Pudleston Court, Albert Heijn's stateley home near Leominster, where it graced the ballroom until 1934 and was then moved here. Too large and imposing for the chancel, the traditional place for a church organ, it was erected in the gallery completely blocking out the west window. A slightly askew, two storey, tower made of grey stone was built in the thirteenth century, the attractive black and white belfry was added during the reign of Elizabeth 1. Originally it was detached, and one of the seven detached church towers around the county. There are six bells, one of which is dated 1609 and bears the embarrassing acclaim 'God bless our noball King James'.

To avoid walking along the A49 for any distance, I turned eastwards and followed a quiet road across the valley. Standing in a field a few yards from the road is a solitary standing stone marked on the map as Wergins Stone. Like many such curiosities, its origins can only be speculated about. One suggestion is that it may be the last remaining medieval marker stone erected to direct ways around the meadow during times of flood. When the Hereford to Shrewsbury railway line was still under construction, a navvy is said to have set up home in a tree in Moreton station. The tree ended up with a thatched roof and a brick chimney, and at sixty two feet in circumference it was large enough to seat up to fifteen people. When the navvy moved on, the tree became a store house and in 1862, the ticket office. In 2003, against all the odds Moreton got a new pub. In these dark days of disappearing ale houses, this is indeed very good news and we should hope the community will enjoy this valuable asset and it will be kept open!

'Now we get a view of the flat topped hill known as Sutton Walls where Offa, the great King of Mercia, built himself a fortified palace.'

Sutton Walls hill fort was excavated between 1948 and 1951 by a distinguished archaeologist, Kathleen Kenyon, with occasional help from another, Sir Mortimer Wheeler. During the dig, many artefacts were found that pointed to the Romans being the last occupiers. In modern times gravel extraction has taken place within the fort and there has been some ill-advised dumping of chemicals, too, but little or no evidence has been found to suggest any occupation by either King Offa or the young King Ethelbert. A mile to the west on the river plain in October 1999, the TV archaeology *Time Team* excavated what was thought to be the foundations of a substantial Saxon building, raising speculation that it might be Offa's lost palace. This find hasn't yet been verified but what they discovered was certainly ancient and apparently a site of high status. As this area is traditionally associated with Mercian Kings, it is tempting to assume it may have been home to one of them. The association of Offa and Ethelbert with Hereford in general, but Sutton in particular, is strong. Offa had begun his reign as King of Mercia in 757 and this ambitious man decided he would put the remaining southern kingdoms of Wessex, Sussex, Essex and Kent also under his management. Less than twenty years later he had succeeded in doing so and proclaimed himself King of All England. To keep the Welsh in check, he completed one of his greatest achievements, his huge defensive system we all know as Offa's Dyke. He considered the northern territory of Northumbria too powerful at this stage to bring under his control but clearly had designs on the East Anglians. There their leader, the young Ethelbert saw early signs of Offa's intentions. For a while, Offa and Ethelbert were at peace but when Ethelbert proposed marriage to Offa's daughter Aelfrida, the stage was set for treachery.

The union was intended to cement peace between the two kingdoms but Offa must have sensed that this would prevent his claim on East Anglia. Worse, Ethelbert's heirs might even inherit Offa's Mercia. The young King travelled to Hereford to discuss matters but accounts of what happened next vary. Whether Offa's wife took a dislike to Ethelbert or Offa himself couldn't resist the opportunity of getting rid of an obstacle to his expansion plans is pure conjecture. What is certain is that Ethelbert was at some stage brutally murdered and his body thrown into a marsh. With one stroke of a sword, Offa had solved the problem. However, it seems he was troubled by his conscience and sought forgiveness from the Pope who had strictly forbidden any usurping of territory. There were a number of conditions attached to his absolution. First, Offa was to build a church at Marden dedicated to the Virgin Mary at a place where Ethelbert's body had been initially buried by the river Lugg. Then he was ordered to build a new stone minster at Hereford and re-bury Ethelbert there. Offa died in 796 and didn't see the completion of the new cathedral at Hereford, nor a united England, but he was the first to have the

Hereford bull, true symbol of the county

dream and his ruthless determination almost made it a reality. When the Welsh destroyed the cathedral in 1053, Ethelbert's remains were lost, except perhaps for the head which according to the Oxford Dictionary of Saints (1978) was said to have been taken to Westminster Abbey. I later wrote to Dr Tony Trowles, a librarian at the abbey, for any evidence that a relic of Ethelbert might be stored there and his reply was emphatic:

'The list of relics recorded by John Flete, a fourteenth century Westminster monk and abbey chronicler, makes no mention of any belonging to Ethelbert and as Flete claimed so many extraordinary relics for the Abbey, it is hard to believe he would have omitted the head if indeed it had been there!'

When Ethelbert's body was exhumed at Marden for transfer to Hereford, it is said a spring formed at the grave site. The well from the spring can still be seen today inside the west end of the church. The church is a mile from the village and travellers can be forgiven for wondering why it is so far from the community it serves until they learn why it was built over that spot. Marden is now predominantly a retirement village and almost entirely modern. The gardens are neat and carefully tended. In spite of the size of the village, it is claimed to be one of the largest in Hereford, the local pub is struggling to survive. It seems to me there is a dilemma here which requires a mention. Marden is very much a stand alone community. It has all the services needed to develop and maintain village life, including the pub. Why then do people stay away?

Situated on the floor of the valley and sheltered from the north by the wooded heights of Dinmore Hill, round hop kilns with their tall slate blue roofs and white cowls rising above the farm buildings of The Vern provide a typical Herefordshire welcome as I made my way along narrow lanes which shut off the property from the outside world. In the early part of the twentieth century some of the most sought after Hereford cattle were bred here by Captain Richard Saher de Quincey, one of the most successful of all the Hereford cattle breeders. De Quincey was a pilot in the Royal Flying Corps in World War I and following his demobilization, he approached Percy Bradstock, then recognized as the leading breeder of Herefords, at Free Town, near Tarrington, and asked to become a student at his farm. His time there must have been well spent because Captain de Quincey bought The Vern estate in 1922 and soon established himself as a successful breeder eventually winning at all the county shows. From then on bulls from the Vern herds were exported all over the American continent. The Captain's champion was a magnificent beast which, when it was born in 1939, he named Vern Robert. This bull lived until 1952 and produced a line which produced other champions. Vern Robert never left his home at The Vern and was buried on the banks of the river which runs through the estate. His reputation was such that when a new stained glass window was commissioned for Leominster Priory in memory of another distinguished breeder, George Butters, who had requested that a Herefordshire bull be included in any memoriam to him, Vern Robert was chosen and, thus, his immortality was assured. Captain de Quincey continued to produce high quality cattle until his death towards the end of 1966, ended an era in Hereford bull breeding history. The whole herd was sold at a disposal sale attended by buyers from all over the world. An attempt was later made to reintroduce a herd at The Vern but, after a short time, that too was sold off. Sadly, the farm and estate have once again withdrawn into themselves and the white faced cattle no longer graze the riverside meadows or shelter from the heat of the sun beneath the great oaks on the upland pastures.

From the gates of The Vern I turned east across redundant grazing fields and meadow and headed towards Bodenham. An old man was resting on a fallen tree by the river, eyes following the water, deep in thought. Next to him, his faithful dog watched his master keenly for any suggestion of movement. The old man's name was John Power and he called his dog Bugsy. Hearing my approach, the old man looked up sharply, his concentration broken. One of the most endearing memories of my journey is the number of times I've been asked by local people whether I was lost, as if visitors to their neighbourhood somehow always take wrong turnings and shouldn't be where they are.
'Are ye lost?" he asked
'No, I don't think so and I don't suppose you are either.' I replied coarsely, feeling more than slightly miffed by the assumption.
'I oughtn't to be,' he said *'I'm seventy four and I bin 'ere forty nine years.'*
Just as I was about to ask mischievously why he had been sat there all that time, he began the story of his life. He told me he was born in London, near Tower Bridge, and after the war ended up in Leominster where he met his wife. They'd settled in near by Bodenham where he got a job at the Cadbury factory at Milbrook and worked there until retirement. His wife had died sixteen years before and he'd been on his own with Bugsey ever since. That was about the gist of it, but it took him a lot longer to tell me, and I didn't have the heart

to stop him. Our conversation eventually strayed back to the dog, a handsome beast of a kind I hadn't seen before, short bodied and shepherd dog-like with varying shades of grey fur, dark grey face, and black eyes.

''ee's a Norwegian helk 'ound, look, named after the helks in Norway', he explained, putting his hands on top of his head, index fingers raised, elk like. *''ee's the third one I've had like 'im, look. Goes everywhere I go. Won't let me out of 'is sight, look. People what know me call 'im me shadow.'* And so he went on. I took advantage of a brief lull in our conversation to excuse myself and moved on, wishing him a long life and hoping Bugsy III would stick around long enough to see him through it.

Mine hosts for the night in Bodenham were Mick and Judy Wells at Vauld House Farm, and my lodging was a converted room in an old hop drying kiln. I hadn't previously stayed on a farm, so I wasn't sure whether I'd be called upon to help out with milking and the mucking out. As it transpired, Mick had enough time on his hands to run the village garage, as well, while Judy ran the B & B business in their farmhouse home. During a relaxing moment before dinner a family of ducklings followed me around the yard, but there appeared to be little else to distract from the rural pleasure of the surroundings. I dined at England's Gate Inn, a fine seventeenth century timber framed pub just down the road from the farm which seemed to be popular with locals and visitors alike. The inn at one time was on a cross roads of the old Leominster to Gloucester road, but since the main route has been prioritized, the inn finds itself on a side road, hidden from the view of passing traffic and thus denied many income opportunities.

The oldest house in the parish is Broadfield Court, parts of it dating back to the fourteenth century. At one stage of the house's history, it belonged to the Knights Hospitallers, a Christian order dedicated to St. John the Baptist but following the dissolution of the monasteries, it returned to lay hands. Architecturally, it is noted for its six south facing gables all added to the original building in different centuries, one in the twelfth century, two in the fifteenth century, and three in the nineteenth. A seventh Edwardian gable was demolished in 1968. Broadfield is now renowned for its extensive vineyards and fine range of white wines. During the Second World War, Captain Keith James spent time in Italy as a prisoner of war working in vineyards there. The experience of working with grapes never left him and when he came to the court in 1968, he started experiments with vines. In due course he discovered that despite being one of the most northerly vineyards in the country, the site had an extraordinary ability to produce fully ripened grapes even in poor summers. Today, the vineyard covers fourteen acres.

The next morning, taking a lane by the side of the England's Gate Inn, I set off in the direction of Dinmore Hill. Beyond Bodenham bridge a bridleway leads upwards and follows the crest of the hill. Here, the track is a sunken lane and for most of the way there is ground evidence that this was an ancient road above the valley connecting Bodenham with the Roman road five miles to the west at Bush Bank. For part of the way, the views are open down to the river Lugg and across to the heights of Hampton Park. In the distance I could see the intrusive Cadbury's Chocolate factory, which although out of town, is an important employer for Leominster people. Then a tantalizing glimpse of battlements and flagpole, the only view now of Hampton Court nestling in the meadow. Here, resting on the crest of the hill, after clambering up through Ashen Grove, Timmins described the scene.

> *'A very warm corner this proves, amidst the sheltering boughs now clad in the freshest green of early summer. The oaks are late this season, the young shoots showing a brilliant orange red in the sunlight; while the open glades are bright with orchids, bluebells and primroses and, here and there, the pale yellow green hoods of the 'lords and ladies'.*

Alighting at Dinmore station, Timmins turned west along the lane passing the Railway Inn. Strangely, he does not mention the inn although it was there at the time. Trains travelling north out of Dinmore station disappear for over a kilometer beneath Dinmore Hill in the direction of Leominster. The original tunnel for a single line was dug in 1853. By then, it is likely that the Railway Inn was up and running, too, and the provider of drink to the navvies, of which there must have been hundreds! Alfred Watkins recorded that his father, after he had just completed his new brewery in Hereford, had told him 'a great deal of beer went into building that tunnel'. In 1893, a year after Timmins' visit, a second tunnel was started and the line doubled. The opportunity was taken to build this additional track on a less steep gradient, producing tunnel entrances not in line with one another.

The modern A49 Hereford to Leominster road cuts through Dinmore Hill at Queenswood where there is now an arboretum and picnic area. In 1953 Richard Cotterell, a local landowner, established a fund to purchase rare tees and shrubs for the arboretum and thanks to his imagination and efforts there are now 450 species including Japanese maples and Californian redwoods covering sixty-seven acres of woodland. The building housing the tourist information centre used to be a tannery in Leominster, and the café at the visitor's centre was formerly the seventeenth century Essex Arms in Widemarsh Street, Hereford. In 1990 the pub had become surplus to requirements and was carefully demolished timber by timber and transferred here.

'Where the old coach-road climbs the shoulder of the hill, there nestles the lonely old farmhouse of Burghope, deep in a hollow. The manor house there was home to the Gooderes, of whom Edward Goodere was a baronet and sometime member for the county. Differences arose between Edward and his younger brother Samuel over ownership of the manor, whereupon Samuel caused Edward to be kidnapped, and brought aboard a man'o-war under his command then lying at Bristol, where, by his orders the luckless Edward was put to death; after which event the house bore the evil reputation of being haunted by the uneasy spirit of the murdered man, and was eventually pulled down.'

After a brief stop for refreshment at Queenswood, I sought out the old coach route that climbed from the Burghope valley up through natural woodland surrounding the park. In the valley bottom was the old manor at Burghope, the scene of family bickering and murder in the eighteenth century. Little remains of the old house but a modern replacement nestles quietly in the valley, seemingly oblivious of it's predecessors turbulent past. Throughout the centuries, Burghope shared this landscape with Dinmore Manor where a priory was founded in 1186 by Thomas de Dunemora for the Knights Templars. It later became one of the most important commanderies of the Knights Hospitallers, who held it until Henry VIII's dissolution. The commandery was their third largest in the country and was responsible for the possessions of the Order in Herefordshire, Worcestershire, Shropshire and south Wales. The present manor house is Jacobean and stands on the site of the old domestic buildings of the Knight's commandery. The estate was bought in 1927 by Richard Hollins Murray, a Manchester businessman who invented reflecting lenses for use on roads, better known as Cat's Eyes. In honour of the man's ingenious achievement, letters on a directional finger post the side of the A49 are inlaid with them. During the course of his tenure, Murray added a west wing consisting of a huge baronial hall which he called the Music Room, and adjoining cloisters with traceried windows in the style of fourteenth century. Facing the house is a chapel which retains some stonework from Dunemora's original twelfth century construction. In 2002 the house and gardens of Dinmore Manor were open for public viewing and it was on my schedule to visit. Unfortunately, the estate closed before I had the chance to see it and regrettably is now in private ownership.

The old road, replaced by the A49, is still metalled at Burghope and I decided to follow it as far as I could. Timmins experienced difficulty negotiating the muddy conditions as the road ascended the high wood. The hard surface I was following was short lived too, and once I had passed the few houses that remain alongside it soon became nothing more than a well worn track and finally disappeared into a section of woodland. Having found a detour via a public footpath through the wood, I regained the old road, metalled again, on the other side as it descends to the village of Hope under Dinmore, where some of the cottages which so delighted Timmins still remain.

> *'We pass by numerous cottages with snug thatched roofs and quaintly-cut yews at the little wicket-gates, more or less dimly suggestive of peacocks and other figures; while from the blossom of the overshadowing apple trees falls a summer snow of delicate white petals.'*

I rejoined the A49 and the junction with the A417 from Gloucester. Half a mile back along the Gloucester road is one of Herefordshire's great gothic mansions, Hampton Court. The great house was built in the early fifteenth century by Rowland Leinthall, Yeoman of the Robes to Henry IV, who had bestowed on him the area then known as Hampton Richard for his services to the Crown. In order that he could afford to build his castle and live in the custom generally expected of Kings' favourites, he was allowed to draw his income from surrounding lands, including Ludlow twenty miles away. The sylvan surroundings of Hampton would have made an ideal location for hunting deer and fishing. In 1415 Rowland was knighted by Henry V for supplying eight mounted men and thirty three bowmen for the battle of Agincourt. After Rowland's death Hampton Court went through a period of relative inactivity until the estate came into the hands of Sir Thomas Coningsbys who would bring the Court back to life and in 1614 build his hospital for old soldiers at Hereford. Thomas's success as a servant of the Crown was overshadowed in life by the tragic loss of five of his six sons and when he died at a great age in 1625, the estate passed to the surviving son, Fitzwilliam. As a result of Sir Thomas's funding for the hospital in Hereford of £200 per year, Fitzwilliam inherited rising debts and in order to boost the depleted coffers, he had to sell property in Hertfordshire that had been in the Coningsby's family for over one hundred years. Furthermore, as Governor of Hereford and High Sheriff for the county during the Civil War, he bore the costs of defending Hereford itself and providing for the troops on each of the three occasions the city was overrun by the opposing Parliamentary forces. Once again, Hampton Court suffered neglect. In the early eighteenth century the estate passed by marriage to the Earl of Essex whose principal house was also in Herefordshire, at Netherwood, so the Court was put up for sale for the first time in three hundred years.

> *'Hampton Court is a truly magnificent structure, combining as it does the features both of a castellated and a monastic building; surrounding a courtyard, and having a stately entrance tower, with gateway and portcullis in the centre of the north front of such goodly size.'*

When Timmins visited Hampton, the owner was John Arkwright,

great grandson of Sir Richard Arkwright of Spinning Jenny fame. The great mansion had been rebuilt in a gothic style and paintings by Holbein, Lely, Vandyke and modern drawings by Turner and David Cox hung on the walls. 'Johnny' Arkwright had the distinction of being only the second Arkwright since the illustrious Sir Richard to excel in an industrial vein. While out walking on the estate one day, his wife, Evelyn, discovered an unusual variation of the common primrose and her husband immediately set about cultivating it. He won prizes with Evelyn Arkwrightii at the Royal Horticultural Society's shows in 1890 and achieved some commercial success. He also designed a rectangular wooden box with corner blocks for the safe transportation of fruit and vegetables, still a familiar sight today.

By the mid-twentieth century, the Arkrights had gone as a result of declining fortunes and the effects of war and recession and, like many of the county's great houses in war time, the house had been used as a temporary hospital. By 1960, it was in such very poor condition that the treasures that had been there since the days of the Coningsbys were sold off to pay for badly needed repairs. Since the Van Kampens took over in 1972, they have invested heavily to create the modern castle we see today and provide gardens and well laid out grounds for the public to walk in. Over the years they have completely refurbished

Hampton Court, near Leominster. A view from the back lawn.

it and although a family home for most of the year, it has been available for residential seminars and weddings. However, in April 2005 it was announced that the present American owners, would accept offers for this imposing manor house and unless someone was prepared to fork out £10 million for the whole property, the 1,000 acre estate could be broken up.

For the second time on my journey, I was within sight of Leominster but first had time for a breezy stroll over Winsley Hill to witness a landmark which, I had heard, was worth the effort. My walk ended in the isolated village of Upper Hill where amidst fine old cottages and quiet narrow lanes is Sheppard's Surplus Store, an ex-government discount warehouse famous locally. In the yard in front of the main building is an old Swift F-4 Supermarine jet plane with undercarriage intact. It is for sale and represents a quirky claim by the owner that you could buy practically anything in his store. Once, nearby there had been another aeroplane on display, a spitfire which stood beside the Spitfire Inn. Unfortunately both are now gone. The pub closed some years ago and the old war plane was bought by a collector, apparently for too low a price according to the store owner, and shipped off to Canada. Determined not to make the same mistake again, the price for the F-4 seems to be higher than anyone is prepared to pay so here, for the present, it stays. The store is a barn of a place stocked to the rafters with clothing, furniture and household goods. The decision to open such a business here in the midst of open fields was either brave or foolhardy. Sad to relate it was proved to be the latter, when in March 2011 the store closed. At the time of writing the F-4's future is uncertain.

After a brief walk round the store (I bought a fleece jacket) the path was onwards and upwards to Ivington Camp, one of the most impressive hill forts in the county. The view to the west and the Black Mountains from the summit is quiet stunning. Not so, though, the view to the north. Strewn across the southern Leominster landscape are row upon row of well publicised poly-tunnels of a fruit farm complex. Strawberries are grown here the modern way – undercover with computer controlled trickle irrigation. The people who run it claim to supply 8,000 tonnes of the class 1 Elsanta strain to supermarkets throughout the UK every year. This year they will employ 2000 people during harvest time, mostly from the European mainland, housed on site in a purpose built camp. There is an even larger complex near Ledbury, where they pick up to 1,000 tonnes of soft fruits between April and Christmas.

Strawberries were first introduced into Britain in their wild form by the Romans who grew them as a crop. The first hybrid variety was produced in 1780, and they have been selected and bred ever since to provide larger and sweeter berries. Most lovers of this exceptionally nutritious and delicious fruit will remember when, for three months of the summer, we were invited to pick our own from, a sunny, south facing, well drained, field strip. All that is changing thanks to the voracious appetite of the supermarkets forever on the lookout for yet more ways to make money. The variety they want us to eat now is a hardy plant with a long shelf life and travels well, we are told. Readers will notice the word 'flavour' is missing from that statement. A similar marketing ploy was introduced a few years back so that we can now eat tomatoes all year round. This results in continuous rows of uniformly round, very red, and very tasteless fruits which have lost all appeal. Personally, I find tinned tomatoes more acceptable now. Even so, every year the use of polytunnels increases as farmers pursue a longer growing season and larger harvests. The far from level playing field is controlled by the supermarkets who demand high yields. Thus, the distinctive Herefordshire patchwork landscape, where first the yellows of rape are replaced by the blues of flax, interspersed with the reds of the soil when growers plant their acres of potatoes, has now to include these highly reflective lakes of silver. In a report by Andrew English in the *Daily Telegraph* in July 2004, it was pointed out that polytunnels create environmental problems of their own. Most significantly, the extensive use of methyl bromide to control verticillium wilt (to which Elsanta strawberries are particularly vulnerable). This highly toxic and pernicious depleter of the ozone layer was to be phased out under the terms of the Montreal Protocol of 1987 but earlier that year the Department of Food, Environment and Rural Affairs (DEFRA) won exemption for the British strawberry industry. It is not surprising that Herefordshire County Council have sought a review of the impact on their countryside. They have now issued a warning that polytunnels should only be used on the same site for a maximum of two years after which planning permission is required. According to John Berry at Haygrove Farm near Ledbury, 'We want three years for strawberries, six for raspberries, and even longer for cherries'. The battle for the Herefordshire countryside has commenced.

Three more miles across the river Arrow plain and I would be in Leominster. I had arranged accommodation, this time for three nights at Copper Hall, just five minutes walk from the town centre. Leominster is Herefordshire's second town and evolved around the Anglo Saxon abbey founded here in 658, another with a claim to being the earliest Christian site in Herefordshire. The Saxons named the settlement after Leofric, the husband of Godiva who we may recall rode on horseback around Coventry 'au naturelle' in support of a reduction in taxes. In the twelfth century a Norman Benedictine priory replaced the abbey and both Leominster and the Priory grew wealthy from the wool trade but were subject for centuries to attacks from Welsh raiders. During his campaigns against the Marcher Lords, Owain Glyndwr captured the town and made the nearby hill fort at Risbury his base. In the middle ages Leominster flourished as a market centre for the surrounding rural area. In particular, the wool from the locally bred Ryelands sheep was greatly prized and was known far and wide as 'Lemster Ore'. However, the dissolution of the monasteries had serious consequences for the town. Large parts of the priory buildings were demolished and the monks dispersed, bringing to an end, almost overnight, centuries of prosperity and stability. In spite of periodic setbacks, the river Lugg and its feeder streams which flowed through the town continued to provide water and power for the mills where wool was still being processed as well as corn. During the seventeenth and eighteenth centuries the town once again went through a time of prosperity, but then failed to adapt to the industrial revolution and slipped again into slow decline. The canal from Leominster to Stourport was never completed and the railways came too late to prevent population migration from the mid nineteenth century up until the 1960s. But, in spite of Leominster's insecure development it remains an important market centre for the farming area of north Herefordshire.

'At length we reach our destination and with time well in hand proceed on a voyage of discovery round about the little town.'

Leominster's buildings are a mixture of architecture from across the centuries. For the most part the shop fronts carry elegant and eloquent higher storeys. Darkened passageways and narrow streets bear names that evoke Leominster's industrial heritage; Drapers Lane, Ironmongers Row, and Cordwainers Street. Timber framed buildings with typical jettied construction abound. The hidden interior of Brook Hall on Broad Street dates from 1590 and recently sixteenth century wall paintings described as remarkable and quite extraordinary were discovered there. On Church Street, there are examples of Georgian architecture at its ingenious best. Many of the houses are older than they look but their earlier timber framed frontages have been removed and replaced with the more fashionable Georgian brick facades. Corn Square, where once, in medieval times, Leominster's corn traders gathered is today the venue for local farmers' markets, and has some of the oldest buildings in the town. On one corner leading out of the square is the sixteenth century Three Horseshoes Inn, one of two outstanding black and white buildings. Leominster has another late sixteenth century pub, The Chequers Inn, on nearby Etnam Street, where there is another mixture of Elizabethan, Georgian and Victorian architecture. High Street eventually becomes a wider Broad Street, the old market place and original site of a splendid market house, another example of John Abel's master craftsmanship. It isn't here now but it is still in Leominster, removed and rebuilt elsewhere and still in remarkable condition. More about this later. Timmins' 1891 sketch depicting *'a bit of old Leominster'* (See Page 160), shows a row of seventeenth century shop fronts. They still survive, nestled amongst the more modern shop fronts of the high street. One stretched my curiosity beyond resistance until I decided to go in. The tiny shop interior was oak panelled and old wooden shelves displayed the current owner's wares – violins. The owner, John Langstaffe, was sitting in his even tinier workshop at the rear amidst the debris of a master craftsman. He was alerted to my entry by the old spring mounted door bell and graciously agreed to talk to me about his business.

'I learnt my skills at the Newark School of Violin Making,' he told me, 'but after I graduated there was more demand for guitars, so I made those for a while. Eventually, though, I recognized that there were already too many guitar makers for me to make much of a living and decided violins would be a greater challenge after all.'

I asked him to explain the secret of a good instrument.

'The body of the instrument has to be made from maple or sycamore and pinewood. The most important part of the fitting up of an instrument is the sound post, that's a small and unremarkable cylindrical piece of pine responsible for achieving full tonal potential. Violins have been made this way in England since the sixteenth century.'

I wasn't surprised to learn from him that he doesn't get many callers and earns much of his crust through repairs and restorations. *'I make just three new violins a year for which I charge around £5,000 each, and then hope for more bits and pieces after that.'*

As we talked about his work, surrounded by Jacobean oak walls below ancient beams with the only light provided by a small window onto a narrow passageway, it was as if time had stood still and the only intrusion was the modern cut of the clothing we both wore. Outside,

School Lane, Leominster by W.A.Green

shoppers were going about their business in the bright sunshine, but it wouldn't have looked out of place if a coach and four had passed the window at that moment.

Leominster Priory Church is a building of cathedral size proportions. The first monastic church was twice as long with transepts, circular apses, a central tower and a lady chapel. Two extra naves were tagged on in the thirteenth and fourteenth century to serve as the parish church and these additions must have presented a vast and awesome building. Displayed in the north aisle today is a ducking stool, a relic of a curious method for punishing social misfits. As its title suggests, the unfortunate villains were condemned to be strapped to a chair and repeatedly lowered into the murky and often ice cold waters of the river Lugg until due penance was carried out or mercy given. Usually it was women of ill-repute or those suspected of being a witch who suffered the most, but men were also subject to this form of justice, especially bad traders who were accused of ripping people off. The last ducking was that of Jenny Pipes in 1809 for persistently nagging at her neighbours, but her correctional dip apparently didn't have a lasting effect as she is said to have continued her annoying habit. At the dissolution, the Benedictine priory buildings were almost completely destroyed, but the magnificent medieval church was left more or less intact though reduced to the two naves that have been used by the parish ever since. Below the remaining west tower is a Norman doorway of the highest quality, yet another superb example of the work of the Herefordshire School of Sculptors. The last remnant of the old priory is still attached to the north aisle of the church and contained the monk's hospital and lavatories, conveniently placed above the Pinsley brook which flowed under the building until just forty years ago. Since the dissolution the old hospital has been used first as a jail, the Leominster workhouse in the eighteenth century, a private house, and is now a youth hostel. Just outside the churchyard is the Forbury chapel, Archbishop Peckham's initial thirteenth century solution to the dispute between the monks and the townsfolk who wanted to use the priory itself for worship. Although the chapel is classed as an ancient monument, it has been completely modernized internally and now serves as a meeting place and coffee house.

'Retrace we now our steps across the spacious churchyard, to a wicket gate which gives us access into the Grange, a bright and pleasant recreation ground where a cricket match is going forward upon the well kept greensward, the children scrambling for a vantage point atop the Russian gun standing at a corner.

Here at last, in the setting of the town green, we have arrived at the old market house which was originally in the town centre from 1633 until 1856 when it was taken down and rebuilt on its present site. It is now called Grange House and is used as council offices. The old building is still supported on twelve massive oak pillars, with ionic capitals and carved brackets with arches in between. Around the whole building above the arches, in characteristic lettering, is an inscription partly in Latin, partly in English.

'Vive Deo gratis, toti mundo tumulatu.
Crimini mundatus, simper transpire paratus.
Where Justice rule there vertu flow.
Vive ut post viva. Sat cito, si sat bene.
Like collumnes doo upprop the Fabrik of
A building, So noble Gentri doo support
The honor of a kingdom.
In memoria aeterna erit Justus. 1633.'

As at Abel's great town hall in Hereford, the original roof was adorned with small dormer windows with gables above them. Sadly, they weren't included in Leominster's rebuilt version becasue it was mistakenly thought they would create instability.

Leominster still has a railway station for trains running north to south between Shrewsbury and Cardiff. There used to be lines east to west, too, but along with many other provincial towns throughout Britain, the town began to lose its trains from the moment the railways were nationalized in 1948. The first section to go was the extension from Kington to New Radnor in Powys. In 1952 the line from Leominster to Bromyard was closed and three years later the remaining section from Kington to Leominster was closed to passengers. Consequently, the 'Kington Coffee Pot', much loved by the local children would no longer thrill them with its whistle at level crossings. When efforts were made in 1964 to sell this line as a going concern for less than £90,000 there were no takers. The tracks were torn up, the land reverted to agricultural use or just left derelict, and the stations were sold off cheaply to be converted into private homes. The railway era had barely touched this part of Herefordshire before it almost disappeared without trace.

Leominster has had few famous sons and daughters to celebrate. The artist John Scarlett Davies was born here in 1804 but although he grew up in the town, he left in 1818 to study in London and never returned, spending much of his short life touring Europe. In spite of his early death at the age of forty one, he was a prolific painter and the art gallery at Hereford, not Leominster, has over seventy examples of his work. One of the town's best remembered benefactors was Sydney Bridge. Born in 1858, he built his wealth by improving property in the town as a painter and decorator. He had a reputation for being charitable and donated generously to the church and the local hospital but lived frugally himself. He died at the age of eighty two after falling from a ladder while helping to redecorate a friend's house. Arguably, the most successful is Stanley Holland, the son of a publican. He spent much of his early adult life drinking in the town's pubs, and after running into debt and stealing from his employers to finance more drinking, he was given the choice of prosecution or emigration and decided on the latter, to the USA. There he finally changed his ways, became a competent engineer, and in time amassed a fortune building bridges. He never forgot his debt to Leominster and regularly sent large donations to charities. Although he had become a citizen of Chicago, he left instructions to be buried in Leominster church, to which he had gifted a new window in 1924.

Just off the high street a grassy footpath follows the Pinsley brook through the suburbs and westward across wide meadows. It was now mid June but the whole country was under a massive area of low pressure and it had been very wet and windy for several days. Although the rain had eased that morning, the seasonal high grasses had been well watered ensuring I got wet pretty well up to my waist as I struggled to leave Leominster behind. Apart from a few fields near an old Mill at Cholstrey, the path was invisible beneath huge swathes of grasses blasted flat in places by the wind. Styles lay hidden behind curtains of nettles and as I followed the swiftly flowing brook behind overgrown hedges and riverside vegetation, I caught only occasional glimpses of it as I pressed on to Kingsland and the Welsh Marches lands beyond.

'Starting away bright and early, we find ourselves, by the time the Londoner is chipping his breakfast egg, amidst broad pastures and ripening cornfields. A branch line leading away towards the hilly west country brings us to Kingsland Station, whence a field path makes a short cut to the village, whose dwellings are marshalled in pretty groups along the high road'

The delightful village of Kingsland is about four and a half miles northwest of Leominster in a valley sandwiched between the Pinsley Brook and the River Lugg. It is a neat pretty place with many fine houses, some in the black and white timber style. The village's original name was Kingslene, Land of the King, the 'King' being Merewald, a seventh century Saxon leader. The remains of a motte and bailey in the meadow close to the church of St Michael and All Angels is likely to have been his palace. In the thirteenth century, the Mortimers owned the land and built the church. Opening off the north porch is a tiny chapel, called the Volka chapel, in which an ancient stone coffin rests below an elaborate arch. No-one knows to whom the coffin belonged, although it was tempting in the past to say it was the Mortimer builder. Speculation remains as to the purpose of a chapel lying outside the business area of the church, or why an important person, particularly a Mortimer, wasn't laid to rest in a more prominent position inside his own church. It is perhaps easier to believe that the chapel was added and used for masses for the dead after the great clash of the houses of York and Lancaster at Mortimer's Cross, a mile down the road.

There is another local story worthy of mention. It concerns Elizabeth Turner, an uneducated widow, who married John Hughes in 1793. One of twins subsequently born to the couple died and Elizabeth was deeply afflicted. She blamed herself as a great sinner and chose a life of repentance and prayer. During this time she claimed to have received the power of healing after seeing visions of angels, and started 'laying hands' on anyone who came to her with complaints of blindness, lameness or other deformities. By 1800 she had become known as the Kingsland Doctoress and pilgrims came from as far away as Kent, Hampshire and Yorkshire. However, her reputation didn't go down too well with the local intellectuals who doubted her powers and denounced her as a fraudster. Following her death in 1849, the records of her burial reflected the opinions of the Reverend R D Evans who described her *'Formerly a celebrated charmer and a great imposter'*. The evidence in her favour is that she never charged for her miraculous services, instead occasionally accepting gifts for her other children. The village, too, no doubt was a beneficiary from the influx of the many visitors seeking cures.

I followed the winding river out of the village, skirting acres of rolling fields of golden barley, a picture of twenty-first century peace and tranquility. The impression is of timelessness, a place where not much happens. There is nothing visible that hints at the scene of violent mayhem that took place on the opposite bank midway through the fifteenth century. This is the arena where the decisive battle of the Wars of the Roses was fought on Candlemas Day, February 1460. In the ensuing carnage, Edward, Duke of York, a Mortimer, defeated the Lancastrian forces of Henry VI in a vicious slaughter in which four thousand men perished. The area became known as Mortimer's Cross, from then on chained to the notoriety of that one almighty battle. Before the conflict, a strange event is said to have taken place. In the sky above the battle field, there appeared a perihelion, a trick of sunlight occasionally seen when the temperature is low and the sky is clear. A chronicler of the time recorded it thus:

'About ten o'clock, before noon, were seen three suns in the firmament shining full clear, whereof the people had great marvel, and therefore were aghast. The noble earl Edward then comforted them and said, 'Be of good comfort and dread not, this is a good sign for these three suns betoken of the Father, the Son, and the Holy Ghost, and therefore let us have a good heart, and in the name of Almighty God go we against our enemies.'
After the slaughter, at the age of nineteen, the victor was crowned,

King Edward IV. Unprepared for the pomp of monarchy, Edward retired to the Mortimer castle at Wigmore where he could be more comfortable in the wild and beautiful landscape and with his rural friends than with the busy capital and the affairs of state.

There is an old mill at Mortimer's Cross which stands, on a secluded stretch of river bank, since 1450, amongst a small collection of similar aged buildings. There would have been a cider mill to quench the thirst of the workers and their families, and a stonemason to maintain and repair the grinding stones and the mill houses too. In ancient times, millers were allowed to deduct part of their customer's grain as payment and they could be very unpopular people. Many would cheat by feeding grain to their farmyard animals and millers were notorious for having the fattest pigs in the district! In 1774, two mills at Kingsland were almost completely destroyed by an angry mob which had decided to take revenge on the millers for their wayward ways. The unfortunate organizers of this particular local rebellion were caught and sentenced to death, later to be reprieved and transported to America to work on sugar plantations. Some millers were more generous towards their workers than others. Florrie Jukes, a young girl of fourteen came to work at the Mortimer's Cross mill in 1919. She lived at Orleton a few miles east and when she was employed at the mill, stayed at the cottage next to it. She was apparently well looked after and seemed content with her life. Florrie visited the Mill again in 1992 and in an account of her life there she recalled:
'I started work at quarter to six in the morning and I used to go to bed at half past eight at night. I had one of those little tiny lamps to go to bed with. You could see nothing! I had two rounds of bread, ham in the middle, and a pint of cider. When I was young before coming to the mill we didn't have much. I used to have swedes and apples to live on and occasionally bread and dripping. We washed in the brook near our home. But here at the Mill, they give me bacon and eggs and I don't know what for breakfast, and a jolly good cooked dinner later. I was part of the family and they were very good to me.'
The last miller to operate at Mortimer's Cross was a woman, Dorothy Biggs, who ran the mill until 1940. She had taken over from her father, when she was twenty two years old, after his arm had been

crushed in an accident with the machinery. Although this mill is a registered monument and subject to a deed of guardianship with English Heritage, it remains in private hands. Until he came here 'Chris' was a new age traveller and lived in a Ford Transit van in lay-bys of Hampshire. When he eventually tired of the outdoor life, he and a few friends bought the mill with the cottage where young Florrie Jukes lived, having decided to repair and run it again in the traditional manner. English Heritage doesn't pay him for his role as a guide, but Chris is allowed to keep the entrance fee and any other income from books, leaflets and any knick-knacks he can sell. Today is a quiet day and I am his only visitor.

'From what I can collect, I have to live on and pay the insurance on this place. It's not much really. To encourage the punters, I usually dress up as an old miller and let them take photographs of me, hoping they won't notice the Matalan trousers!'

Having told him not to bother with the smock on my account, he introduced me to his 'assistant' Aloysius, a very lifelike dummy positioned behind a small window by the mill entrance.

'So that people can see I'm not alone.' he said, with false confidence.

After I had paid my entrance fee, Chris showed me around.

'Everything is made of timber and can be operated by one person,' he started enthusiastically. *'The mill wheel is driven by water coming down the leat from the weir on the river, and produces twelve horsepower. We could make up to four hundred weight of flour per hour, if only we were allowed to.'*

I waited for an explanation, and it came with what I thought was a forced smile.

'Unfortunately, once we settled in,' he continued mournfully. *'We discovered we weren't allowed to operate the mill in the traditional ways for fear of igniting the dust and causing an explosion. And then there was the likelihood of rats contaminating the grain. I was told to convert to modern stainless steel equipment or stop production. So I now find I own nothing more than a museum.'*

Then, as if to emphasize the fact, we climbed to the top of the building where he showed me his battlefield collection, a small descriptive explanation of the carnage which took place in the meadow below

more than five hundred years ago.
'How do you make ends meet in the winter?' I asked, expecting him to say he'd close the place and head back to the Hampshire lay-bys for a month or two.
'Plastic Snowmen!' was his response, and delivered with such gusto. *'Hundreds of them, all shapes and sizes. I dot them around the yard and the river bank. The kids love 'em!'*
I was relieved when he said he had long term plans for the site in case the plastic snowmen idea didn't work out and receipts from the mill tour remained low.
'For next year's attractions I'm thinking of displays of old fishing rods and pictures of famous Manchester United footballers as part of my new Museum of Life.'
At that point, I thought I'd heard enough and it was time for me to slip away.

> *'Crossing elevated slopes, the eye commands a vast stretch of country ranging the whole extent of Herefordshire, the horizon bounded by the graceful Titterstone Clee, the serrated line of the Malvern Hills, and the broad terraces of the Black Mountains, beyond which grey-blue in the remote distance soar the twin peaks of the Brecon Beacons, those monarchs of the South Welsh hills.'*

From Kingsland, Timmins had taken the back lanes northwards, missing out Mortimers Cross. I would cross his path a little further on, but in the meantime taking a field path to avoid the busy B4362, I arrived within a short time outside the locally renowned Lucton School, an independent day and boarding school for boys and girls founded by John Pierrepont, a prosperous London vintner, in 1708. The main building is a magnificent piece of Queen Anne domestic architecture. It is a beautifully proportioned dignified house of red brick with stone dressings, a tiled roof, and a central pediment to give it an air of greater dignity. In an arched alcove above the front door, a statue of the founder stands in magisterial poise. For all that, this being a school and not a gentleman's residence, internally there was no great attention to artistry, only simple joinery and plain unambitious panelling. The wealthy Pierrepont was a contemporary of the equally wealthy Bristol merchant Edward Colston, and must have been aware of the famous school there that bore Colston's name. The desire of both men to promote the cause of the Church of England and support the evolution of charity schools where children of families living in town and city squalor were denied education was a key point in what they planned for their principal good deeds. As Pierrepont discovered at the time, North Herefordshire was ill provided with places of education so he persuaded the owner of land at Lucton, Sir Hubert Croft, to part with the plot where he wanted the school to be built. The builder of the resulting fine school house is not identified, but Frederick Kempson had a hand in later Victorian extensions.

I left Lucton school along a well worn footpath which climbed gently back towards the road where I had an early glimpse of my next destination, Croft Castle, which stands on an ancient site overlooking the north Herefordshire plains. The Croft family has been in residence here, more or less, for nearly a thousand years. The present building looks older than its eighteenth century origins and may not even be on the site of the first castle. Excavations have taken place in the grounds recently to discover where that was and results have more or less proven the existence of an earlier medieval house. Further discovery of traces of burnt materials suggest a fiery end to that residence sometime during the Civil War. After the Second World War, in common with many large estates Croft suffered from a lack of investment, neglect, and crippling death duties, and since 1957 the estate was been in the hands of the National Trust. The castle is approached by an avenue of oaks and beeches, and in Timmins's day *'magnificent chestnuts with mighty, curiously twisted trunks.'* Next to it is a small quaint sixteenth century church which not surprisingly houses memorials to various Crofts down the centuries. In the grounds, the trees are the splendour of the estate. As at three other Herefordshire manors, Shobdon Court, Hampton Court, and Brampton Bryan, Croft is renowned for its mighty oaks, but here there are also splendid avenues of limes and Spanish chestnuts. Lord Bernard Croft and his cousin, Caroline Compton still live in the private quarters, and before planning my visit to this remote part of the county I had wondered whether they would break the habit of a lifetime and agree to talk about life in their stately home. The chances of Lord Croft doing so, I was told, were less than zero, but I was thrilled to receive a letter from Caroline.

'The days of regular picnics on the lawn and parties in the ballroom attended to by teams of servants belong to history,' she wrote. *'Nor do we live any longer in our great state rooms. Our quarters are now the old kitchen.'* Caroline told me she hadn't been brought up at the castle. Instead, she had lived in Hampstead with her mother who had been running an art gallery in the West End.

'My grandfather inherited the Croft estate but when he died shortly after the Second World War ownership seemed to have been a hot potato and passed through a number of branches of the family. In 1956, the widow of the last owner, another cousin, found she had no need of the castle and wanted to demolish it and fell all the trees, so my mother agreed to work to save the estate. She slaved away in the garden for several years removing hundreds of bricks from a demolished wing and later paid for the castle's upkeep until her death in 1999.'

Caroline's words continued to emphasize the normality of their present existence at Croft.

'There are no diamond tiaras. I have no-one to clean the flat here or my London home, and we spend hours every day during the summer months getting our hands dirty weeding the garden and painting benches.'

Croft escaped the formal garden layouts immortalized by Capability Brown, and the parkland surrounding the castle is little more than gentle sloping pasture. Within the boundaries of the estate is Fish-pool Valley, a deep combe of man-made pools created in the eighteenth century to provide fresh fish for the Croft's dinner table. The combe is an excellent example of the theories of Richard Knight and Uvedale Price, the Herefordshire squires who pursued the splendid confusion and irregularity of their Picturesque Movement. Over the years though, nature has become the beneficiary of neglect, and as the pools have been allowed to decay waterside plants and vegetation have spread encouraging a wildlife takeover.

A footpath threads its way through this now tangled wonderland, gradually gaining height towards the top of the valley and an iron-age fort called Croft Ambrey. Some say this ancient British camp was occupied as long ago as 1050BC. The name Ambrey has been associated with the great Celtic warrior leader Ambrosius Aurelianus, but there are doubts that he ever made his home here as he lived four hundred years after the fort was said to have been abandoned. However, its massive defences and complex structure suggest a settlement of great importance. Excavations by Birmingham University in the 1960s discovered elaborate entrances, which persuaded the researchers to conclude that it must have been one of the most heavily fortified hill forts known anywhere in Britain, and certain to have been occupied by a high ranking military figure. For the time being, we know not who.

> *'Next morning we are up betimes, and bidding farewell to mine hostess at the farmstead, we pursue our way between the hedgerows, a brisk breeze driving the cloud shadows helter-skelter across the meadows in the broad vale beneath. We steer a course which leads us over the broad reaches of Bircher Common, pushing our way through waving bracken, beneath stately oaks, and passing an occasional quarry of grey-brown limestone of which these hills are built.*

Beyond Bircher common, the land drops away onto the north Herefordshire plain where the villages of Yarpole, Orleton and Ashford Carbonel nestle in the lea beside the river Teme flowing down from Shropshire. Orleton is a large village of some antiquity. Although there is no evidence that a castle or military base was ever built here, there are many old tracks criss-crossing the area, some of which appear to be Roman in origin. The position of the village on raised ground with a good water supply and abundant timber suggests this was a site with self sustaining qualities. Nikolaus Pesvner describes it in his *Buildings of Herefordshire* as having *'a pretty winding street with a number of black and white houses.'* Standing comfortably amongst them is The Boot Inn, recorded as being a pub in 1851. Even at the beginning of the twentieth century, Orleton had most of its own facilities and there was little need to travel to Leominster or Ludlow, the two nearest market towns. The village was the birthplace of Adam de Orleton, Bishop of Hereford during the reign of the weak and ineffectual Edward II. Adam was a loyal friend of Roger Mortimer, Edward's bitter enemy, and after the King's capture and imprisonment in Berkley Castle, Adam wrote the infamous letter to his keepers which they interpreted as an instruction to murder Edward. The bishop protested later that they had misread his message *'Edwardum occidere nolite timere bonum est'*, pleading that he had mistakenly omitted a comma. Thus the message *'Refrain, not to kill Edward is right'* was taken to read *'Refrain not, to kill Edward is right.'*

ORLETON COURT.

The twelfth century church of St George contains within its walls, a history lesson in stone. Around the chancel arch are several carved stone heads said to represent Edward II, his favourite, Piers Gaveston, his wife Queen Isobella and the misunderstood Bishop Adam de Orleton. At the top of the arch and casting an eye on all of them is Roger Mortimer, Lord of the Marches, lover of the Queen, and responsible for plotting the King's overthrow. But the star of the church, as in many other churches on our journey, is the magnificent limestone font, unusually bucket shaped and carved with nine bearded figures. This is more excellent work by the Hereford School of Sculptors and has been here since the church was built over eight hundred years ago.

Orleton Court is a handsome sixteenth century building with only limited modern touches to make it habitable. The entrance at the front is through a gabled porch on top of which is a rare polygonal oriel window. The court was in royal hands until 1609 before it was eventually sold to the celebrated Herefordshire historian Thomas Blount in 1655. Blount was the author of *'Glossographia'*, a glossary of difficult words. The book contains eleven thousand explanations and was the first dictionary of its kind. It has been reprinted several times, the last being in 1969, and modern academics still regard it as a treasure trove of lost words. Blount trained as a lawyer but because he was a Roman Catholic, and therefore barred from public office, could not practice. Instead he used his literary talents to help the burgeoning non-academic middle classes who were ascendant at the time, and of which Blount himself was a member. He remained an amateur scholar of law throughout his life, and in 1670 published *Nomolexicon,* a dictionary of legal terms, as a contribution to the profession he was unable to practice. Although Blount is not as well known as later dictionary writers such as Johnson and Webster, he was a pioneer and scholars of today owe him a debt of gratitude. The poet Alexander Pope was a frequent visitor to Orleton Court in the early part of the eighteenth century, and local legend tells of Charles II staying at the manor after his defeat at Worcester. However, history records that the King's escape route from the battle of Worcester was north towards Stafford before turning south for Dorset, via the Cotswolds and Somerset, and it is unlikely he would have chosen a diversion into north Herefordshire.

Fourteenth century pigeon house at Orleton

Inside the Fourteenth century pigeon house at Orleton. Note the revolving ladder used to collect squabs.

The day draws on and I have one more mile to go before reaching the Shropshire border. Turning off the B4361 at the Richard's Castle Inn, a minor road climbs straight and gradual towards the border heights of High Vinnalls and Haye Park wood. In no time at all I passed the handsome fourteenth century home which Timmins described as an *'hospitable farmhouse.'* and in whose grounds stands an unusual circular dovecote now scheduled as an ancient monument. Having stayed the night here, his description of his discovery after breakfast requires no improvement by me.

> *'Strolling into the garden, where the sweet scents of old fashioned flowers suggests the housewife of a bygone generation with her stillroom and press of homespun linen sweet with sprigs of lavender, the path leads us to a fine example of those curious pigeon houses which have ere now attracted notice during our peregrinations. That this one is of early date is proved by the great thickness of is stone walls; the circular roof is relieved by three pretty dormer windows with a lantern above, whereby its feathered inhabitants gain entrance; and numerous holes inside can be easily reached by a revolving ladder constructed for the purpose.'*

The straight road ends on a high hillside amidst a scene of medieval splendour; ancient cottages, a magnificent church, and the brooding remains of a pre-conquest Norman castle. This is Richard's Castle built by Richard Fitz Scrob, a noble of the court of Edward the Confessor, himself a Norman. Its construction could have been a response to the Welsh raids of 1050-55, the same attacks which destroyed the castle at Hereford. By all accounts this castle was a considerable building and strong enough to withstand many attempts to take it, including that by Owen Glyndwr. However, according to the antiquary John Leland, it was in poor condition by the sixteenth century and was finally destroyed during the Civil War. Today, there is a significant piece of curtain wall still standing, but the Keep mound is almost completely overgrown and a few timber supports holding up scant stone remains of a tower are barely visible amidst the rampant vegetation. A small part of the gatehouse is enclosed in metal scaffolding to prevent further decay. The signs indicate that this castle is not often visited, many presumably preferring the much larger and historical significance of the great castle at Ludlow just three miles away. The position of the church next to Richard's Castle and the surviving Norman architecture in the nave, suggest ancient origins. Much of this building is fourteenth century, although the bulky bell tower might be even older. Unusually, the tower is at the east end of the church, presumably because being so close to the castle defences, they would have hindered construction, or the tower might have become a security risk, being used by an attacker to get a in a few close shots. In the north transept is a chapel with an empty burial recess. It is tempting to suggest it might have been made for the founder of the church, Hugh Mortimer, but why the tomb itself is missing is a mystery.

> *'Standing once again in the churchyard, we gaze upon the widespread view extending afar over woods, pastures, and mellowing cornfields. Towards Ludlow, the broad glades of Haye Wood skirt the base of the hill, where in 1634 an adventure which befell the children of the Earl of Bridgwater, who lost their way and were benighted in the forest, suggested to the poet Milton the motif for his play 'Masque of Comus.'*

Milton's play was performed that year at Ludlow Castle, in front of the Earl. The roles of the children in the play were performed by the

Earl's fifteen year-old daughter and her younger brothers. The play concerns a young lady who is walking through the forest with her brothers to reach her father's castle. She meets an evil spirit called Comus (the son of Circe and Bacchus) who is disguised as a simple shepherd and offers her the hospitality of his humble cottage for the night. He tries to persuade her to drink from a magic chalice which turns all who drink from it into beasts. Comus argues that nature has filled the world with pleasures, and that it is ungrateful to refuse the gifts of nature. The young lady replies that the right choice is the wise use of nature's gifts in accordance with how God created them. The evil spirit is defeated, the lady freed, and she and her brothers are led safely to the castle.

Ludlow is not, alas, on our schedule for this book, it being over the border in Shropshire. So turning west, away from the forest and evil spirits, I followed a footpath along the combe below the old castle's ramparts and attached myself to a splendid wooded section of the Mortimer Trail for the four miles to Aymestrey and its delightful inn.

> *'Trudging along between the hills which close around on every hand as we advance, we call to memory that this was one of the favourite hunting grounds of that great geologist, Sir Roderick Murchison. The limestone rocks of this district yielding some of the most valuable results of his researches which were recorded in his great work 'The Silurian System'.'*

Murchison was born into wealth in the Scottish Highlands in 1792 and, after a spell in the military, spent much of his early life fox hunting. He took an interest in science at the ripe old age of thirty two and dedicated the rest of his life to geology, earning in the process a directorship of the Royal Geographical Society. He wrote over one hundred scientific papers in his lifetime. His most famous, *The Silurian System* in 1839, was the result of the extensive research into rock formations here in north west Herefordshire and the Welsh borders. He named it after the old British Silures tribe who had inhabited the area. His reputation as an authority on geological discoveries was held in high regard around the world (The Murchison Falls in Uganda and The Murchison River in Australia are named after him). Deep in the heart of the north Herefordshire countryside, the A4110 passing through Aymestry was once the Roman Watling Street, connecting the great Roman forts of Wroxeter in Shropshire with Caerleon in south Wales. Here too, the river Lugg has forged a path between high wooded slopes to access the northern plains as it meanders onwards south east to Leominster. After a hearty breakfast, I left Aymestry's Riverside Inn and headed north west for a while, following the quiet river valley, before climbing over Woodhampton and into Wigmore.

The ancient village of Wigmore three miles north of Aymestrey can trace its history back over a thousand years. Its Norman church built on the site of an earlier Saxon building stands high bove the village and dominates the surrounding areas. Higher still on an adjoining spur is a romantic ruin. Wigmore castle was the ancestral home of the great Mortimer family who settled here after the Norman conquest and ruled the borderlands between England and Wales which became known as the Marcher lands or Marches, the Saxon word for border. The Mortimers' castle was originally built in 1070 by the first Marcher lord, Earl William Fitz Osbern but after a failed rebellion by the Earl's son against William the conqueror in 1075, Wigmore was granted to Ralph de Mortimer. From then on Wigmore castle became the Mortimer family seat until 1424 when the last Mortimer, Edmund, died without issue. By then, the great castle at Ludlow had become the major royal house in the area for the Tudors, so Wigmore became redundant and left to decay. Over the centuries this historic site has become overgrown and has been preserved virtually in that state by English Heritage, breaking away from traditional excavation and landscaping. No digging has taken place, only stabilisation of the structure and a general tidy-up. Any historical treasures reflecting life under the Mortimers that might have come to light had excavations been carried out will remain buried.

Amidst its many ups and downs, a tragic episode in the history of that once great family of Mortimer is touched upon in Shakespear's *Henry IV*:

'Yesternight: when, all athwart, there came
A post from Wales, loaden with heavy news
Whose worst was, that the noble Mortimer
Leading the men of Herefordshire to fight

Against the irregular and wild Glyndwr,
Was, by the rude hands of that Welshman, taken
And a thousand of his people butchered.'

The reference is to the battle in 1402 at Pilleth, further to the west in Welsh Powys, where Edmund Mortimer was captured by Owain Glyndwr. Edmund died during a later battle at Harlech, although by then he was fighting for Glyndwr not against him, having married his daughter. Just to the east of Wigmore is a large natural basin which 20,000 years ago was a lake, fed at its southern end by the melting ice sheet which covered most of Herefordshire. The water then flowed out towards Ludlow through the spectacular Downton Gorge, as does the River Teme today. Over the centuries, Wigmore 'lake' has been extensively drained and used for agriculture, although even now it regularly floods in places. The original line of Watling Street crossed the lake's western side and was the main route servicing the Roman frontier during their occupation.

Before leaving Wigmore, I had arranged to meet a local couple who have dedicated their retirement to the study of the county's historical make up and know more about this particular area than anyone. Jim and Muriel Tonkin have lived in their low red brick bungalow next to the church for nigh on forty years, ever since they abandoned their beloved Cornwall to live in Herefordshire. Jim is a gentleman of the old school, and having invited me into his home, keen to observe the rules of etiquette, insisted on donning a jacket in my presence. They had settled here in 1963 when Jim was offered the job of Headmaster at the Wigmore School, but in recent years their names have become synonymous with the Woolhope Naturalist Field Club, based in Hereford, to which they have devoted their spare time as committee members. As I discovered, their home has become choked with files and documents concerning the Club's work and activities recorded in the renowned *Transactions* journals. Even in their spacious lounge, I was hard pressed to avoid tripping over the evidence of their commitment to the WNFC. An example of their dedication in providing records for future students of geography was their recording of every field name throughout Herefordshire, the undertaking of such a task surely beyond most people, which had taken up much of their time over an eight year period since 1986. Now in their mid eighties, they told me they were anxious to off-load the responsibility for such work to younger members.

'The problem for the Club these days', Muriel told me, *'is that there are few new recruits qualified to make a contribution. The age of people joining means 'younger members' are sixty years of age or more'.* Jim and Muriel's voluminous collection impressed me, as did the stunning view from their bungalow's vast picture window looking out towards the remains of Wigmore castle and across the 'lake' to the heights of Downton and the Shropshire hills beyond.

> *'Starting afresh in the cheery morning sunshine, we take up once more the even tenure of our way, casting a lingering glance behind at old Wigmore, with its castle ruins bulking bravely above the homely dwellings of the villagers. No sooner do we fairly settle down to the rigours of the highroad, than the trusty map suggests a detour, where a by-lane gives access to another relic of mediaeval days.'*

During his Wigmore visit, Timmins paid much attention to the abbey. It was founded in 1179 by Hugh Mortimer for Augustinian Canons who had first established a priory at Shobdon not many miles away, then at Aymestry, and finally here on the edge of the 'lake'. Given the close proximity of the castle, from which the Mortimers controlled the Marches for four hundred years, it is to be expected that some of them would have been interred at the abbey. The general belief among historians is that Hugh was buried here along with twelve other succeeding male Mortimers. Excavations in the past have not confirmed as many burials, but some as yet unidentified graves have been discovered in a prominent position where the nave would have been in the abbey church. Amongst the few monastic buildings remodelled over the centuries for farming

The Mortimer burial stone at Wigmore Abbey. The line ended when the last Mortimer, Edmund, died unmarried.

purposes, the magnificent gatehouse remains more or less intact.

> *The noble gatehouse is entered by a lofty stone arch, beneath a timber framed building supported, as our sketch shows, upon mighty oak brackets. The ancient guest-house, now converted to the use of a farm, retains the original open-timbered roof, albeit in somewhat forlorn condition; and a beautiful traceried window, with the old leaded panes; besides many fragments of beautiful carved work from the ancient monastic buildings.*

Leaving Wigmore, I discovered a footpath which would lead me across the 'lake' in a north easterly direction towards the village of Burrington on the far 'shore'. Even after millions of years the flat lake bed needs deep side drainage channels to prevent surface water accumulating. That summer has been wetter than usual and the ground was soft and spongy as if walking on a water bed and I wondered just how close to the surface, even now, the water table really was. Occasionally the meadow grass was chest high, giving me the strange feeling that I was drowning until eventually the ground began to rise as I reached the site of the opposite 'shore' line. As I looked back at Wigmore clinging to the hillside to the west, the castle keep peering over the trees and the thick vegetation protecting the old walls from crumbling, I felt relieved and absurdly foolish for imagining a sudden and cataclysmic return of the ice age floods before I had reached the higher ground. Leaning against a field gate and taking in the sunlit scene, I decided that at that moment, I didn't want to be anywhere else. High above me hidden by broken white clouds, the deep drone of a jet aircraft receded as it carried its human cargo to places where they, presumably, would rather be, and rejoiced in the fact that the evolutionary plan had earmarked me for this simpler, less hectic life.

Burrington is an ancient settlement dating back to Domesday. Its present church was built in 1864 to replace an earlier building, and boasts the finest collection of seventeenth and eighteenth century cast iron grave slabs in the country. These rare memorials displayed outside the church are dedicated to members of local iron founding families, including the Knights of nearby Downton. The absence of any memorial inside the church, to them and to the Knights in particular, is down to an almighty spat with the vicar at the time of the church's rebuild. The cost of constructing the nave was met by the Mr A.Boughton-Knight, the then owner of Downton Castle, while that of the chancel was provided by the vicar and several other subscribers. The fall-out between the two parties occurred because each chose different architects and the two sections of the finished church differ to the point of distraction. For the nave, Boughton-Knight employed the Shrewsbury architect Samuel Pountney Smith, who had already built him a new church near to his castle. The vicar asked George Frederick Bodley, whose outstanding talent for interior design, particularly in churches, was employed to stunning effect at Kinnersley. The vicar appears to have had the final say by banishing the Boughton-Knight's ancestral graves to the churchyard.

Downton Castle is a castellated mansion standing above the river Teme at the head of a narrow and at times spectacular gorge. It is one of the most important major houses in Herefordshire. There is a road to it up through the gorge but I was taking the scenic route requiring a stiff climb to Burrington Hays and over Hunstay Hill. A few cottages and a fine half-timbered farmhouse nestled in the early autumn sunshine at the end of a secluded lane where a bridle path led me out of the Wigmore basin and onto the heights above Burrington. Hunstay Hill is part of the ancient Saxon forest of Bringewood and from now on I was passing through the Downton Estate. Pheasants hiding in the still lush undergrowth darted everywhere on my approach. Fresh wide-tyred tracks stretching across the tree lined hill slopes indicated a recent shoot, field gates still open following the pursuit of the prey. In spite of expectations, the sudden view of the castle with its dramatic position above the river below was an awesome sight. The footpath crosses the river Teme by a stone hump backed bridge built as an early access point to the castle itself. Downton was designed and built by Richard Payne Knight, the grandson of a wealthy Shropshire ironmaster who had bought the estate in the early part of the eighteenth century.

Payne Knight had spent much of his youth travelling through Italy, and the outline and battlements of his new home were inspired more by the semi fortified houses of Europe than by English castles. The style is Gothic, composed of square, circular, and octagonal towers, and the result is one of the earliest castellated houses of the new revivalism. It was here, surrounded by wild and romantic parkland above a narrow gorge through which the river Teme squeezes, that Payne Knight, together with his neighbour, Uvedale Price of Foxley, sponsored the Picturesque Movement. They contested the orthodox thinking of the day that symmetry was the basis of all architecture, and instead promoted the idea of freedom of styles. Consequently, Downton became the first estate in England to beak away from the regular classical format. The essence of the Picturesque Movement was that the beauty of the natural landscape was the proper source of aesthetic inspiration. However, its exponents admired the beauty of the real world only if it looked like a painting. The word 'picturesque' comes from the Italian 'pittoesco' meaning 'in the manner of a painting'. So it was not surprising that gardeners such as Humphrey Repton, a follower of the ideas of Payne Knight and Uvedale Price, would improve the landscape, if it wasn't landscaped enough, by levelling or creating hills, filling in or excavating lakes, and uprooting trees to plant them elsewhere. Another exponent of the Picturesque Movement was the Reverend William Gilpin, who made his now famed boat trip down the river Wye in 1792 and celebrated the tour by publishing a book complete with sketches and engravings of what he saw. His book *Observations on the River Wye* became not just a bestseller, but served as an introduction to all that this was an essential experience for those in pursuit of picturesque beauty. In recent years, the Downton estate has fallen on hard times but was rescued in 1979 by a confusing arrangement between an absentee landlord living in Switzerland who bought the castle but hardly ever visits, and the French Perrier family of mineral water fame who own the estate and manage the extensive parkland for corporate shoots. The woodland south of the river at this point is a nature reserve managed by English Nature. Small and large leaved limes grow in abundance. Alongside the river itself the humid and unpolluted conditions allow a profusion of lichens, mosses and ferns, and rare fossils of early forms of fish have been found in the rocky cliffs. Set on the hillside in an exposed location on the Downton estate and overlooking a deep section of the gorge is the church of St Giles. Andrew Boughton-Knight, had it built here in 1861 beside the western approach to his castle to replace an older abandoned church in the village of Downton-On-The-Rocks one mile further west. Presumably, the mile walk to attend services was the price the parishioners had to pay for his financing the replacement. The added bonus for them was a much larger church, constructed in Early English style, and the architect, Samuel Pountney Smith, created a rare example of Victorian sensitivity in church building. The view towards the gorge from the church's position on the hillside is quite stunning.

With daylight fading, I took a hill path behind the ruined old church in the village and climbed over Church Hill before descending steeply to join a lane into Roman built Leintwardine, the most northerly point of my journey.

'Before us spreads the placid vale of the Teme, with the tower of Leintwardine church rising above the surrounding woods. Looming darkly beyond, the broad mass of hills known as the Clun Forest stretches away, fold upon fold,

> *till lost in the shades of the falling dusk; while nearer at hand the level rays of the setting sun pick out in brilliant touches the rugged contours of Coxall Knoll; whose deeply trenched lines of vallum and fosse conjure up to the imagination the heroic deeds of the ill-starred Caradoc in his strenuous efforts to overcome the Roman legions advancing across the Teme from Brandon Camp.'*

Leintwardine is the largest village in North Herefordshire and is situated at the confluence of the rivers Teme and Clun, both flowing down from the Welsh hills. Up to the end of the nineteenth century this area was part of Shropshire until a local dispute in 1894 ended by transferring the parish to Herefordshire. The Romans set down their third station along Watling Street here in 70AD and named it Bravonium. The bridge they built over the river was a little to the east of the present one, itself a fourteenth century construction, but no trace of the Roman bridge remains. The Roman road ran through the centre of the settlement and is preserved now as a back street separating pretty cottages and delightful houses, many of which are medieval survivors. The suffix 'wardine' of the later re-name suggests Saxon origins but the town layout is strictly Roman. The church of St Mary Magdalene is built partly over the ramparts of the settlement, and has Saxon and Norman foundations. The present Lady Chapel was formerly the Mortimer Chapel built by Roger Mortimer, and the choir stalls are early fifteenth century brought from Wigmore Abbey after the dissolution. Near the church, Leintwardine House lies hidden behind high hedges, silently protecting the memory of a forgotten hero of the American War of Independence. Sir Banestre Tarleton, the son of a Liverpool merchant, decided in 1775 to purchase a commission and join the fight to hang on to the colonies. He was known for his bravery and impetuosity and it wasn't long before he made his mark. During the campaign to capture New York, Tarleton, as officer-in-command of the advance guard, surprised and captured the American General Charles Lee as he was relaxing behind his own lines. Lee was taken back to New York as a prisoner and later exchanged. After the war, Tarleton returned to England, became a close friend of the Prince of Wales and married the daughter of the fourth Duke of Ancaster. Sometime around the beginning of the nineteenth century, this, by now retired, Major General of the King's Dragoon Guards left the high life of London and settled with his wife here in the north Herefordshire borders.

Having discovered my overnight stay was to be in one of the pretty village cottages, I decided to book an extra day to look around, and found it a friendly and vibrant outpost. It's not a large place by any means, but fifty years ago, Leintwardine was a thriving market centre supporting the surrounding agricultural area. In its heyday, there were two grocers, two bakers, two butchers, a draper, watchmaker, pharmacy, a shop selling household goods and another, bicycle accessories. More importantly, there were five public houses satisfying the local thirst for beers and cider. The Swan Inn is now closed but was never de-licensed and some of the locals remain hopeful that it may yet re-open. During the 1940s, Lotte Amos was a regular at the Swan. She would play the fiddle and a Jew's harp, and sing in return for a glass of ale. She was also known for her herbal remedies for aches and pains which she brewed up in her isolated cottage at the back of the town. The Lion Hotel, by the river bridge, is still open for business, and due to the postcode, proudly advertises itself as being in south Shropshire. However, against all odds, the ancient Sun Inn still survives as a rare example of a parlour pub. Nothing more than a terraced cottage, this relic from an age long gone is an original ale house where ale was brewed on the premises, firstly due to the absence of water to satisfy a basic need of the tenant, and then when there was a surplus, sold to passers by. The owner at the time of my visit was Flossie Lane, at ninety years of age perhaps one of the country's oldest landladies. I'd just eaten at the The Lion and was considering the short walk to the Sun when the hotel manager warned me that I might not be allowed in!

'I'd get friendly with a local quickly if I were you, and then ask for an introduction. Flossie won't allow anybody in unless she knows them.'

'I tried earlier,' a voice murmured from a corner of the bar. *'In spite of the door being open and the lights on, she told me the pub was closed'.* After the man, whose name was Terry, and I had introduced ourselves we agreed to give it a go together. Entry was accomplished this time without incident and a few nods and hellos to those already seated in the settles seemed to be enough to ensure our visit would last a little longer. Flossie's attention was

taken by a lady sat next to her and both were deep in conversation. *'The beer's in the kitchen, gentlemen,'* someone said.

Terry sprinted in that direction out of Flossie's vision, and I followed almost as quickly. Beer in hand, I was then able to take in the surroundings. The three very small ground floor rooms all had furnishings making up Flossie's domestic quarters, and in her lounge two wooden benches and a table for her customers. As we sat down, Flossie smiled tentatively but made no move to have us evicted. Before the end of the evening, I had got to know many friendly locals, including Chris, the adopted mayor of Leintwardine, a round jovial character who insisted on making the many trips to the kitchen to refill our glasses. His office came with no regalia or gold chain, his election a result of a bit of fun repeated annually during the dark cold nights of winter. I learned that Douglas Griffiths, the village butcher, supplies hot food for the regularly held celebration suppers, when the menu might include 'squirrel casserole' or 'rook pie'.

Peter Faulkner, the coracle man of Leintwardine

Peter Faulkner teaches children with special needs in Ludlow and was one of those friendly faces I met that night. He also makes coracles, those curious walnut shaped river craft which you steer with one hand, and he has developed quite a reputation as a master craftsman. The morning after my inauguration at the Sun, I found him sat on the steps of his delightful cottage, strumming a few tunes on his guitar and chatting to the occasional passer by. He invited me to his workshop in the old schoolhouse to show me how his boats are made. The walls were lined with his stock of timbers, some already in the process of being shaped under tension, and in one corner a coracle was in the early stages of construction. *'The essence of old time craftsmanship is the use of locally sourced materials,'* he told me, *'I use hazel for the frames and ash, which I collect from woodland hereabouts, for the seats and paddles. The cowhide coverings come from Douglas's slaughter house next door!'* Since making his first boat in 1987, Peter has emerged as a leading specialist, and his customers come to this tiny corner of Herefordshire from all over the British Isles and Europe in order to purchase one of his skin boats. I asked him what led him to embark on this road to fame. *'Being at the convergence of two rivers, Leintwardine has traditionally been a favourite spot for water related pastimes. When I was a lad, I spent much of my time messing about on the river bank, when I wasn't actually in the river itself. One day, I met the great coracle maker, Eustace Rogers, and after seeing him at work near his home at Ironbridge in Shropshire, I decided I'd have a go. My first attempt must have been good because some of the local lads asked me to build one each for them and it took off from there. Now, in addition to single seaters, orders are coming in for multi-manned sea going Currachs.'*

Along with his wife, Vivienne, Peter has attended craft fairs and boating festivals to exhibit his crafts, travelling as far as Scandinavia in the process. He has featured in Country Life magazine and appeared on TV. Eustace Rogers died two years ago, and Peter has taken over the mantle of master coracle maker and is currently chairman of The Coracle Society. When not producing coracles, he is paddling in one. Between 1987 and 1992, he rode the rivers Teme, Wye, and Severn, and parts of the Shannon in Ireland, a total of four hundred miles. In August 2003, starting at Cricklade he paddled the Thames as far as Teddington Lock, covering the one hundred and thirty five miles in eleven days. All this in a small single seater round boat with one paddle!

Flossie Lane died in June 2009 but thankfully the Sun Inn is now being run by Gary Seymour who owns the Chip Shop next door to the pub, along with Nick Davis from Hobson's brewery. Beer and Chips! Long may that combination continue to be offered.

My memorable stay at Leintwardine at an end, I whispered a sad farewell to no-one in particular as I took a riverside footpath following the river Clun for the first time. After a half mile or so I crossed a footbridge and chose a field path west towards the Teme again and the iron age fort of Coxall Knoll looming above the village of Brampton Bryan. Some historians believe that this was the site of the British chieftain Caractacus's last stand against the Roman advance lead by Publius Ostorius Scapula in 51AD. The Romans saw their adversary as a resourceful enemy. However, in spite of their resolution, the Britons had no chance against the superior strength of the Roman legions. They were heavily defeated and Caractacus himself was treacherously delivered up to the Romans soon after by Catimandua, the Queen of the Brigantes, a rival British tribe with territory in the north east of England with whom he had sought protection.

On his website battlefieldanomalies.com, Graham Morris argues a case, not for Coxall Knoll as Caractacus's final stand which he considered indefensible to a determined attacker, but for Caer Caradoc, not suprisingly it being the Welsh for Caractacus's Fort, four miles west. Aerial photography taken in 1983 discovered two large Roman military camps, one at Brampton Bryan, the other at nearby Walford. The Brampton Bryan camp is enormous, covering some sixty four acres. The heavy presence suggested a major military objective and it was known that Caradoc used both Coxall and Caer Caradoc as bases. Morris contests that the clear fallback line towards Caer Caradoc becomes progressively steeper, and at the summit near Stow Hill a mile or two east of the Welsh border town of Knighton, a fighting withdrawal could be made. The site chosen appears to fulfil all the criteria of a sound military position. In spite of the vast amount of resources and effort to capture him, Caradoc was kept alive and taken to Rome where he was allowed to live out his days and walk freely, a sign surely that Rome had a great deal of respect for their resolute British opponent.

> *'Sallying forth betimes in the morning, we glance at the much restored church of St Bartholomew, and then devote our attention to the compact ruins of Brampton Bryan Castle, a fortress which in former times kept watch over the valley of the Teme. Though the shell of*

the building is, as will be seen from our sketch, in a fair state of preservation, few traces have survived to indicate its ancient importance.'

Crossing a lively stretch of the river below Coxall Knoll, I arrived at Brampton Bryan or 'Bron' as it is called locally, a delightful village in the northernmost corner of the county where it borders with Powys and Shropshire. The fast flowing Teme runs along its northern side and the quaint mixture of black and white cottages assembled around the tiny village green paint a picture of ageless charm. One of the cottages used to be the Oxford Arms from where Timmins sallied forth. The village is the ancestral home of the great Harley family and a branch of the family still lives in the eighteenth century hall built next to the ruined castle which was the family home up to the Civil War. The dynasty was started by Robert de Brampton who settled here and built a castle in 1070. The last of the de Brampton's, the fourth Sir Bryan, died in 1294 but in 1309 his eldest daughter Margaret married Sir Robert de Harley who then moved in, and the Harleys have remained here ever since. It was the great-grandson of the Civil War Sir Robert who gave his name to the famous London Street of medical consultants. Throughout the centuries there have been many in the family who have achieved great things, not least the heroic defence of her castle home by Lady Brilliana Harley in March 1643. While her husband was attending Parliament and her son was also away fighting for Cromwell, a Royalist army under the command of Sir William Vavasour arrived at Brampton and ordered that the castle be surrendered to the King. When Brilliana refused, Vavasour began a siege. Brilliana held out for seven weeks until the Royalists left to carry out other war duties. In June that same year, the Royalists returned and a second siege began during which the unfortunate, and by now exhausted, Brilliana caught a bad cold and died. The castle finally fell in April 1644 and was destroyed in the aftermath, along with the church and most of the village dwellings. St Bartholomews was rebuilt in 1675 as were some of the houses, and now with the ruined castle hidden away behind high yew hedges of the hall, it is hard to discern that any destruction took place at all. The thriving village shop and post office and a buoyant community spirit remain in harmony with their current Harley landlord.

Brampton Bryan Castle and first home of the Harleys

> *'But we must be up and away, for many a mile of rugged and unfrequented country lies upon our line of march to-day. Crossing the village Green with its wide spreading lime trees and groups of tidy cottages, we turn south-westwards and enter the park, climbing steeply upwards by a tortuous path amidst gorse and bracken beneath clumps of great Spanish Chestnuts now in full bloom.'*

Brampton Bryan park is one of the oldest deer parks in the county and is an area of great beauty rising to over one thousand feet. Many of the Spanish chestnut trees described by Timmins are three hundred years old and the view at the top of the park westward to the Welsh border is spectacular. I covered the next five miles of rough cart tracks and silent meandering lanes in easy fashion around the broad flanks of the appropriately named Harley's Mountain, which on its eastern side looms over the secluded village of Lingen. At the foot of these lonely hills, guarding the entrance to a remote section of the Lugg valley from its lofty knoll, are the remains of another castle at Stapleton. This ruin is that of an Elizabethan manor house, built on the remains of a twelfth century Norman castle which was yet another Mortimer stronghold. As at Brampton Bryan, the Civil War took its toll on isolated defences and Stapleton wasn't strong enough to survive. There is no public access to this romantic ruin, which is just as well since a large chunk of what was left collapsed in 1999.

Less than a mile across the river plain on the southern bank of the Lugg is the border town of Presteigne. Pronounced Presteen, meaning 'household of priests', the town is actually in Powys but is surrounded on three sides by Herefordshire and I have to pass through it to continue my journey. Its early occupation by Offa's Mercians who captured the town from the Welsh accounts for its position on the English side of his defensive Dyke. In the fifteenth century, the upper Lugg valley was noted for the quality of its wool. A cloth industry developed here on a considerable scale and as in Leominster, Presteigne went through a prosperous period. However, fortunes took a nasty turn in 1681 when much of the town was destroyed in a disastrous fire. The visitor today will see a town full of early Georgian replacements, some with blue plaques identifying previous important residents. One such is Joseph Baker, a third lieutenant on the merchant ship 'Discovery' which explored and charted the American north-west coastline in the late eighteenth century. Lieutenant Baker was a skilled draughtsman and drew maps and charts as a result of the exploration. Baker Island in the Great Columbia River between the US states of Washington and Oregon, and Mount Baker in Washington were named in his honour. Curiously, the second lieutenant on the same trip, Peter Puget, also lived for a time on the same street as Baker. Another plaque celebrates Joseph Murray Ince, a successful painter of landscapes in watercolour who lived here in early childhood. He received private tuition from David Cox in Hereford before moving to London in 1826 where his paintings of rural Wales and Herefordshire went on show at the Royal Academy. Although he returned to Presteigne in 1830, he maintained contact both with the galleries in London and the wealthy purchasers of his works. In 1983, the Welsh composer and pianist Adrian Williams founded a Festival of Music and the Arts here which has since become a major event in the cultural calendar of the United Kingdom. The Presteigne Festival has attracted numerous acclaimed performers in its lifetime, including the BBC National Orchestra of Wales, and soloists Evelyn Glennie and Julian Lloyd Webber.

Presteigne's church of St Andrew is a fine medieval structure with Saxon and Norman remnants. Its greatest treasure is a Flemish tapestry of Christ's entry into Jerusalem dating from 1510. A window in the Lady Chapel contains fragments of stained glass collected after the Parliamentarians smashed all the windows during their occupation of the town in the Civil War. Before then, the windows had contained the coats of arms of the great families of Mortimer, Harley, Cornewall, and Vaughan, as well as the royal arms of Prince Arthur, the eldest of Henry VII's sons. In earlier times still, being then on the English side of the border, the church had the unfortunate distinction of being sacked first by Llewellyn the Great in the twelfth century, and then again by Owen Glyndwr in the fifteenth . But it was in the churchyard where I discovered a memorial to the town's darkest secret and everlasting shame. In 1805, a slab was erected near the south porch telling the tragic tale of Mary Morgan, a young servant girl who was hanged for killing her illegitimate child. Mary was in the employ of Walter Wilkins Esq., the Member of Parliament for Radnorshire, at Maesllwch Castle near Hay-on-Wye when she gave birth to a daughter whilst alone in her room. That she then killed her baby is, apparently, not in doubt and no amount of conjecture can help explain her reasons or her state of mind at the time. Illegitimate births in the early nineteenth century were commonplace but executions for infanticide were rare, and these circumstances make the story a particularly sad one which still attracts attention today. At the inquest, the coroner found that Mary Morgan:

> '...being big with child, afterward alone and secretly from her body did bring forth alive a female child, which by the laws and customs of this kingdom was a bastard....moved and seduced by the instigation of the devil afterwards on the same day, feloniously, wilfully and of her malice aforethought did make an assault with a certain penknife...."

Vicious stuff, you might think, and you can almost hear the damning voices already bellowing for more blood. At her trial here in Presteigne, the jury, influenced by Mary's apparent disregard for human life not surprisingly found her guilty of murder. There was only one penalty and a large crowd watched as the tragic figure was taken by to the site of execution. In that unsympathetic world, few would have considered any injustice had taken place, though the victim was a sixteen year old girl and poorly educated. The identity of the father of Mary's child never came to light though the simple explanation would be that he was the squire's son or one of her fellow servants. As was the fashion of the alpha males of the day, whoever it was would give little thought to her fate. Even Judge Hardinge's summing up at the trial was later described as *'consisting of pious platitude....without pity or understanding'.* His tone was repeated in the sanctimonious words of the memorial stone erected by one of the judge's associates.

> 'To the memory of Mary Morgan, who young and beautiful, endowed with good understanding and disposition, but unenlightened by the sacred truths of Christianity, became the victim of sin and shame and was condemned to an ignominious death on the eleventh April 1805 for the murder of her bastard child. Rous'd to a first sense of guilt and remorse by the eloquent and humane exertions of her benevolent Judge, Mr Justice Hardinge, she underwent the Sentence of Law on the following Thursday with unfeigned repentance and a furvent hope of forgiveness through the merits of a redeeming intercessor. This stone is erected not merely to perpetuate the remembrance of a departed penitent, but to remind the living of the frailty of human nature when unsupported by religion'.

Nearby, a second stone was erected by an unknown hand who clearly thought that sentiment too much and responds

> 'He that is without sin among you, let him cast a stone at her'.

Amen to that.

Presteigne is a remarkable town, unspoilt by overdevelopment, and many of its historic town houses are little changed. There are shops here that could have graced a nineteenth century Dickensian setting and are collectively still capable of providing for the everyday needs of the twenty-first century. I found it wholly self-contained with little need for its people to travel far for anything. During the two days I stayed there, I became aware of being thoroughly happy and oblivious to the greater world elsewhere. There was a kind of mystique, an overwhelming impression of Shangri-La, where folk were going about the daily lives with a permanent smile, as in a trance. It is no mystery therefore why musicians, artists, and painters have come here to work, and why many have stayed. My accommodation here was the sixteenth century Radnorshire Arms sitting practically on the English Welsh border at the edge of the town and where I received a warm welcome in the bar from local farming and landowning folk eager to proclaim their neutrality over a few pints of beer.

From Presteigne, the Lugg winds its laboured way between wooded slopes towards Shobdon. Three miles east and sitting on a buff high above a narrow densely shrubbed gorge is Kinsham Court, an elegant, three story, mainly Georgian brick house, once part of the great Harley estate and a rural retreat from one of their main houses at Eywood, near Kington. In 1812, it became a temporary love nest for Jane Elizabeth Harley, wife of the fifth Earl of Oxford, and Lord George Gordon Byron. In September of that year, Byron had taken residence in Cheltenham, within sight of the Malvern Hills he had come to love as a child during holiday visits. There he would mix with the political set and take the waters. In November, he was invited to stay with the Harleys at Eywood where he remained until the following spring. When not ensconced in Lady Oxford's affections, Byron spent much time in her well stocked library. He also found delight with Lady Oxford's children, taking them on rambles around the north Herefordshire countryside, including to the Roman camp at Wapley Hill just outside Presteigne. At Lady Oxford's suggestion, when things got too hot at Eywood, he moved into Kinsham Court. Kinsham is now the home of Commander and Mrs Wood, and having expressed a loose interest in the life and times of the poet, I was invited to Kinsham to see a couple of reminders he had left behind. Mrs Wood is herself an Arkwright whose family moved in here after selling Hampton Court in 1911. After a warm welcome, she showed me around the secluded grounds which included the remains of a cedar she called 'Byron's Tree'. He is said to have composed two cantos of his poem 'Childe Harold' while sat beneath its spreading branches. The tree is now dead and the stunted greying trunk is filled with concrete to prevent collapse. After the affair with Lady Oxford ended, Byron is said to have etched his name on a small pane of glass in an upstairs window. Mrs

Wood showed me the alleged signature but though the evidence was exciting to behold, whether it was by him or anyone else cannot be conclusive.

Lord Byron's signature scratched on a bedroom window at Kinsham Court

Timmins didn't stop to admire Presteigne as I did because it being in Wales would have meant him diverting beyond his strict plan to keep within the Herefordshire border. Apparently it mattered not to him, that to progress towards Kington he would have to cross the Hindwell Brook from the Welsh side. My two nights stay in Presteigne necessitated criss-crossing the border several times in the space of twenty four hours while I looked around the town and surrounding area. After a final full Welsh breakfast, I set out along the quiet B4355 road in my erstwhile companion's footsteps over the Hindwell in the direction of the Rodd.

> *Just within the Herefordshire border, upon the high road between Presteigne and Kington, stands a noble specimen of a seventeenth century manor house; the original home of the Rodd family whose name it bears. Built of brick and stone with wide mullioned windows, some with lattice panes, and doorway set deep within a massive arch, the exterior of the mansion is adorned with festoons of ivy and creeping plants, while quaint pigeon-cotes set against the huge old chimney stacks add a picturesque feature.*

Although the Rodd family may have lived here for many centuries, they have long gone from Herefordshire. In the eighteenth century the house had been home for a while to James Rennell who, at the ripe old age of twenty, had been appointed Surveyor General of Bengal under Lord Clive of India. After exhaustive work mapping first Bengal then later the whole of India, Rennell became known as the Father of Indian Geography. He was also instrumental in founding

The Royal Geographical Society which was eventually formed just two months after his death in 1830. The Rodd estate was bought in 1983 by Sir Sidney Nolan, Australia's most internationally celebrated modern artist who first came to prominence in 1946 with a series of atmospheric paintings on the theme of the famous bush ranger Ned Kelly and the ill-fated outback explorers Burke and Willis. Although Nolan's work mirrored his feelings for his homeland and its history, he decided to settle in the Welsh borders where he continued to develop his unique work. After his death in 1992, his wife Lady Mary, who was a painter in her own right, stayed on at the Rodd where she still lives and was instrumental in setting up a Trust in her husband's name.

> *'Time flying, we reluctantly bid farewell to The Rodd and its interesting associations, and pursue a narrow lane which leads along the valley beneath the escarpments of Garraway Hill and Nash Scar. We follow a green trackway so narrow that the luxuriant undergrowth sweeps against us as we pass.'*

Retracing my steps along the B4355, I turned west at the Hindwell Brook and followed it through a peaceful valley flanked by Nash Wood and Little Brampton Scar, probably the same Scar in Timmins's account. In common with other parts of pre-historic Britain, the land of this border region was glaciated, and at the end of the last ice age there was a very rapid melt resulting in the formation of a huge lake between steep sided hills around what is now the town of New Radnor in Powys. When the lake burst out between Burfa Bank and Herrock Hill, it formed the valley through which the Hindwell Brook now flows. In places, the banks of the now tiny river are wide and steeply terraced, reminders of its destructive and energetic birth. Hindwell Pool, alongside the B4357 two miles further west is the last remnant of that great lake. Ahead now was the idyllic hamlet of Knill. A large modern house nestling by the brook below the church has replaced what was once the spectacular five bay, half timbered Knill Court which was burnt down in 1943 while being used as a school. The records show that the old court was medieval in origin but was largely rebuilt in the nineteenth century with an Italian garden and leisure areas added. After the fire, the remains of the court and the gardens were abandoned to become a statistic in the ever growing catalogue of lost great houses of England. The new house was built on the vacant plot in 1980. The ancient manor of Knill, came into hands of the Walsham family in 1599 and remained so until the last of the line to live there, Sir John Walsham, died in 1900. Sir John was MP for, and Lord Lieutenant, of Radnorshire in 1843 at which time he was called to give evidence to the Commission of Enquiry on the Rebbecca Riots. The 'Rebbecarites' dressed as women and attacked and destroyed tollgates around mid Wales. Their grievances centred on the high toll charges levied at turnpikes and the discontent that was generated amongst poor farmers who found it increasingly expensive to move stock to market. The use of the name 'Rebecca' appeared to have biblical origins. It took the intervention of the Metropolitan Police and eventually the army to quell the disturbances. The ringleaders were deported, but the aftermath saw a reduction in toll charges and gives an early indication of the effects of people power.

> *'Crossing a stream by a footbridge, we scramble up a steep path to the top of Garraway Hill, and obtain from its level grassy ridge a glorious view for many miles around, which is only obstructed by some loftier heights to the westward. Traversing the moorland runs old Offa's Dyke which winds a circuitous course around the side of Herrock Hill and passes onwards towards Kington.'*

On Herrock and Rushock Hills, Offa and Mortimer almost meet as the trails in their names parallel each other and tumble down the hills' southern flanks, while on adjacent Bradnor Hill, golfers now enjoy spectacular views across the greens and fairways of England's highest course. Far below, Herefordshire's most westerly town lies in wait in the late hazy afternoon sun.

> *'The path across the mountain is somewhat obscure, but a south westerly course should be followed, which will lead around Bradnor Hill, until the town of Kington comes into sight in the valley below. A footpath now leads steeply down, affording glimpses of the rugged scenery by which this favoured little town is surrounded.'*

Kington is the smallest of Herefordshire's five market towns and lies in that part of the county west of Offa's Dyke known as *Herefordia in Wallia,* Herefordshire in Wales. It is a fine town full of old world charm which shows great reluctance to be overmodernized. Believed to have been named after King Edward the Confessor it, in time, become part of the Welsh principality of Brecknock. The town was captured by Harold Godwinson in 1055 and has been English ever since, although the town's loyalties have always been as much Welsh as English. Its position at the approach into Wales between Bradnor Hill and Hergest Ridge made the town defensible against further Welsh attempts to reclaim it. Here, too, well established trackways from New Radnor, Presteigne, Leominster, and Hereford converged and was an ideal place for a market. The fledgling borough grew first on high ground around the protection of a castle and church with its substantially constructed tower until, in the thirteenth century, the castle was abandoned and a new Kington began to appear at the bottom of the hill. There are many buildings in the town which date back three hundred years, and a few even earlier.

Kington's strategic position as a market town and a centre for droving meant it was regularly crowded with cattle and sheep. The narrow streets would be filthy and smelly especially in the heat of summer. Before the Public Health Act of 1875, the streets of the town were regularly choked with raw sewage. The Hereford Times reported in 1853 that 'the stench arising from ill-constructed or blocked up drains is intolerable in nearly every thoroughfare.' A visitor to the town wrote that the churchyard was 'too full of mouldering remains to appeal to any save an anatomist.' The early roads of Herefordshire were notoriously poor, little more than mud tracks, and very few were fit for wheeled traffic, especially in winter. At the beginning of the eighteenth century, a gentleman's carriage was rarely seen in Kington. In Georgian and Victorian times, as the town grew and new fronts were added to high street shops and offices, the rears and interiors were left alone and remain still in the past. Five of its old tollhouses survive. The original market hall, sadly replaced, was another work of the great John Abel's.

The emerging industrialized world almost missed out Kington altogether in the nineteenth century. A horse-drawn tramway from Brecon and Hay which had reached Eardisley in 1816 took a further four years to connect the extra six miles to Kington, and even then only because it was on the way to its eventual target, the limestone quarries at Burlingjobb north west of the town. A canal planned from Kington to Stourport in the West Midlands didn't materialize. The trains from Leominster finally arrived in 1857 and from Hereford in 1874, then disappeared again one hundred years later. Nevertheless, Kington developed its own thriving businesses. One such was that of James Meredith & Co, in the nineteenth century a major employer. In his book *The Meredith Family of Presteigne and Kington*, John Southwood describes the business in 1877 as 'wholesale and furnishing ironmongers, iron and brass founders, agricultural implement makers and agents, nail manufacturers, furnishings and woollen drapers'. Clearly this was a sizeable business. The foundry was sold after the First World War but the shop on the High Street continued, expanding to concentrate on the new technology of electrical and wireless equipment. The famous department store of A.W.Gamage in Holborn, London, started life in Kington in 1866 when the twenty one years old Albert Walter Gamage opened a shop devoted to ladies wear. He moved to London in 1874 and opened the Holborn store four years later. The business prospered and Gamage became an extremely wealthy man. His son Leslie, a solicitor, married into aristocracy and eventually became the Vice-Chairman and Joint Managing Director of The General Electric Company.

In 1960, an old clock was discovered in a shed in Bridge Street. It had been made by Henry Carleton Skarratt, in his clockmaker's shop in Kington in 1841 and was the first and last of its kind. Around that time, local historian Richard Parry wrote of seeing the clock displayed outside Skarratt's shop, '*.... with an illuminated dial....which is an exquisite piece of craftsmanship and shows the time equally as well by night as in day time*'. The secret was gas. Henry Skarratt's clock had a gas jet, similar to a pilot light, which turned up full during hours of darkness and died down again during daylight hours. The gas clock remained on display in the Kington shop until 1920, and since its rediscovery has been kept in the archives of Hereford Museum. Although only a small town, Kington's many shops sell local produce and all that is needed to survive a catastrophic collapse of society elsewhere. At one time it boasted thirty one inns, and still has nine within its town centre streets. The Oxford Arms is said to be the oldest and may have medieval origins. In the eighteenth century, a coach and horses ran from outside this inn each Friday to London via Hereford and Malvern. Kington seems to have an air of indifference to the present and a disdain for the future, and could at any moment retreat even further, if the townsfolk so wished.

I had booked my accommodation at the Burton, a large but modest Hotel in the centre of the town so on the folowing day I set out to explore this interesting place. The remains of the castle stand on a crag twenty metres above the Back Brook which flows down the valley from Old Radnor, and overlooking now the A44 by-pass. Built sometime at end of the eleventh century by Adam de Port who had been granted the land by William Rufus, it seems to have been nothing more elaborate than a palisade and tower. Adam's descendants had held it for about one hundred years before Roger de Port joined a Welsh rebellion which was quickly put down by Henry II. The castle was then forfeited to the crown and it remained in royal ownership until King John gave it to William de Braose of Radnor, a Marcher Lord, in 1201. This seems to have been a mistake because John took it back and started a dispute between the crown and the de Braose family lasting more than ten years. When the de Braoses captured the castle again the King attacked their Marcher territories, including Hay on Wye, and Kington castle was destroyed. It had lasted less than one hundred and thirty years.

Below the ramparts but on its own elevated position, the church of St Mary the Virgin was built a short time after the castle. Its substantial bulky tower has an attractive broach spire which was added in the eighteenth century. Inside is the tomb of Thomas Vaughan who died supporting the Yorkist cause at Banbury in 1469, and his wife Ellen Gethin, once known as Ellen the Terrible. Her reputation was the result of the manner in which she avenged her brother's death. An archery contest had been arranged to which the accused, another, unrelated Vaughan, John of Tretower, was invited. At an appropriate moment, Ellen, disguised as one of the archers, turned her bow and shot him. Thomas, too, had a reputation for being mean and intolerant towards his people and was known in life as Black Vaughan. After death, legend has it that his heart was thrown into the moat that surrounded his home at Hergest Court. Whether this would have been a deliberate act by his enemies or an accident is not disclosed, but his spirit is said to have roamed the countryside in the form of a black dog, the original source of Sir Arthur Conan Doyle's idea for *The Hound of the Baskervilles.*

As I made my exit from the church, Valerie Housley was changing flowers in the churchyard and we talked for a while about the town and the people she knew. She remembered a story told to her by her father who lived near Hergest Court.

'One day when he was cycling home along the Hergest road after work, he came cross a large black dog standing in the road. My father was an avid dog lover, and stopped intending to stroke it. Instead, the dog which he said later had sharp red eyes and terrifying teeth, attacked him. My mother forbid father to tell anyone about the incident in case he was ridiculed. To this day, I've always believed that what he saw was Black Vaughan, though why he chose him to appear to is a mystery.'

The Vaughan legacy intrigued me and I was looking forward even more to my visit to Hergest Court to meet the current Vaughan owner which was planned for the following day.

From the churchyard, the view to the west is across the fertile valley of the river Arrow, one of the county's tributary rivers which joins up with the Lugg just south of Leominster. Across the road from the church is one of Kington's main schools named after the foundress, Lady Margaret Hawkins. She was a Vaughan, and the second wife of one of Queen Elizabeth 1's great seafaring heros, Sir John Hawkins. Although she spent most of her later life in the Queen's service in London, she never forgot her roots and when she died in 1619 left £800 in her will for the founding of a free school in Kington. It opened on the feast of St Michael and All Angels, 29 September, 1632 with sixty two pupils, and every year since on that day the school has celebrated Founder's Day.

In the early part of the nineteenth century the narrow gauge tram road connecting Brecon with Hay-on-Wye and Eardisley was extended through Kington to the lime quarries at Burlingjobb, five miles to the north west of the town. As a result, the horse drawn wagons transported coal, foundry products and farm produce to a growing population along a forty mile corridor. The tram road was a great success during its short life and was one of the last to operate in England. It survived until 1863, in spite of the opening of the Leominster to Kington railway six years earlier, mainly because the railways had no plans at that time to extend beyond Kington when transport was needed for the quarries at Burlingjobb. However, when the railway finally did arrive, a more ambitious plan was introduced by the Kington & Eardisley Railway Company to open a route to Preseigne making use of the line of the tram road. That line opened on the 3 August 1874 but struggled financially. In 1897 the K&E Company was taken over by GWR which closed the line in 1916 and took up the tracks to meet the war effort. They relaid it in 1922 to fulfil a promise to the community that they would do so as soon as materials became available but it lasted only until 1940 when the tracks were once again taken up and the buildings and land sold off. I decided to follow the old tram track bed out of Kington for a while and then eastwards across the meadow by the river. The track turned south through Lyonshall Park Wood, cutting through a section of Offa's Dyke before turning south west around an ornamental lake, ironically called Tramway Pool, before passing in front of the old castle and church at Lyonshall. Unusually, the park has no modern house associated with it but seems to have been crown land connected to the twelfth century castle.

Again, Timinns' schedule appears to have been tight and it didn't allow for a stay in Kington. Having descended Bradnor Hill, he caught the still available train immediately, to return to Hereford to prepare for the next stage of his journey.

> *With a glance at the well preserved church, and interesting school-house dating from the Elizabethan period, we hasten along the busy main street, just in time to catch the evening train, which carries us swiftly back through the rich woodland scenery around Pembridge and Leominster, until the familiar landmarks of the cathedral city are discerned, silhouetted against the lemon-coloured sky of an autumn sunset.*

Hergest Court is a very old house indeed. It stands on an elevated spur above the river Arrow two miles to the west of Kington directly opposite a much earlier motte and bailey. The original building dates from around 1267 and was built by Hywel ap Meurig, a local hereditary reeve. Meurig was a Welshman certainly, but more than likely a Norman vassal, too. Although probably of modest beginnings, Hergest Court grew considerably in time and by the late fifteenth century was being described by the Welsh poet, Lewis Glyn Cothi, as 'A house on the plan of the towers of Alhambra.' By the fourteenth century, the Meurig family name had been Anglicised to Clanvowe. At that time, Sir John Clanvowe was a contemporary of Geoffrey Chaucer and a close friend, and there is a long held belief that one of Chaucer's creations *'The Boke of Cupid God of Love'* was in fact written at Hergest Court by Sir John, who was a poet in his own right. At the beginning of the fifteenth century, Hergest Court passed to the Welsh speaking Thomas Vaughan, the younger son of Roger Vaughan of Bredwardine Castle. It was from then on occupied by the Vaughan family until the late eighteenth century when it passed through marriage to become yet another addition to the Harley estates. Not far from the old Court is Ridgebourne House, a large Grade II listed eighteenth century building on the lower eastern flanks of Hergest Ridge. Originally a secondary Vaughan house to Hergest Court, Ridgebourne is

Hergest Ridge centre left above Kington where Offa's Dyke and the Wesh border meet

now owned by Lawrence and Elizabeth Banks, as is the nationally renowned Hergest Croft Gardens next door, but their roots make their ownership surprisingly relevant to the Vaughans story. The first member of the Banks family to appear in Kington was Richard Banks who came from Kent in 1814 to join James Davies, an heir of the Harley family, in practice as lawyers. Davies lived at Ridgebourne. Richard Banks eventually married James Davies's niece of Bronllys Castle near Talgarth. The Davies' of Bronllys claimed descent from the same Welsh princes of Brecon as Hywell ap Meurig, hence the Vaughans and their Harley heirs, the Davies' and now the Banks' who own Ridgebourne and the Hergest estates, are all joined in lineage.

And so, on a bright mid autumn day, I arrived at Ridgebourne to meet Lawrence Banks and his wife, Elizabeth. I had telephoned Lawrence prior to arriving in Kington to express my interest in looking around Hergest Court. I felt fortunate when he told me he was more than happy to drive me the two miles distance and explain the origins of the various buildings of the court, and show me the bits and pieces that formed the earliest structure. We arrived at a sad looking house of white walls and dark timbers that exudes a weary air of detached indifference, but undoubted ancient significance. It is now a shadow of its former glory but in the days of Thomas 'Black Dog' Vaughan, Hergest would have been a much grander and more heavily fortified property than the house that greets visitors today. Yet long before the arrival of Meurig or the Vaughan's, something was going on here. As Lawrence explained, *'Hywell ap Meurig's choice of this site on high ground surrounded on three sides by a dry moat is intriguing, especially as there is a motte and bailey on the hillside opposite which predates the court. Why move across the road from an already well defended site? I believe there seems more to Hergest than is yet known.'*

As we scrambled around in ancient darkened rooms, musing on ghostly apparitions of dead men and black dogs, he explained his own desire to learn more about what he now sees as his ancestral home. *'In 1995, I asked Richard Morriss, the author of The Archaeology of Buildings, to search for some answers which I believed lay hidden behind these dusty walls and he subsequently reported that Hergest is one of the most important sites in the Welsh Marches. It is important because of its comparative rarity value. It's not a castle but a large fortified settlement belonging to influential local magnates, and there is a parallel with Owen Glyndwr's home at Sycarth near Oswestry.'*

Lawrence's intense interest in the history of the house and its occupants persuaded him to write a contribution to the 2002 edition of *The Transactions of the Radnorshire Society,* a sort of Woolhope Club of the Marches, outlining the known history of the court and adding his own discoveries. When the Vaughan family arrived at Hergest in the fifteenth century, they became the guardians of the area.

'It was about this time,' Lawrence told me, over coffee back at Ridgebourne, *'that Lewis Glyn Cothi wrote The Mabinogion, ancient tales of Welsh legends and myths with close Arthurian connections and which became known as The Red Book of Hergest.'*

The original Red Book is in the Bodleian Library in Oxford, but I wasn't surprised to discover the Lawrence had a copy on his well stocked bookshelves.

Another Banks' house, Hergest Croft, has been converted for facilities for visitors to the now famous Gardens. It was built on the approaches to Hergest Ridge in 1912 as a home for William Banks, a banker and passionate gardener, and together with his wife Dorothy they created the first magnificent garden. William's son, Richard, planted a huge number of maples and birch trees, and now giant rhododendrons nestle amongst ancient oaks in a secluded valley. The gardens are open to the public and extend over fifty acres with over four thousand rare shrubs and trees, described as one of the finest collections anywhere in Britain.

I was thrilled to have met Lawrence and Elizabeth and privileged to have had the opportunity to get up close and personal with their historic family and their legends. I gave them my thanks and left them to catch up with their busy daily affairs of estate.

On a previous visit to Kington, my attention was given over entirely to walking the local section of Offa's Dyke Path, a walk I had started many months earlier at its southern end near the mouth of the river Wye at Chepstow, intending to finish eventually at Prestatyn in north Wales, all one hundred and seventy seven miles of it. The everlasting memory of that visit was not of Kington itself but of Hergest Ridge, the magnificent massif dominating the western side of the town. This time, on my last day, I would make a long-awaited return to the summit with its unforgettable panoramic views. The boundary between England and Wales passes over the Ridge north-south while the Offa's Dyke Path crosses the full east-west length of this spectacular hill. The Victorians constructed a racecourse on the summit which with views to hand was popular with the local gentry and farming community up to 1880. The course is still used today by local horse owners although for more leisurely canters. The instrumentalist Mike Oldfield had a house nearby and was inspired by the topography to compose two of his record albums, *Hergest Ridge* and *Ommadawn*, At the end of *Ommadawn* is a short song entitled 'On Horseback'. The last lines of which are: *'So if you feel a little glum, to Hergest Ridge you should come. In summer, winter, rain or sun, it's good to be on horseback.'* The Ridge is four miles long and access is particularly steep from the western end so the need for appropriate time and stamina should be considered if one is to complete the walk both ways in one go. On this occasion, I did not have time for a full crossing but sat by the racecourse for a while before returning to Kington in time for lunch.

Later that day, I walked a lonely road below the southern flanks of Hergest a few miles westwards out of Kington to the tiny isolated hamlet of Huntington, on the very edge of England. It is a silent place where time stands still. After King John had destroyed the castle at Kington, Richard de Braose built another one here in 1221 hoping it would become the chief castle in the area. Unfortunately, his plan didn't work. Being so isolated, the township which grew up at Huntington couldn't compete with the market prospects of its neighbour, and both castle and township had been abandoned by the middle of the fifteenth century. However, there is still a small community here very much rural, and agriculture is the only industry. The remains of de Braose's castle are impressive and parts of the stonework of a fourteenth century rebuild can still be seen. There isn't much to see of the old township, baring a few cottages, a farmhouse or two, a pub, and the most delightful little church of St Thomas Beckett. It has been suggested that it was constructed on the site of an earlier, Saxon, church, itself part of a lost Saxon village overlooked by another, much older castle on the hillside nearby. The present church is reputed to have been built as part of the penance of Richard de Brilo, one of Becket's four murderers, in 1170. At the Reformation, Henry VIII declared that the great Archbishop's death was not truly martyrdom and so he was de-canonized, thereafter referred to only as Bishop Beckett. As if in defiance, this isolated gem has remained unchanged and unchallenged, and continues to declare Thomas's sainthood.

De Braose's castle was a medieval baronial centre where he entertained his friends with sport and hunting. An area now described on the OS map as Huntington Park would have been enclosed for that purpose and there, another of Herefordshire's great families, the Romillys, set up home in the nineteenth century. Sir Samuel Romilly became Solicitor General in 1806 and during his time at Westminster was a leading Whig law reformer. He was one of a small parliamentary group who campaigned against the death penalty for minor offences, supported catholic emancipation and the abolition of slavery. In 1818, at the peak of his career, tragedy intervened when his wife Anne suddenly became ill. He accompanied here to the Isle of Wight where they stayed with their friend, the architect John Nash. However, Anne didn't recover and died there in October of that year. Just four days later, grief stricken, Samuel committed suicide by cutting his throat with a razor. Their six sons all became successful men, serving as MPs or called to the bar. A great grandson, Bertram Romilly, married the eldest sister of Clementine Churchill and accounts for the many visits the Churchills made to Huntington Park. Bertram's son Esmond eloped and married one of the Mitford girls, Jessica. When Diana Mitford married Oswald Mosley, thus becoming Esmond's brother-in-law, the Romillys had covered the full political spectrum. Eventually, though, the house in the park went the same way as Huntington castle, it was just too far away from London. The family dispersed to other more accessible manors and the house was demolished in 1966.

The following morning, I left Kington early, treating myself to a short bus ride back to the village of Lyonshall from where I could restart my journey. The original village of Lyonshall grew up around the

Remains of the Earl of Oxford's Eywood Manor

castle built around 1090, but after the devastation of the black death in the fourteenth century it moved to a new site straddling an ancient road three-quarters of a mile to the south east. Now the B4362, this quiet cross county back road was one of the great highways used by the Romans to link their camp at Croft Ambrey with their outpost at Clyro near Hay-on Wye. Lyonshall castle, built by Marcher Lord Roger de Lacy, around 1090, was home to the Devereux family for centuries. They arrived in England with William the Conqueror and were given land in Herefordshire for their assistance at the Battle of Hastings in 1066. Substantial fragments of stone walls of the original building remain though overgrown, and part of the moat is still wet. Frustratingly, the site is privately owned and although a footpath skirts close to the southern section, there is no access to the castle for the public. In the chancel of the church is a particularly sad tribute to the two young sons of Aston Edward McMurdo, who were both killed in the early years of the First World War. To the west of the village, I came across an impressive section of Offa's Dyke which rises to twenty one feet in places. It disappears altogether a mile or so further on at Holmes Marsh and can't be seen again until the lower southern slopes of Ladylift Clump beyond Weobley, some seven miles distant.

There is a story told by Vera Harrison in a publication for the Kington History Society about a young girl from Lyonshall by the name of Ann Pugh. She had been deported to Australia in 1799 after being convicted of stealing £2.12.6d from her employer. The journey took two hundred and six days. When her ship carrying female convicts arrived, it was boarded by men who chose servants and wives from the wretched cargo. Ann was chosen by John Nichols, a convict who had served his time and was on the way to becoming a successful farmer. The partnership apparently survived whatever tribulations arise from such circumstances. When Ann died in 1849, she had lived in New South Wales for forty eight years of her life and her greatest legacy was her family. She left behind her eleven children and sixty-six grandchildren. Today there are an estimated quarter of a million Australian descendants from Anne Pugh and John Nichols, roughly two percent of Australia's population.

After a rare period of road walking, two miles or so, I was on the outskirts of Almeley (pronounced 'Amlee'), a small village with great historical significance to England and to the United States of America. It is a pretty place and many of the houses in the village are seventeenth and eighteenth century timber framed. One such house, Almeley Manor, is medieval in origin. Curiously, Almley has not one, but two ancient castle mounds. It also has one of the earliest Quaker meeting houses in the country which still survives just outside the village. In 1672, a local landowner and farmer, Roger Prichard, donated a converted cottage for the Friends of Almeley to hold their prayer meetings and it has been continuously used ever since. On display at the meeting house is a document, signed in 1948 by Governor Duff of Pennsylvania USA, recording that two signatories to William Penn's charter which established the state in 1682 came from Almeley, one of them being Roger Prichard's son. A second meeting house was opened at Woonton two miles away in 1881 and used for ninety years. That building is now a private house but while still active, two branches in the same parish must have rated as a unique achievement by the Quaker movement. Curiously, the name 'Pennsylvania' appears as a field name along the road I had just walked from Lyonshall.

Long before the Reformation of the Roman church, in the time of Richard II, a group of courtiers began to question conventional religious beliefs and to follow the protestations of John Wyclif, a scholar and teacher of divinity at Oxford University. These dissenters became known as Lollards, a Dutch word meaning 'mumbler', which described the way Lollards read from the scriptures. Wyclif favoured abolition of papal taxation, lay control of the Catholic Church in England, and a sequestration of its assets by the crown. Later, he deviated further from catholic teaching by denying transubstantiation - the real presence in the Holy Eucharist, and the validity of Papal power and of the church hierarchy. One of the stalwarts of this movement, Sir John Oldcastle, was born at Almeley in 1360, most likely in one of the two castles. In the wars against Owen Glyndwr, Oldcastle fought alongside the young Prince Hal, and it is said that Shakespeare took the jovial Oldcastle as the model for Falstaff in his Henry V. Although Wyclif never actually preached his beliefs, there were those at Oxford who had agreed with his theories and became the early movers in the heresy. Nicolas Hereford, the builder of Old Sufton House at Mordiford, was one such associate and was recognized as the first leading promoter of Wyclif's writings. Lollardism thrived here in rural north west Herefordshire, and another of its early followers was Sir John Clanvowe of Hergest Court, friend and contemporary of Chaucer. John Wyclif died in 1384 and without the guidance and leadership of the founder Lollardism was a fragmented body with no form or constitution. Nor did it have any support among the ruling classes, and from then on degenerated into a grass-roots movement relying on personal and small group contact, including the likes of Sir John Oldcastle. He continued to defy the established Church and ignored pleas from his good friend Hal, now the monarch. Oldcastle was eventually imprisoned in the Tower in 1413 for supporting and sheltering Lollard priests but escaped the following year. His fanaticism finally drove him to plot against the King but without sufficient support the revolt failed. Having gone on the run, hiding for a time in the isolated Olchon Valley below the northern flanks of the Black Mountains, he was eventually captured at Montgomery in Mid Wales in 1417 and executed. In the end, Lollardism was more an irritant than a threat, a distraction for a bored few of the middle classes, maybe. Even so, it was difficult to eradicate and survived well into the sixteenth century before being absorbed into the emerging Protestantism of Henry VIII's reign.

Little is known about the earliest Almeley castle which rises by the confluence of two streams in what is known locally as the Dingle, except it is more than likely to have been Saxon in origin and might have been built as an outpost when they pushed further west in the eighth and ninth centuries. I followed a path below the castle hill which then rose steeply out of the Dingle. At this point, I was surprised to see a few pieces of green carpet had been laid on the path to aid traction on the wet slope. I have not seen such thoughtfulness anywhere else. Less than half a mile away, across the village, I could see the earthy remains of the second castle built by the persistent castle builder, Roger de Lacy, in the early thirteenth century. Its south facing position represented a move in the defensive arrangements from the earlier one on the western side of the village, though why this took place is a mystery. The high point of the de Lacy castle's short existence was the visit of Henry III on his way to Hereford after checking further advances by the Welsh in the Marches. Almeley never figured in any attacks by Glyndwr, or anyone else, so it is likely that the castle had been abandoned by 1400. Adjacent to the site is St Mary's church, started shortly after the castle it was finished in the early part of the twelfth century. The original building didn't last long because a hundred years later the chancel and nave were rebuilt, probably with stones from the by then defunct castle. The roof of the nave was replaced in the sixteenth century and an end section of it was unusually panelled and painted with Tudor roses.

I stayed with Tessa and Jeremy Plummer, both originally from Hampshire, in their delightful black and white home, Oak Hall, in the nearby village of Woonton. Jeremy is a freelance guide for the

Tourist Information and was filmed 'guiding' Russell Grant in his *Postcard from Hereford* programme in 1993. Their grade II listed cottage with its heavy timbering and old oak panelling dates back to the late fifteenth century and started life as an open medieval hall.

'We used to holiday occasionally in Herefordshire and knew Oak Hall as a B&B place. It was called Rose Cottage then,' Jeremy told me over tea and biscuits in their tiny book lined lounge.

'We first stayed here in 1991. Years later, it was a colleague in the Hereford office who told me the cottage had come on the market, and we jumped at the chance of buying it.'

Since they moved in Jeremy and Tessa have landscaped their two acre garden impressively, the neatly cut lawns bordered by flowers of every description. There is a small orchard and a rose garden with a small pool, and even a secluded garden surrounded by high hedges offering only glimpses of the outside world. It is quite the most perfect example of Englishness, the kind of country cottage home city dwellers fantasize about owning. I am thrilled to have experienced the reality, if only for one day.

Another intriguing dwelling in the parish of Almeley is Newport House, a large imposing red brick mansion built to replace an earlier manor house which some historians say could have been Sir John Oldcastle's birthplace, if not in de Lacy's castle. In Vera Harrison's compilation for the Kington History Society, she suggests, plausibly, that 'New Port' may be so named in contradistinction to 'Old Castle'. The word 'Port' in such rural surroundings is a surprise and might therefore suggest another interpretation for 'Manor' but this does not appear anywhere else in Herefordshire. Newport House was bought by Thomas Foley, the Worcestershire ironmaster, in 1712 and it remained one of that prodigious Foley family's estates until well into the nineteenth century. For a short time, it was home to one Benjamin Hall, the Commissioner of Works under Lord Palmerston, after whom the great bell of Westminster is named. But in 1953, Newport became the centre for the Latvian Society and a venue for their national gatherings. Basil Coleman remembers the earlier years of the celebrations as he explained to me over a pint in The Bells Inn.

'The Latvians would arrive from all over the country knocking on doors

in the village asking for accommodation. We lived in a council house at the time but we would always find room for them. They would be singing and dancing all night. The music was different, as you might expect, but it was lovely to hear. In later years, though, they became Anglicised and the music turned to modern disco rubbish. It was a shame, really. I suppose it was inevitable. Still, we were sorry to see them go in the end.' The centre closed in 1998, but one or two Latvians stayed on and still live in estate cottages. Recently, the Slavic theme continued when Newport was purchased by Richard Goode, a businessman who specializes in importing aerobatic aircraft from Russia.

Almeley has always been a relatively remote area, and its charm lies in the fact that it is not on a route to anywhere. It seems incredible that the village had to wait until 1966 for mains water supply and a further eleven years before it was worth mentioning in the local press that 'more houses now have inside sanitation'. For hundreds of years, most of the parish roads were little more than cart tracks. Even today there remains none much wider than a single track carriageway. One of the delights of this small community is the well manicured common which is home to the village cricket team. The club enjoys one of the few village green grounds in the county, one with an unsurpassed view of the Black Mountains and beyond to the Brecon Beacons. Just west of the village the track bed of the old tramway to Kington, the ivy-clad ruins of the old station, and parts of the platform can still be seen in the corner of a field. When the trains replaced the trams, you could catch the 7.24am train from nearby Titley Junction to London, arriving at Paddington shortly after 11.00am. It left Paddington again for Almeley at 5.15pm and arrived at 9.27pm. The return trip cost 19s 8d, (98p). Food for thought.

Three miles south west of Almeley, the village of Eardisley abounds with black and white timber framed buildings dating from between fourteenth and sixteenth century, most of which are still in use. It is one of the stops on a Herefordshire tourist attraction, The Black and White Trail. Motorists driving along the narrow A4111 on their way through the village can only glimpse the close-packed cottages but will remain oblivious to the gardens, remnants of Saxon land schemes, hidden behind them. To get to Eardisley, I started due west across country, not only to avoid the main road but to visit one of Herefordshire's hidden gems. Holywell Dingle nature reserve occupies a narrow steep sided wooded combe cut by the fast flowing Holywell Brook. The surrounding woodland is dominated by oak and ash with occasional silver birch and limes, and the indications are that the flora is rich and varied. Unfortunately, it was late autumn when I was there and I could only imagine what treasures might be seen in spring.

Nevertheless, it is a magical place at any time of year. At the centre of the village, two inns face each other. The New Strand Inn, built in 1902 to replace an earlier timber framed building which burned down, has recently been renamed. As well as being a pub, it is also a post office, a cafe, and a book shop, fulfilling HRH Prince Charles's much publicized wish that 'the village pub is the hub'. Opposite the New Strand is the black and white Tram Inn with a piece of rail preserved in the bar as another reminder of the area's short lived courtship with early rail transportation. During the Second World War, the radio propagandist Lord Haw Haw announced that the starving English were driven to eating foxes. The enterprising landlord of the Tram decided to include fox pies on his menu. They weren't, of course, made with fox meat, but he must be admired for latching on to a good idea in order to attract more business. Unlike its smaller neighbour, Eardisley has just the one castle, but it was infinitely more significant than either of Almeley's two. Castle and surrounding parkland became the stronghold of the de Basquevilles soon after the Conquest, and this great and ancient family lived here and until 1684.

The Anglicised Baskervilles have a truly royal ancestry. They first arrived in Britain as a family of high rank, related closely to Duke William of Normandy. Robert de Basqueville, who settled at Eardisley, married the daughter of Rees ap Griffith, Prince of South Wales, and kick started a dynasty which, through both male and female lines, retains influence in the border region of Herefordshire to the present day. The last Baskerville seems to have died in poverty in the remains of the castle gatehouse after his grandfather, Sir Humphrey, fell out of favour by backing the wrong horse at the restoration of Charles II in 1660. As a result of his ill advised opposition, he became a target for the mob which attacked the castle and destroyed most of it. Sited next to the castle, is the church of St Mary Magdelene. Its jewel is the extraordinary twelfth century font carved by the Herefordshire School of Sculptors. Though it is of outstanding quality, it has posed problems of interpretation. There have been many attempts at explaining the confusing scenes depicted on the stem and around the bowl, but the consensus now is that the main theme is The Harrowing of Hell, a well-known motif in Romanesque art depicting Christ rescuing a child from the Devil, but the font at Eardisley stands alone as the only example of its kind in England.

Less than a mile to the west, along a quiet lane, stands a fine, newly built, large Georgian style house. Eardisley Park is a superb recreation of an original house destroyed by fire in 1999 and rarely have I seen such a re-build satisfying to the eye. The well preserved outbuildings, consisting of a dovecote, cider house and impressive timber framed barns, parts of which are said to be remnants from the Baskerville's castle, appear to be justification enough for the decision to rebuild the house. The Eardisley Park estate was purchased by William Barnsley after the last of the Baskervilles died in 1684 but when Barnsley died, his family fought legal battles over ownership lasting thirty four years. The lengthy court cases are said to have inspired Charles Dickens to write *Bleak House*.

There is a rare tree on the outskirts of the village known as The Eardisley Oak which is very old indeed, some say eight hundred years old. It stands by the side of a lane half a mile west in the hamlet of Great Oak, which took its name. At the time of Domesday, oak forests still covered much of the rising ground away from the river Wye and this magnificent specimen is the sole surviving giant. There are other older oaks in Herefordshire, protected in ancient parkland where no human is allowed to interfere with their ecological progress, but this magnificent beast has managed to keep going, exposed to all and sundry, for longer than most. One of my lasting memories of Eardisley is of that tree, how, I wonder, has it survived?

Moving on at speed to make up lost time, I set off across fields with open views east towards Kinnersley, where I would find another rare building, this time a castle which has survived a full millennium, evolving from a Norman motte into a twenty-first century home. The first building erected on this site was one of many motte and bailey castles constructed in the area. Kinnersley was converted into a fortified medieval manor house during the early part of the thirteenth century. During Richard III's murderous campaign to usurp the throne in 1483, the Duke of Buckingham arranged for the young Henry Tudor to be kept here in safe keeping whilst the Duke plotted to thwart Richard's plans. Towards the end of the sixteenth century, the medieval house became an Elizabethan mansion for Roger Vaughan who moved in from his family base at Kington, and it remains little changed to this day. The present building is L shaped with a four-storey tower at the apex of two wings. Nikolaus Pevsner believed that the lower storey of both wings and tower are original and the additional height and shape was created from the stonework of the rest of the medieval castle after Vaughan had demolished it. Some of the surviving stone still bears his signature and crest, a youthful head resting on a wriggling serpent. Argument persists over what this unusual theme represents. One suggestion is that the head is that of the newly born Roger Vaughan and the serpent is the umbilical cord which was wrapped around his throat before he succeeded in tearing it away, thus saving his own life. After Roger's death, ownership of Kinnersley passed to Francis Smallman, Sheriff of Herefordshire and MP for Leominster, and later to Sir Thomas Morgan, second in command to Colonel Birch during the civil war battle for Hereford.

The famous privateer, Henry Morgan, later Governor of Jamaica was Sir Thomas's brother. Unlike many of the county's old estates, there was to be no long term family ownership but a sequence of changes right up to the present day, which may account for the many attempts to impose various styles and designs on the interior. One of the castle's more infamous owners was the grandfather of the present Lord Brocket. Although an active member of the Conservative Party, Arthur Ronald Nall-Cain, the 2nd Baron Brocket, was a notorious Nazi sympathizer with extreme right-wing opinions. In 1939 he travelled to Germany to celebrate Adolf Hitler's fiftieth birthday and continued to sympathize with the Nazis well into the Second World War. For a while he was confined to Kinnersley where he could be kept quiet but he urged a negotiated peace settlement with Germany and worked closely in trying to arrange talks with Hitler. He eventually sold Kinnersley Castle in 1944 and returned to the family home at Brocket Hall in Hertfordshire. When he left, he hired an entire train to move his belongings and took practically everything with him.

Now, after years of indifferent occupation, it is a family home once again, run by Caius Hawkins and his wife Kate.

'This is not just our home, it's our life.' She explained to me as we strolled around the well kept lawns. *'We work here, too, hosting residential courses in music, catering, and gardening. We have wedding parties here, and in the summer open-air theatre. All the proceeds go towards the maintenance and improvement of the castle.'*

Passing through this old building's many oddly shaped rooms and corridors, I was struck by the confusing styles of previous incumbents and the changing preferences through different centuries. There is no shortage of panelling in most rooms, but apart from rare oak arches above the tower staircase and two curious oak chimney breast carvings showing both European and South American influences, there is little else to enthuse seekers of Tudor or Jacobean treasures. However, this being a very old building, there have been a few exciting discoveries. Under a bathroom floor is a priest's hole and in the cellar is a blocked passageway which appears to lead below the lawn towards the church next door. In the garden, there is a rare Japanese Gingko tree which, in its native Japan, is believed to give protection from fire and were often planted next to Buddhist temples. Kate's Ginko was planted as a mature tree in the early 1900s and is now said to be the largest known specimen in Britain.

St James's church next to the castle is yet another rarity. The dedication might well have been influenced by Herefordshire School stonemasons returned from Santiago de Compostela in the twelfth century. The scallop shell motif of St James has long been adopted as a reward to pilgrims for their journey to Santiago, and here, on or near St James's day 25 July, the motif banner is carried in procession around the churchyard as a reminder of the great processions still held in the Galician city. The surprise, inside the church though, is the eccentrically decorated walls, chancel ceiling, reredos, and organ case, the result of a late nineteenth century commission by George Frederick Bodley. Bodley was a leading interior designer of the Victorian era. Much of his work was carried out in churches at a time when there was a call to restore, decorate, and care for the country's ecclesiastical heritage a lot of which had fallen into disrepair since the Reformation. Bodley's bold use of colour, particularly red, green, and gold was highly sought after, even in America where he was invited to design cathedrals in Washington and San Francisco. In 1872, Bodley married Minna Reavely whose family then lived at Kinnersley Castle, a fortunate union for the parish as Bodley most likely would not have otherwise chosen St James for one of his major works. His influence here then indicates a personal interest rather than a commercial undertaking. Unfortunately, although Bodley's unique style may have been sought after on both sides of the Atlantic, it was short lived and many of his schemes have disappeared under whitewash and modern restorations. St James's represents a rare glimpse of Victorian imagination and artistic endeavour. Bodley died in 1907 and is buried in the churchyard alongside members of the Reavely family.

Throughout my journey, I have made many references to the work of John Abel, carpenter extraordinaire, builder of many of the county's wonderful black and white timber market halls. He was born in 1577 at Sarnesfield, my next destination just two miles from Kinnersley, and died there ninety-seven years later. During his time he developed a reputation for designing and building in wood and is regarded as being responsible for starting the widespread use of timber as the chief building material in the Marches. Abel was brought up a Catholic, and at a time of religious intolerance, he was liable to persecution. That he survived for nearly a hundred years, prospered openly, and after his death buried honourably in an established churchyard is remarkable. The black and white gabled structures on top of sturdy oak pillars became his signature and his skills were much in demand to build market halls first at Brecon, then at Kington, Ledbury, Weobley, Leominster and Hereford.

The example in Ledbury alone remains in its original position. The only other market hall to survive is at Leominster, but as we have seen that was taken down and moved to make way for road widening. The jewel in the crown, without question, was at Hereford, sadly demolished in 1862, it was a huge twenty-two gabled monster that would, had it survived, now be the city's greatest attraction. Abel's skill as a carpenter was in no way restricted to market halls. In his long life, it is thought that he had a hand in more than a few timber framed cottages around the county, though none have yet been discovered that can be directly attributed to him. However, one contract that was definitely given to him was the reconstruction of the chancel at the ruined Abbey Dore, in particular the great heavy screen which can still be seen in all its majesty. During the Civil War in 1645, Abel was in Hereford which at the time was being besieged by Parliamentary forces. At a crucial moment the defending Royalists under Barnabas Scudamore lost their powder mill and could not produce gunpowder for their ammunition. John Abel saved the day by making hand mills so the fight for the City could continue. The siege failed, Scudamore was knighted, and Abel was made King's Carpenter. Later that year, Abel was again asked to assist in the Royalist cause by building a siege engine for an attack on the castle at Canon Frome, eight miles north east of Hereford which was still in Cromwell's hands. His design resembled a timber tank, consisting of dual lofts above a retractable drawbridge, and was apparently a formidable structure. However, in a curious parallel to the Greek's Trojan horse, the tank was inexplicably left unattended on the night before the attack, was captured by the Parliamentarians and never used. John Abel's last work was his own table tomb, which stands beside the porch of Sarnesfield Church. The epitaph is also his own.

'This craggy stone covering is for an architect's bed,
That lofty buildings rais'd high yet now lies low his head.
His line and rule, so death concludes, are locked up in store.
Build they who list or they who wist, for he can build no more.
His house of clay will hold no longer,
May heaven's joy build him stronger.'

And so to Weobley, the most photographed of Herefordshire's black and white villages, visited by many thousands each year.

Without a camera, Timmins did not spare the pencil but produced his finest drawings in and around the village and the surrounding area. I had booked two nights stay at the delightful Salutation Inn and despite the ordeal of having to fight my way through several acres of tightly packed rape which by now had gone to seed, high expectations carried me onwards in fine spirit.

> *'Westward Ho! A sunny morn invites us to quit the crowded pavements and traffic-laden streets of old Hereford, for the shady hedgerows of the country lanes; or anon to strike across the meadows, e're long we find our road a steep one, but the stiff pull is rewarded by a varied prospect; ranging from the towers of now distant Hereford, overtopped by the blue line of the Malvern Hills, to the picturesque heights of Ludlow, and the more remote mountains of Wales.'*

Weobley is twelve miles north-west of Hereford and is one of England's finest medieval villages. It lies in an area of great natural beauty brimming with fine historic houses, ancient farms and cruck-timbered cottages, and is arguably the best preserved of Herefordshire's famous black and white villages. Henry Timmins was so attracted by what he saw around him that he sketched virtually every building. Weobley was founded by Wibba, the son of a sixth century Mercian king, as a defensive outpost against the Welsh and became known as 'Wibba's ley'. A moated castle once stood here built by the ubiquitous Roger de Lacy in the eleventh century and the ramparts and ditches that remain suggest it must have been quite a substantial building. Like Leominster, Weobley shared in the prosperity of the area and in particular from the proceeds of the wool trade. It was a market town trading well into the seventeenth century and, which until the Reform Bill of 1832, had two MPs but then lost both of them at a stroke as well as its status as a borough. One of Weobley's more famous residents was Colonel John Birch, who fought on both sides during the Civil War. Birch was a Lancastrian by birth with no formal education he moved to Bristol where he set up as a merchant. His introduction to a military career began in heroic fashion. The story goes that Birch fell in with a band of Roundheads who attempted to rob him of his goods, but he fought so valiantly that when Cromwell heard of the affair he offered him a commission. In recognition of later achievements, Cromwell made him governor of Bristol but then fell out with him. Birch eventually sided with the Royalists and after playing his part in restoring the monarchy he retired to Weobley in 1661, built himself a fine house at Garnstone on the outskirts of the town, and became one of the town's MPs.

Richard Tomkins was another well known Weobley character who it is claimed fathered thirty-three children in the same room of the same house! The house was part of a block of black and white timber buildings in the centre of the village and was the end house pictured

in Timmins's sketch. Sadly, the block has long gone - burnt down on 4 November 1943. The fire apparently started in a bakery, reviving memories of the Great Fire of London in 1666. Missing from the scene is one of John Abel's market houses which was demolished in 1845. A rose garden now covers the spot.

Weobley's glory is its abundance of black and white buildings reflecting an ageless character. The old manor house, built in 1320, despite its implied seniority, seems to blend in with other timber framed houses around it. It is now an Hotel, as is the Red Lion Inn close by built about the same time. A house called Throne Farm became an inn midway through the seventeenth century some time after Charles I stayed there in 1645, when fleeing from the battle of Naseby. Sadly, it is no longer an inn.

> *'Across the road, the visitor's attention will be drawn to the charming little half-timbered front of the old school house with projecting porch and carved spandrels; now uninhabited, and the doorway hedged across by trailing sprays of neglected rose bushes, recalling in its humble way, the palace of the Sleeping Beauty. It is devoutly to be hoped that this characteristic remnant of old Weobley may be preserved from untimely destruction.'*

Indeed it was, dear Henry, and is yet as pretty as you would have wished it. Black and white was in fact a Victorian introduction when the timbers were coated with tar for protection and the infill panels whitewashed. In contrast to those dwellings in the centre, on the edge of the village there is one which is brown and pink. Before the nineteenth century, houses were limewashed all over and frequently coloured with ochre, from yellow to red. The pink house therefore gives an insight into how houses looked in earlier times. At the end of the splendid Broad Street, the spine of the village, dominant in every painted or photographed view of Weobley, is the tall spire of the church of St Peter & St Paul. The first stone church was built here by Hugh de Lacy in the early part of the eleventh century. His church replaced an earlier Saxon timber one but the present building dates mainly from the early part of the fourteenth century. The tower is at an odd angle in relation to the main church and suggests it was built on the foundations of a previous detached tower.

In 1640, the spire came down in a storm and the replacement, erected in 1675, financed by Colonel Birch is the second highest in Herefordshire (the tallest being that of All Saints in Hereford.). Among the church's many memorials is a full length marble statue of Birch himself beneath a handsome Corinthian canopy with an inscription describing this remarkable soldier's virtues and achievements.

To the south of the town, Garnstone Wood forms the edge of an ancient deer park, which was presumably part of the old castle. In 1806, Colonel Birch's house at Garnstone was replaced with a castellated Gothic mansion designed by the Regency architect John Nash for Dr Samuel Peploe, whose descendants still live at Garnstone, although not in the mansion. That was pulled down in 1958. In the early part of the twentieth century, Garnstone's lord of the manor was William Verdin, known to the locals as Ol' Billy. He employed half the village as gamekeepers, gardeners, woodmen and domestics, and once a year he would open his grounds to the public. Each year, too, as was his liking, pheasants were raised in substantial numbers for he and his guests to shoot. Architecturally, Garnstone wasn't one of Nash's greatest successes and few regretted its eventual demolition. Now only a few overgrown remnants remain along with the walls of the ha-ha beneath the overhanging branches of a magnificent cedar.

A mile west of Weobley, is a large timber framed house of stunning quality. Timmins's Romantic sketch would do justice to it, even to-day.

> *'The present mansion is a beautiful example of the timber dwelling of the English yeoman of the sixteenth century, with its finely curved beams, ornamental plasterwork and diamond paned windows. A charming feature is the boldly projecting entrance porch which has a massive nail studded door, and over it the quaint device and motto of the founder bearing the date 1589.*

The Ley was built for the Brydges family, sometime Dukes of Chandos and descendants of the Mortimers. In 1783, Lord Eldon, one time celebrated Lord Chancellor but at that time plain John Scott, came to visit the town as a Parliamentary candidate for the borough, and is believed to have stayed here, when it was owned by a Mr Bridges, a clergyman. There is a story worth retelling: Mr Bridges had a daughter who asked the honoured guest should he become Chancellor and she should marry a parson, the Chancellor would give him a living. Lord Eldon later described what happened:

'Years rolled on and I came into office. One morning I was told

> a young lady wished to speak to me, and I replied that young ladies must be attended to, so they must show her up.'
>
> Up came a pretty young lady who curtsied and said she thought I did not recollect her. I answered I certainly did not, but perhaps she could recall herself to my memory. So she asked if I remembered the clergyman at Weobley and his little girl to whom I made a promise. 'Oh, yes I do', I said, 'and I suppose you are the little girl?' She curtsied again and said yes.
>
> 'And I suppose you are married to a clergyman?'
>
> 'No', she said blushing, 'but I am going to be married to one, if you my Lord, will give him a living.'
>
> And then I looked at my list and found I actually had a living vacant which I could give him. I told her she should return home and get married as fast as she liked, for her husband would be presented with a living, and I would send the papers as soon as they could be made out.
>
> 'Oh, no!', she exclaimed, 'pray, my lord, let me take them back myself.' I was a good deal amused, so I had the papers made out, signed them, and she took them back the next day. Is it not remarkable that I should have given that promise in early life, and that it should actually have been fulfilled?

If only that were true today.

After a lengthy period of closure, The Red lion was reopened in 2005 so today, Weobley has three inns again, all of them have been around for more than 500 years. The Unicorn is the oldest, but my choice for this visit was the seventeenth century Salutation Inn, run for the last five years by Mike and Julie Tai. My room looked out across the village centre with the church dominating the scene. Mike was a consultant in a London Hospital and when he and Julie came to Weobley during a holiday break, they stopped at the inn for lunch, liked what they saw, and decided immediately to buy it. Anthony Hoyle liked what he saw in Weobley, too. He is a Dentist and practices near Grimsby and he, too, was a guest at the Salutation. He told me he had decided to do some walking in the Brecon Beacons and had

Broad Street, Weobley

stopped off in Weobley on the way. He had never been to Herefordshire before and was so taken aback by the beauty of the landscape generally and the charm of Weobley in particular, he decided to stay on for two days longer than planned. I got the feeling he would not be in a hurry to return to Grimsby.

> *'A delightful stroll of about two miles across open meadows, where cattle graze half hidden in the deep pasture, leads us by pleasant paths to the village of Dilwyn, prettily situated in a hollow near the ancient Watling Street. The massive tower and wooden spire of the venerable church rise gracefully above the village, standing amidst the well-tendered churchyard where, surely, the forefathers of the hamlet must rest in peaceful seclusion.'*

At first glance, the village of Dilwyn appears more black and white than Weobley. However, while Weobley is historically and architecturally pleasing, Dilwyn is just plain georgeous. Alongside the stately manor they call the Great House, pretty timber framed cottages line up along the lane to the village green in chocolate box fashion, and

The Crown Inn, white only the last time I saw it, stands proudly at its centre defying recent trends to be de-licensed and turned into a private dwelling. There are equally delightful red brick cottages here too blending handsomely, while the great sandstone church of St Mary the Virgin looks down from its grassy pedestal like a shepherd tending his flock. Its massive squat tower with tiny slit windows resembling a castle keep mirrors that of many border villages subject to constant Welsh attacks in ancient times.

The church was built by the monks of Wormsley priory, the site of which lies off a back road to Hereford, and a canopied tomb in the chancel is thought to be that of a member of the great Talbot family who founded the priory. An ancient custom still practised in many villages of Herefordshire is wassailing, and Dilwyn is one of them. The word comes from an Anglo-Saxon 'waes hae'l, meaning good health, and the tradition is performed to ensure a good cider apple harvest. Originally, the wassail was a drink made of mulled ale, curdled cream, roasted apples and spices, and traditionally, wassailing is celebrated on New Year's Eve and Twelfth Night. The apple is king in Herefordshire and songs in praise of 'Auld Cider' were common. There were other curious customs, too, like planting a plum cake onto the horn of a bull which was then encouraged to toss its head. If the cake went forward, the harvest would be good. If it went backwards, a poor harvest was forecast. Although it has close connections with Christmas, wassailing is more a celebration for hopes of a fine crop come spring.

'Here's to the champion of the white horn
Here's God send the master a good crop of corn,
Of wheat, rye and barley, and all sorts of grain
If we live to this time twelvemonth, we'll drink to his health again.'

It seems likely, though, that customary distinctions throughout the county were few as wassailing carols developed into another way of wishing each other a Merry Christmas.

'Here we go a-wassailing, among the leaves so green
Here we go a-wandering, so fair to be seen

Love and joy come to you, and to you wassail too.
And God bless you, and send you a happy new year
And God send you a happy new year.'

Thoughts of seasonal celebration are not far from my mind either as the year has progressed to late autumn days and shorter walking hours. A further two mile walk along narrow lanes towards Pembridge suddenly brings the rambler upon the picturesque timber framed Luntley Court glimpsed behind high hedges. Although the house, built in 1674, has tell-tale geometric signs of a modern makeover, it still preserves some of its ancient features and remains a good example of a seventeenth century mansion. In an adjoining meadow is a four gabled pigeon house said to be built at the same time as the Court.

'We trudge merrily on, and turning a sharp corner, come suddenly upon the little town of Pembridge, sedately ensconced in a quiet nook near a pretty stream called Arrow. Right before us stands an ancient hostelry (The New Inn), with over hanging gables, whose equally venerable vis-à-vis is a timber built market hall.'

Pembridge, nestling in the rolling North Herefordshire countryside, is one of Britain's finest mediaeval boroughs. Every street contains mediaeval buildings that in any other location would be individual attractions in themselves. Few new houses have been built, existing buildings have remained unaltered and, over ninety listed buildings still survive, making this fine place the jewel in the crown of the Black and White Trail. This was a prosperous borough until the sixteenth century having been granted a charter in 1240. Its prosperity was based on its role as a market centre, being the furthest point west English traders could go because of the unsettled conditions that prevailed in the Welsh borders. Trading took place in the old market hall which recently received a lottery grant towards badly needed restoration. The old stone tiled roof of the hall built in 1520 is supported by eight oak pillars, and is reputed to be the oldest market hall in the country. Alongside, and sharing a cobbled frontage, the New Inn is one of the oldest 'New Inns' in the country. It was apparently re-built in 1311 after the original building burnt down.

Together they form a corner of this old village that is unchanged from medieval times. What a pity the scene is nowadays spoilt by motor cars cluttering up the narrow approaches to the square, and often parking higgledy-piggledy in order to secure the best spot in front of the inn, whilst ignoring the free car parking area just yards down the main street. A narrow flight of stone steps off the square gives access to the church, a fine building and an indication of the prosperity that was prevalent here. There are few signs now of its Norman origins but the fabric of the building has changed little since the fifteenth century. The star though without doubt is the detached bell tower, the finest of all Herefordshire's detached bell towers, whose enormous timbers are known to be twelfth century. Its structure consists of four sections starting with a low stone ground storey of irregular octagonal shape, followed by a high truncated pyramid roof, then a weather boarded bell turret with another truncated pyramid roof and the whole topped with a smaller boarded stage with short spire and weather vane. Inside the belfry, behind massively thick walls, is an immense oak bell frame surrounded by a stone walkway. This impressive building was started

BELFRY AT PEMBRIDGE.

in the thirteenth century and has been added to and restored in every century since.

Unlike other Bell towers built as refuges against attack, this one appears to have been just a tower for bells. It has even been suggested that the bells were originally suspended by the huge timber frame alone and the walls and roofs were added after it was decided not to build a tower onto the church. Across the busy A44 and a short distance along the road down to the river is an ancient three arched bridge through which the Arrow glides silently past on its way to meet the Lugg at Leominster. Pembridge is a joy and the tourists flock every year to enjoy it. How much better and safer it would be strolling among theses ancient dwellings without having to keep one eye out for the traffic which thunders along the main highway towards mid Wales. Is it too much to hope for pedestrianization and a by-pass in the future?

Back along the lane to Dilwyn is Dunkerton's Cider Company, started in 1979 by Ivor and Sue Dunkerton after they moved here from London. Ivor had been a senior TV producer with the BBC and, with a seventeenth century house on the river at Richmond, enjoyed a comfortable living. After their wedding, Ivor and Sue had spent their honeymoon at Pembridge, both visiting the county for the first time. *'I have always loved the countryside'*, Ivor told me over coffer in his ogee windowed office, *'Even as a youngster growing up in London, I used to head out of town on my bicycle as often as I could. But when we came to Herefordshire it was love at first sight and we decided that this is where we wanted to be.'* They bought an eighteen acre smallholding at Pembridge and tried their hand first at raising goats and a few cattle but soon realized it wasn't enough.

'We had no idea at first how we were going to survive. But then I read John Seymour's 'New Complete Self-Sufficiency', a book for dreamers and realists alike, and we agreed to have a go at creating a 'Good Life'.'

At that time, Bulmers was the dominant cider producer in the county, so after approaching the Apple Research Centre in Long Ashton near Bristol the Dunkertons saw an opportunity to make cider organically. Why organic?

'Because we care about the countryside and the wildlife,' Ivor explained passionately. 'Organic means no pesticides, no fungicides, and no herbicides under the trees.'
They have now been producing organic bottled cider as well as perry, produced from pears, for over twenty years, and are supplying outlets throughout the county and to London. Before I left, Ivor showed me around the cider house and bottling plant, and after coffee in their new visitors' restaurant, it was time to move on.

> *'Free of the houses, we take to the fields, and so go merrily over stiles, passing through broad meadows, and ere long come to Eardisland, a bright pleasant village through which the Arrow meanders in a clear stream, running here over rippling shallows, anon into shady pools.'*

Eardisland is another essential part of the Black and White Trail followed by many tourists who find themselves drawn to the rural charms of Herefordshire. The picturesque aspect of this village can be seen almost in its entirety from the hump-back road bridge over the river Arrow which flows through the centre. Even at this, by now, late autumn time, there has been little rain since spring, and little to reveal that the river here is subject to flooding, creating serious problems for those living in the idyllic cottages along the river bank and in the immediate vicinity. Close by Eardisland is Burton Court erected before the reign of Edward III. It is a typical squire's house built on the site of an ancient fort where Henry V stationed his troops to keep an eye on the movements of Owain Glyndwr. The present house is late eighteenth century, but in the seventeenth century, by all accounts, the house was a multi-gabled affair and the fourteenth century great hall is the only surviving part of the original structure. The court's hayday was the early part of the twentieth century when there were twenty three servants looking after the needs of the Clowes family. During this time, the frontage of the house was redesigned by Clough Williams-Ellis who later created the enchanting village of Portmeirion in north Wales, the setting for the 1960s cult TV drama series *The Prisoner*. The Great War of 1914-1918 put an end to the good times at Burton when the Clowes' only son was killed during the defence of

Amiens. By 1950, the estate had been split up and the house had become neglected and in danger of going the way of many great houses at that time. It was eventually bought by Lieutenant Commander Robert Macaulay Simpson who halted the decline and set apart a major portion of the remaining land for growing fruit and now uses the house to host weddings and the occasional film set.

> *'Pushing on the gloaming, we catch a distant glimpse of Weobley's tall steeple beyond the nearer spire of Dilwyn. A sharp turn downhill takes us through the village, and so by more field paths, we re-enter Weobley as the labourer is plodding homewards, pipe in mouth, from his day's work upon the plough lands, or amidst the far stretching avenues of the hop yards.'*

After returning to Weobley and another splendid chatty night with locals at the Salutation, I set off across Roger de Lacy's deer park and laboured up steep wooded footpaths to join the back road to Hereford, known as Raven's Causeway. It descends spectacularly between tree clad hills on either side with the impressive iron-age fort of Credenhill as a backdrop. In spite of the obvious inconvenience of traffic, this is a rare beautiful stretch of road walking. Apart from a few terraces and banks hidden in the undergrowth, nothing remains of the thirteenth century monastic buildings at Wormsley founded by the Talbots for Canons Regular of St Augustine. Close to the site, though, is Wormsley Grange, an early Georgian house of considerable importance as the birthplace of Richard Payne Knight and his brother Thomas. While Richard was building his castle at Downton and immersing himself in his Picturesque Movement, Thomas was following his own interests and experimenting with new strains of apples. One of his noted successes became known as 'The Downton Pippin'. Since 1932 Wormsley has been the home of the Herefordshire Golf Club and there can be few courses boasting eighteen holes set in countryside of such beauty. A correspondent once began his article in a golf publication: *'If you find Glen Eagles too expensive to visit, do the next best thing and treat yourself to a day at the Herefordshire course'*

Nestling beneath the northern flanks of Credenhill is the medieval moated manor house of Brinsop Court, a part of which dates to the early thirteenth century. The picturesque house of red sandstone and timber additions was remodeled in 1913 but still preserves some of the ancient features, in particular, the windows of the original Great Hall. For centuries, the house was owned by the Dansey family, and for a short time by David Ricardo, a nineteenth century political economist of some renown. But in 1825 Thomas Hutchinson, brother-in-law of poet William Wordsworth, moved in as tenant. Both William and his sister Dorothy were attracted to the romance of Brinsop and the woodland and pastoral surroundings. They visited the house regularly between 1827 and 1845, often with their daughter Dora. On one occasion, Wordsworth wrote a poem for a distraught George Hutchinson, Thomas's young son after his dog Prince had been put down by hanging by a servant called Jerry Preece.

' Stop passenger, and drop a tear.
A most ill-fated Prince lies here.
His reign in youth was wild and pleasant.
He hunted rabbit, hare and pheasant.
Grown old, he bid adieu to sport,
And mildly ruled at Brinsop Court.
But shame on these reforming times
Of revolutionary crimes;
This harmless, old and good Prince loyal,
Was vilely used by hands disloyal;
His noble neck was hempen collared
And stretched upon a willow pollard:
O wicked traitor Jerry Preece!
Repent, if would die in peace.'

Today, Brinsop is a holiday complex offering exceptional surroundings in which to relax or explore the Herefordshire countryside.

Lower down the valley are the scant remains of a fortified medieval settlement. A few modern cottages keep company with mounds, ditches and the lovely old church of St George, which author Simon Jenkins has listed in his acclaimed *England's Thousand Best Churches*. This little church stands beneath the wooded slopes of Credenhill, and the unas-

suming exterior hides a wealth of culture both old and new. Within, on the north wall, is an ancient stone tympanum carved with the figure of St George slaying the Dragon, from the Hereford School of Sculptors. The stained glass south window in the chancel is dedicated to William Wordsworth and the north window to Dorothy, Mary and their daughter Dora, a surprisingly moving tribute, and emphasizes the poet's connections with Herefordshire. Not far across the meadow from St Georges church is St Mary's, parish church for the village of Credenhill. There are no tracks to connect the two and it required an uncomfortable walk along the busy A480 before turning into a quiet approach lane. St Mary's is a mixture of stonework and refurbishments through centuries from the twelfth to the nineteenth , but it was not the church that I was there to see. In a quiet corner of the churchyard are several rows of rotting wooden crosses marking the graves of fifty Polish men who lived at Credenhill Court next to the church when it was a rehabilitation centre for veterans of the Second World War. The sad state of these graves is a reminder of the debt we all owe for the price these men paid in assisting England in the conflict. I am told that the Polish Consulate based in the West Midlands is hoping to raise funds for a memorial plaque which will say: *'Their bodies rest here, their souls reside with God, but their hearts are in Poland'.*
Let them be blessed for the sacrifices they made.

At the rear of the church a shaded track zigzags steeply to the summit of a slumbering giant. Credenhill is crowned by the remains of an ancient camp larger than Dorset's famous Maiden Castle, and is one of the most important and impressive iron age sites of its kind. As recently as 1960, ancient oaks, beech, and ash trees sheltered under the terraces of the hilltop fort. It was even possible then to look out from the 221m (720ft) summit over Hereford as far as the Cotswolds to the east and along the Wye valley towards Hay and the Black Mountains of south Wales in the west. But then a clearance of many of the old trees and an introduction of conifers to the site was allowed, and now the ancient earthwork enclosure that encircles the hill top is mantled by a dense blanket of firs hiding its massive ramparts. More than two thousand years ago 'Creda's hill' was a tribal capital, a township of some four thousand people dwelling in thatched huts and protected by a wooden stockades. In the second century A.D., when the fort was in decline, Credenhill's importance as a strategic central position was not lost on the Romans who chose the area below the fort to build their area capitol at Kenchester. That, too, was abandoned in the eighth century in favour of a new site on the river at Hereford. In 2003, the fort and the surrounding woods were purchased by The Woodland Trust who pledged to cut down the offending conifers and restore the spaces on the summit for future generations on which to walk and marvel once again at the spectacular views.

> *Passing through the pretty village with snug well-to-do cottages bowery with honeysuckle and roses, a crossroads leads on the one hand to Kenchester where the Roman settlement once stood.'*

The site of the town at Kenchester which the Romans called Magnis lies at the end of a road of modest red brick houses, in a large empty field. Beneath twenty-two acres of cattle trod turf are the hidden footings of a once bustling administration centre, the most important Roman station in the county. Arches, walls and pillars were still visible as late as the nineteenth century, but all have now been removed. Some say though, that the ghosts of Roman soldiers can still be seen on moonlight nights marching across the field along the line of the old main street. The last surviving evidence that there was a walled city here is a small part of the ramparts in the garden of a cottage, appropriately called 'The Walls'.

The village of Credenhill that Timmins found very pretty, overlooked by the imposing bulk of the hill of the same name, is now very different. It has now, for some time, been home to an Army base. The huge red brick camp called Stirling Lines is famous for being the headquarters of 22 Special Air Services, better known as SAS. The founder of this elite force was David Stirling, a Scottish Laird who during the Second World War was first with the Scots Guards, then volunteered for 8 Commando, a special forces command which was disbanded before the young Stirling could experience any serious covert action. However, he had by then seen the possibilities for special operations behind enemy lines and reckoned that a group of highly-trained, highly motivated soldiers could wreak havoc on enemy supply lines, bases, and morale. When he eventually joined up with Jock Lewes, an officer with the Welsh Guards who had similar convictions, their association would prove to be the nucleus of the Special Air Service Regiment. In true SAS fashion, Stirling avoided the strict protocol of chain of command and took his ideas directly to the Commander-in-Chief, General Auchinlek.

Unbeknown to Stirling at the time, the High Command had been planning an offensive against Rommel's German Afrika Corps, and Auchinlek immediately saw an opportunity to use the new unit. Thus, on 17 November 1942, the first ever SAS mission was activated. During that first campaign, their most successful operator was Paddy Mayne, an Irish rugby player whose fierce determination and courage accounted for dozens of Rommel's planes being blown up on the tarmac with 1lb 'Lewes' bombs which had to be planted manually. He is said at one point, having run out of bombs, to have ripped control panels out with his bare hands. Mayne is a legend in the Regiment today and typifies the rugged individualism sought when recruiting SAS personnel. Before I set out on my journey, I had not planned or even contemplated approaching anyone connected to the Special Forces Service, but Stirling Lines is very much part of Herefordshire life, albeit a discrete one, and to ignore it was to refuse that the base exists. Anticipating that any request for an informal chat with the camp Adjutant would be instantly rejected, I had asked where I might find a retired soldier from the unit who might be willing to talk about life in the regiment. I was given a name.

Mike Colton runs the Allied Special Forces Association from a small office in Hereford and I was a little nervous as I knocked on his door. The interview had been arranged a few days beforehand but it is not every day you come face to face with a someone who's seen action with the army's most renowned and respected fighting force.

'I was based at Credenhill from 1973 to 1978,' he told me by way of introduction, *'And I spent time in Northern Ireland and did two tours in Oman.'* Before serving in the elite army group, Mike joined the parachute regiment after watching the Royal Tournament at Olympia in the late 1960s.

'I was so impressed with their display,' he explained, *'that I decided to join them as soon as I could. For much of my early days in the Army, I seemed to be stuck up a mountain, or clinging to a rock face somewhere.'* During a training exercise in Canada, Mike was instructed by a group of serving special forces soldiers and once again the experience left a mark. So it was that in 1973 he joined the Army's toughest unit.

'They put me in Mountain Troop and once again I was clinging to rock faces, only this time I was more often than not, being shot at!'

He went on to explain that in spite of the occasional excitement of the chase, life in the SAS isn't the stuff that some of the current batch of books would have you believe.

'Once, when I was on a jungle watch in Belize, one of our guys developed an eye infection which needed urgent attention so we called a helicopter in. We cleared a patch for it to land and when it did we were puzzled to see the pilot shut down the engines, something you don't do on a rescue mission in case you need to get away in a hurry. When I asked him what he had in mind if he couldn't start up again, he said "You start walking, and I follow you out." Fortunately, he was able to restart the engines and we were able to get our man to a hospital. Life in the SAS was often like that. Action was rare and then avoided wherever possible, especially in the face of overwhelming odds. Shoot and scoot was the by-word of my day!'

It seemed odd considering the number of Special Forces people who gave their lives in World War Two, not to mention Northern Ireland and the Gulf, there are no official reports of their sacrifices and there was no association supporting them before Mike started one after he retired from action.

'A memorial does exist and most of them appear on it,' he explained, 'but it's on the clock tower at SAS HQ at Stirling Lines which is out of bounds to the public. I thought they deserved something better than that, so when I left the service I decided to campaign for a remembrance site where the public could pay their due respects.' I asked him whether he had considered that the cloak of secrecy might be too strong, and did he think he was taking a risk.

'On the contrary, the support from ex Special Forces people from around the world has been overwhelming. You can see from my website just how many other Associations have agreed to become part of the project. The ef-

fort has all been worthwhile because we now have a plot in the National Memorial Arboretum near Lichfield where we've started erecting memorials to our own people.'

The SAS have not been the only military presence in Hereford since the Second World War. Another unit, the 1st Battalion Hereford Regiment, which used to be based on the east side of the city, claimed their own little known but significant scalp of the war. Following Adolf Hitler's death, Grand Admiral Karl Doenitz became Fuehrer of the Third Reich. His appointment lasted just seven days between the first and the seventh of May 1945 when Germany surrendered unconditionally. Doenitz, however, didn't give himself up but was captured on 23 May by the Herefordshire Regiment during 'Operation Blackout', the last action in the European campaign. They took the pennants from the short lived Fuehrer's car into safe keeping, and after the war ended, the pennants were returned to and remain at the Regiment's Harold Street base.

Leaving Credenhill behind, I crossed the busy Brecon Road and continued my walk into Hereford, soon to meet the Wye once again as it snaked towards the city. Alongside a minor road leading to the river, half timbered Sugwas Court slumbered behind a heavy screen of trees. It was formerly a manor house of the Bishops of Hereford and a favourite retreat for Thomas Cantilupe in the thirteenth century but had become ruinous through neglect and was demolished in 1754, along with a chapel dedicated to St Thomas. A new mansion was built on the site in 1792 but that too appeared to be in decline now, and gave off a spooky aura in the late afternoon gloom as I passed by.

Crossing high ground above Breinton, the peaks of the far away mountains of mid Wales were in full view, snow covered from the winter's first fall and shimmering in the clear cold air. Behind me now was the massive bulk of Credenhill fort and, two or three miles further west, the tree clad eminence of Ladylift and Garnons Hill blocking any last look at Weobley in the plain beyond them. Below, the Wye meandered lazily through a narrow gorge where once a ferry boat connected Breinton with the village of Eaton Bishop on the south bank, then on below Weir Cliff passing the site of a Roman bridge carrying an old road from Abergavenny to their local capital, Kenchester. Breinton is a quiet hamlet of redbrick cottages and large country houses where generations of the Bulmer family chose to set up home, not far from the cider business in Hereford which they had built into the largest in the world. In the churchyard, buried beneath a Celtic cross, is Charles Vincent Gorton, priest and honorary Canon of Manchester who apparently died in mysterious circumstances. Gorton was a close friend of Elgar and assisted him with at least one of his musical scores and had another dedicated to him. There are plans to drive a new by-pass from the Leominster road north of the city, through these fields and across the river to rejoin the A49 south of the city and the industrial area of Rotherwas. If the plan succeeds, the isolation and solitude that living in a village like Breinton brings will be compromised, and as usual in these matters, a community's preferences will be sacrificed in the name of progress.

At the end of a narrow lane the path drops down through woods and hugs the river bank through wide meadows hemmed in on either side by the high grounds of Belmont and Broomy Hill. Even as daylight faded, it was busy with joggers and dog walkers. Several canoes and a couple of double skulls from the Hereford Rowing Club ploughed back and forth through the almost still water. An instructor watched a team of four carefully from what appeared to be a tin bath with an outboard motor. Being one of Britain's great fishing rivers, this part of the Wye is a particularly popular spot. Today all the 'pegs' have been taken, but none of the fishermen appear to be having a good time of it. Andy had already been there for three hours (you are allowed six) without a bite.

'The water's too cold now', he said *'And when the water's cold, the fish stay on the bottom. Mine's not a good peg either. The bank here is too high, and even if I did get a catch, I couldn't net the damn fish!'*

Andy comes here every Sunday, and occasionally Wednesdays, too.

'It all depends on the pitch. Up river there's Barbel, lots of 'em. Here it's mainly Bream, Chubb and Roach, sometimes the odd Grayling.'

I asked him if were there any Salmon.

'Hardly any this far up river. Generally, what Salmon there are these days are caught by the big money boys on their estates long before the fish can

get to Hereford.'

Now with the familiar bulk of Hereford Cathedral's tower in sight, I followed the river path across an old railway bridge, a remnant of the tram road to Abergavenny, and as the last rays of the wintry sun set behind a mackerel sky another memorable part of my journey was at an end.

PART FIVE

The Road to Hay on Wye

ARTHUR'S STONE.

'Once more turning our faces to towards the setting sun, we make our way zigzag fashion, up the broad valley of the Wye to the confines of the county; noting many characteristic features amidst the rural district through which our journey lies.'

The Christmas break over and the dreariness of January and February already driven from memory, I returned to Herefordshire for the final leg of my walk through this wonderful county. I did, this time however, cheat a little as I didn't fancy a depressing eight mile walk through the Hereford suburbs along the A438; so took the bus to my starting point at The Portway Inn, where the Roman road from Kenchester exits the landscaped park at Garnons. For those who regularly drive out west from Hereford, the rather stunted grey Gothic style mansion sitting neatly on the hillside will be familiar. Garnons was re-built in 1815 for Sir John Cotterell, with assistance from James Wyatt, John Nash, and Humphrey Repton. At that time the Roman road was still the main highway and Repton advised that it be closed and a new road built further south in its present position nearer to the village of Byford. In the centre of the lounge bar floor of The Portway is a brass plaque with the legend 'The Portway Inn's Horses Heads'. It commemorates the gruesome discovery by workmen in 1879 of forty horse skulls nailed to the joists under the floor. Investigations led to Sir John of Garnons, who in 1800 ordered the skulls to be fixed under the floor to improve the acoustics for a music room! One wonders what skills he could have acquired at the start of the nineteenth century to have persuaded him to do that!

A stone's throw from the inn, Monnington Court is one of several sites reputed to be the last resting place of Owain Glyndwr. Unfortunately for the supporters of such a claim, the owner of Monnington at the time was a Baron Audley who fought for Henry IV against Glyndwr, so it would seem unlikely that the Welsh chieftain would choose Monnington as a refuge under the circumstances. The Cornewalls of Moccas Court on the opposite bank of the Wye were certainly at Monnington in the eighteenth century and built a bridge connecting their two houses. When this was badly damaged in the winter of 1960 access became impossible so Monnington Court was sold. It is now the home of John Bulmer and his wife, the sculptress Angela Conner, some of whose work can be seen in the garden. Not long ago they started breeding American Morgan horses here and now have the largest Morgan Horse Farm in Europe. Next to the court, St Mary's is a pretty little church though of mainly plain design. There were extensive renovations in 1995, but even so it is surprising that diarist Francis Kilvert found the church 'lacking in Gothic features and wanting in prettiness'. At the end of the drive to the Court, I picked up an old friend, the Wye Valley Walk and followed it along a mile long stretch of Scots pine planted in 1623 by the then resident, James Tomkyns, the MP for Leominster, to commemorate the restoration of the monarchy after the Civil War. The path rose steeply until at Brobury Scar, a lofty sloping sandstone cliff, I glimpsed the river far below, and in another mile I thought I had come close to heaven. The delightful hamlet of Bredwardine lies in an area of steep wooded hills, narrow lanes, broad sunny fields and deep shady hollows. The river Wye at this point is spanned by a narrow redbrick six-arched bridge built in 1759 connecting Bredwardine and her 'twin', Brobury. The church of St Andrew's perched prettily on a high bank on the Bredwardine side now serves both communities. It was here that the Reverend Francis Kilvert, though still a young man, spent his last few years living in the Old Rectory next to the church.

When a clergyman at Clyro near Hay-on-Wye in 1870, Kilvert kept a diary, written for his own amusement, which recorded his work in great detail, the people he served and the landscape, but written in such a charming way that it immediately grabs the attention and interest of the reader. As a snapshot of everyday experiences in a remote border community, his diaries have become a classic work of biography and, because of the elegant way they are written, as a work of literature in their own right. His story though is short and ends tragically. On the 30 November 1877 he was appointed curate here at St Andrews. There he met and married Elizabeth Rowland two years later on 20 August 1879. On Monday 23 September he died at the rectory from peritonitis, just three days after returning from his honeymoon. In the churchyard, a distinctive white cross marks his grave. After his death, his widow inexplicably destroyed

Francis Kilvert's distinctive white cross grave stone in the churchyard of St Andrews, Bredwardine

much of his work, which would have run to over thirty notebooks. Happily though, what was re-discovered was published in a three-volume selection by William Plomer in 1938. Elizabeth survived Francis for thirty years and on her death could not be buried next to her husband, as all the plots had been filled, so she lies in an isolated spot in the extended cemetery across the road.

My accommodation was the Red Lion Hotel in Bredwardine, a fine seventeenth century red brick inn which apart from offering simple but comfortable accommodation and good food has been used for village meetings for groups of various interests for many generations. I wasn't aware at the time of making the booking that I would be sharing my room with a ghost who had apparently been thought to have inhabited my converted bathroom! The Red Lion is also a haven for visiting fishermen from all quarters of the UK and, as I discovered later, many from Europe who each year test their skills against the Wye salmon. I felt it would be worth an extended stay to meet up with some of them and decided to delay my departure for a couple of days. That year, crowds of anglers were flocking to Herefordshire to take advantage of an unexpected but welcome increase in salmon stocks. Some 'beats' along the river had recorded up to four times more fish than in recent years. However, there was still some concern that there weren't enough adult salmon to allow future stock to rise further. A voluntary catch and release policy has been in place for some time to help the salmon stocks recover and it is hoped this will lead to a thriving fishery once again along the Wye. But it's not just the salmon the fishermen come for. The river at Bredwardine is home to many other species, trout, chubb, grayling, and the infamous barbel, an introduction to the river to increase the sport but hated by salmon fisherman because they eat precious salmon eggs.

John and Charlotte Jensen from Copenhagen in Denmark first came here ten years ago.

'This is a special place for us,' John told me over a pint of beer in the Hotel bar. *'After Charlotte and my five year old son Emile, fishing is my life. I've fished in many wild and beautiful places, but we come back to Bredwardine every year to coarse fish and meet up with friends we've made here over the years. Charlotte used to sit on the river bank with a*

book, but then she caught a huge Barbel at her first attempt and now has her own rods. The locals call her The Barbel Queen now. We love it here, and the Red Lion is such a friendly place. When we're not fishing, we walk the hills and the lanes. What more can you ask?'

I have never understood why someone would want to sit on a river bank for hours, and often days, waiting and hoping to catch something and then have to throw it back, so John agreed that I could accompany them the next morning to their beat, as long as I shared the back seat with the stinking bait. We were joined by Andy Pearson, a fishing companion of John's who told me that he was planning to give up work and go fishing around the world. At thirty six and single, Andy said he had given up any hope of meeting the right woman.

'The girlfriends I meet don't hang around too long. I think it's the smell of bait; it gets in your clothes, hair, fingernails, everywhere. I don't notice it, myself, but the girls obviously do. No, I can't see myself getting married. It will be just me and the fish'

Another visitor to the inn that week, Simon Rolph, is from a similar stable. I had arranged to spend time with him, too, on the river in the afternoon, and he had chosen to fish in a seclude spot a short distance down stream. As we climbed down the bank to the river edge, we had to fight our way through Himalyan Balsam, an attractive plant with pretty pink blooms, and Japanese Knotweed with white feathery flower heads. I'm told both are vigorous growers and are gradually taking over from our native riverside flora. Simon told me he believes he was born to fish, and, like Andy, remains unattached as a consequence. A railwayman by profession, Simon spends up to ten weeks of the year at Bredwardine, as far from railway tracks as you can be.

'I work the Great Western line out of Paddington station in London,' he told me while attaching a fly to his hook, *'but I hope one day to get a transfer to Hereford so that I can spend more time here than I do now.'*

Unlike John and Andy who cast their lines from the dry bank, Simon's sport is game fishing.

'I put my waders on and go looking for the fish. Hunter against hunted. It makes fishing more interesting than sat on the river bank waiting for fish to come to you. But sometimes the fish can sense what I'm doing and they live to fight another day.'

As I sat on the river bank, the overhanging trees at the base of Brobury Scar cast their mirror image on the almost still, deep water in a curious confusion of colour and texture, the dividing line between the two visions impossible to determine. When messrs Fenn & Fenn passed this way while *Walking with a Greyhound in Herefordshire in Wales*, they made reference to Wordsworth describing his own journey along the Wye : *'O sylvan Wye! Thou wanderer through the woods. How oft has my spirits turned to thee!'*

According to Simon, the day was not ideal for fishing, nevertheless he only just lost out to a fair size trout and would be back on the river in the morning to hunt again.

All those fishermen and women who I met over the two days spent in Bredwardine had one thing in common, a fanatical desire for a catch, whatever it might be. There was an unspoken assumption that salmon, the king of the Wye and crowning glory of all catches, would not be on their list but that was no matter, the Bredwardine beats and the Red Lion Hotel were a catch in themselves, a glorious retreat for country pursuits, and a damn good meal and a beer at the end of it.

The site of Bredwardine Castle built in the thirteenth century by Ralph de Baskerville lies in a field next to St Andrews churchyard. It was rebuilt by Roger Vaughan in the seventeenth century but was never of any strategic importance. One hundred years later the stone remnants, by then owned by Sir Geoffrey Amyand Cornewall, were dismantled and used to build a new home just down the river at Moccas. Today, Moccas Court is Grade 1 listed and widely regarded as Herefordshire's finest Georgian house. Unique in its stunning surroundings, the court offers perfect peace, perched above terraced banks over the river. The strange name, Moccas, may originate from the Welsh word 'Mochros', meaning a place of pigs. According to legend, this place was where the celtic monk Dubricius founded his first settlement in the late fifth century after being instructed by an Angel to find the place with 'a white sow and a litter of pigs'. He didn't have to travel very far as he was born at Madley, less than five miles from Moccas. By the end of the sixth century, the small community of monks at Moccas had been driven out by Saxon raids and Dubricious had founded another cell at Hentland. The Moccas estate has been

Knarled Oakes of Moccas Park

owned by just four families since the thirteenth century. If the claims of Dubricus are discounted, the first recorded occupation was that of Walter de Fresne who built a fortified house here in 1160. At that time the Vaughans were occupying the castle at Bredwardine and the Cornewalls lived at Berrington, near Leominster. Over the centuries, these three families became intertwined through marriages culminating in that of Catherine Cornewall, then heiress to the Moccas estates, and Sir George Amyand, a London banker who took the name and arms of Cornewall after their union. By now the original house was considered too old fashioned so in 1775 a new house, the present Moccas Court, was built to a design by a Gloucestershire architect, Anthony Keck, with influence from Robert Adam. The gardens were laid out to plans by Capability Brown with further, later, alterations by Repton. The Cornewalls remained there until after the Second World War when Sir Geoffrey Cornewall who never married, sold the contents and let the house. In 1969, the Chester-Masters family, cousins of the Cornewalls, moved in and have turned their home into one of the finest country Hotels in Herefordshire.

On the hillside across the fields from the Court is Walter de Fresne's twelfth century deer park, considered still to be one of the most important primeval parklands in Britain. The ancient oaks were immortalized at the end of the nineteenth century by Francis Kilvert, a frequent visitor, who said of them:

> 'I fear those grey old men of Moccas, those huge, strange, gnarled, long-armed, low-browed, knock-kneed, bowed bent, deformed, hunchbacked, misshapen oak men that stand waiting and watching century after century, biding God's time with both feet in the grave..., they look as if they had been at the beginning and making of the world, and they will probably see its end.'

During a visit in 1870, a commissioner of the Woolhope Club noted: 'The park is far too much crowded with trees' and decided that a programme of planting by Sir George Amyand Cornewall towards the end of the eighteenth century seems to have been overdone. The Woolhope Club called again in 1891 (being a guest of the club by then, was Henry Timmins there too?). At that time, the Moccas Oak, the oldest tree in the park, was recorded as being nine hundred years old with a girth of thirty six feet at a height of five feet from the ground. By 1933 there was no further mention of this great tree and presumably it had gone by then. The largest and oldest oak today is the Stag's Horn Tree, a mere six hundred years old with a thirty foot girth and named after the Moccas beetle which lives off the dead wood in the park and is found nowhere else in UK.

At the top of the deer park, besides an ancient high road overlooking the Golden Valley, are the remains of a Neolithic burial chamber known as Arthur's Stone, which dates from around 3000 BC. A mound of earth would have originally covered the tomb but this has eroded away and the great roof stone has collapsed. A settlement has been discovered not far from here on Dorstone Hill and this chamber may be where the occupiers buried their dead. The connection with King Arthur is most likely another piece of ancient folklore intended as a fanciful explanation for the stones.

My two enjoyable days at the Red Lion were at an end too soon, but distance and difficult terrain needed to be covered before my next stop in Hay-on-Wye. Behind the Red Lion, a very steep footpath climbs Knapp Hill rising seven hundred feet, and behind that, higher still, is Merbach Hill. Both stand at the end of the long line of hills forming the northern side of the Golden Valley. Below them to the west is the Welsh town of Hay, where the river Wye enters England after a seventy mile tumble from its birth on Plynlimon in west Wales, and begins a gentler journey to meet its big sister, the Severn, as it enters the Bristol Channel near Chepstow. In the opposite direction, the glorious Golden Valley, not looking quite so golden today under the threatening skies, stretches towards far horizons on which is the strange jagged outline of the distinctive Skirryd Mountain, barely visible in the mist. To the north, the central Welsh hills form a barrier as far as the eye can see. On the English side of the Marches, the Clee Hills of Shropshire seem still to defy invasion from the Welsh, and the Malverns and Cotswold hills complete the defensive barrier further to the east. This all round view from the summit of Merbach was truly awesome in any direction, and I was not in any hurry to leave.

The path drops steeply off Merbach's western flanks and reaches the Hay road beside a lonely inn whose owner closed it some years ago and refused to reopen as hardly anyone called. Nearby, at secluded Clock Mills, there are no clues at the entrance as to the connection with a previous resident famous more for his stories than his name. During his prolific writing career, Raphael Sabatini, born in Italy in 1875 from an Italian father and an English mother spent some time here. His name will be a mystery to most until mention of his books: *The Black Pirate, The Black Swan,* and *Captain Blood.* He wrote more than thirty books, plays and short stories in the early 1900s, and the films based on these novels brought world famous actors to the fore, Errol Flynn, Douglas Fairbanks, and Tyrone Power, to name but a few. Raphael Sabatini was a master of six languages, but he wrote his masterpieces in English because he believed *'all the best stories are written in my mother's tongue'.* He spent his most productive period at Clock Mills creating novels that eventually brought the swish of blades and spilling of blood to the silver screen. Arguable his greatest contribution was *Scaramouche* which he wrote in 1923 and set in the turbulent years preceding the French Revolution. Why Sabatini chose this remote part of Herefordshire is a mystery, but the fact that Sir Arthur Conan Doyle also came here for inspiration for his *The Hound of the Baskervilles*, and Bruce Chatwin wrote *On the Black Hill* near here, gives me incentive enough to be here too. Unfortunately, Sabatini was dogged for much of his life with ill health and eventually returned to Switzerland in 1940 where he died ten years later.

A footpath skirts the grounds of Clock Mills and crosses the hillside overlooking the Wye winding through the plain below. On the far side of the valley above the river is Whitney Court, a large house built in neo-Tudor style in 1898, standing on an elevated shelf of land. It is the third Whitney Court, each one built higher than its predecessor to escape the encroaching river. Previously, there had been a Jacobean house, replaced by a Georgian version. When the peacefulness, warm sun and broken white clouds enhance the beauty of this corner of Herefordshire, there is nothing to indicate that all is not well here. The name 'Whitney' means 'white water' and reflects the sometimes sudden and destructive floods that have swept away parts of the village in the past. The remains of Whitney Castle went downstream during one such flood. So too did the church – the present one was built to replace it in 1740. At least three stone bridges have been washed away, but the part stone and part timber toll bridge there today carrying the B4350 back road across the river to Clifford was built in 1802 and appears to have lasted well. The latest Whitney Court was built for the Hope family who had connections to the Coates thread making firm of Coates-Vyella fame. However, the estates origins reach back fifteen centuries when the de Whitneys lived first in the castle then later in the Jacobean house. A branch of the Whitneys ended up in America where centuries later, in 1793, Eli Whitney made a name for himself by inventing an automatic process of cleaning cotton fibre. He called it his 'Cotton Gin' (short for engine) and, at a stroke, Whitney's invention had eliminated a huge bottleneck in cotton production. Unfortunately, because it was so simple to make it was copied by anyone with a few basic skills, and he was forced to spend his profits fighting lawsuits. By 1797, he had been forced out of business and the US Congress refused to renew the patent when it expired ten years later.

The village of Clifford on the back road to Hay is a scattered community which seems to lack a focal point. Although it boasts two churches, neither is close to the centre. In recent years it has lost its village shop, post office, policeman, and no longer has a pub. The Golden Valley railway once went through but only short stretches of the old track bed remain. A favourite local tale is of a village character, an old man partial to his cider, who used to ride his bicycle to Hay to do his weekly shopping. On each visit, he would consume his usual amount in the Three Tuns, before setting off to return to Clifford, and each time, he would reach home minus some of his groceries which had fallen out of his basket as he meandered his way back. However, caring neighbours would collect the discarded items and leave them on his doorstep while he slept in his armchair.

RHYDSPENCE INN.

The romantic ruins of Clifford's ancient castle are clear to see to all who drive along the toll road, and in 1165, romance played a part in a clever piece of manoeuvring by Walter Fitz Richard. At the time, Fitz Richard had been appointed steward of the castle which belonged to Roger de Clifford and refused to hand it back. When Henry II visited the castle during a Welsh campaign, the wiley Walter introduced him to his daughter, the 'fair Rosamund', a liason which pleased the King and thus ensured the castle would not be returned to its rightful owner. Rosamund's affair with Henry was long and culminated in her mysterious death in 1176 at Woodstock near Oxford, possibly at the hands of Henry's jealous Queen Eleanor. By 1311, the castle at

Clifford had passed into the hands of those great medieval land grabbers, the Mortimers, and not being short on castles they left Clifford unoccupied and allowed it to decay. It was eventually destroyed by Glyndwr in 1402.

> *'A pleasant field path leads hence beneath noble groups of beeches and presently we join the high road, passing by a wooded hill whose summit is crowned by an early British camp. Another mile and we enter the border town of Hay, perched upon the steep bank of the Wye.'*

I walked the last three miles to Hay along the Wye Valley Walk footpath which separates the low level B4350 and high level B4352 road routes and passes close to the curiously named Mouse Castle earthworks. This heavily fortified Saxon ringwork and bailey is similar in construction and size to the citadel of British Camp on the Herefordshire Beacon near Malvern, and would have been a major defence system overlooking the Wye valley and the Welsh border region for considerable distances in all directions. Hay-on-Wye lies on the Welsh side in the county of Powys. However, as far as the Royal Mail is concerned, it is better, apparently, to use the county of Herefordshire for posting purposes. Thus 'Hay-on-Wye, via Hereford'. Throughout its history, the English and Welsh have fought over ownership of the town, and probably for that reason it seems even now still neither wholly one nor the other. Today, though, Hay is a centre for recreation. Thousands visit the area every year to enjoy the splendid scenery. This is great walking country with many miles of dramatic changes from mountain to valley. The long distance footpaths, the Offa's Dyke and the Wye Valley Walk cross each other as they and pass through Hay, and of course there is the great river Wye, itself carving its way through the landscape. For two weeks in May each year, the Hay Festival comes to town, opportunities to indulge in an orgy of music, art, literature, story telling, comedy, food, drink, and of course books. Hay is famous for its second hand book shops, thirty nine of them at the last count.

The second hand book trade was started here in 1961 by Richard Booth, whose family has lived here since 1903. After graduating from

Oxford the young Richard was expected to join the family's accountancy firm in London. Instead, having already developed a penchant for old books, he decided to set up shop where *'instead of playing a minor role in a major business, I could play a major role in a minor one'.* He was fortunate in that his hunt for 'bargain whole libraries' coincided with the destruction of unwanted country houses, and also at that time in Wales, there were no second hand book dealers to bar his way. Booth was persistent in his pursuit of the idea that a town full of bookshops could be an international attraction. By the late 1970s, Hay had indeed become the first book town and was said to already contain over a million books. It quickly achieved national and international fame, partly due to the novelty of the book town concept but equally due to Booth's flamboyant personality. Being situated in mountainous unpopulated mid Wales he believed that Hay could adjust to its international market, its very remoteness protecting it from domination by London. On April 1 1977, in a moment of astute marketing tinged with wild eccentricity, Booth declared 'Home Rule for Hay' and appointed himself 'King'. What started as an off-the-cuff joke was taken so seriously by local councilors and the media, that he decided to develop the idea into a printed manifesto, 'Independence for Hay'. The stunt achieved world-wide publicity and at the same time aggravated an increasingly fragile relationship with the Welsh Tourist Board eager to capitalize on Hay's growing popularity.

Through Booth's influence in the early 1990s, similar book town ventures were copied in France, Belgium and the Netherlands. In 1995 the Scottish Tourism Research Unit at the University of Strathclyde initiated a project, supported by Scottish Enterprise, to investigate the economic effects of book towns in peripheral rural areas. The first research report showed how the growth of Hay had had an astonishing economic effect on it's region, and to some extent on Wales as a whole. Two years later, a Scottish book town was started at Wigtown in the south west lowlands. In his constant search for the rare and the unusual, Booth travelled extensively throughout Europe and America, encouraging others to start their own second hand book enterprises. Following a visit to America and the Black Hills of Dakota, he once again took full advantage of the enthusiastic response and promptly declared himself a Welsh American Indian. In his over zealous quest to establish an international market for book towns, he had earned his inclusion in Margaret Nicholas's *The Worlds Greatest Cranks and Crackpots.*

In 1971, wealth from his success allowed Booth to accomplish his ambition as 'King', to own the castle in Hay which he purchased from a fairground magnate. The castle comprises a large Jacobean mansion next to a crumbling Norman keep. Throughout it's history it has suffered three serious fires. The first was in 1231 when King John set it alight after falling out with William de Braose, and a second fire in 1939 destroyed one of the finest seventeenth century oak staircases. The third was in 1978 when the eccentric new owner overstacked the open fireplace before retiring to bed. Fortunately, Booth survived but the old mansion house didn't and sustained serious damage. He now lives in the family home at nearby Cusop and is intending to completely renovate the mansion as time and funds allow. In the meantime the castle grounds are home to his Honesty Bookshop, where customers are asked to put payments for their purchases in the boxes provided. Despite his critics, few would deny his claim of being the instigator of the book town movement, and so as a direct consequence in 2004 Richard Booth was awarded an MBE for his services to tourism.

OLD MARKET-HOUSE, HAY.

For many years Hay-on-Wye was seen as an odd little book town and nothing more, but in 1988 travelling theatre impresarios Norman and Peter Florence chose Hay as the venue for their first arts festival. Every year since, the festival has drawn increasing numbers over ten days at the beginning of June to see and hear big literary names from all over the world, boosting the town's already booming book tourists to well over half a million. There is nothing 'King' Richard should regret about those figures, or the big bookshop businesses which have opened worldwide. There have been occasions when his high and mighty presence has irked some of the townsfolk, even to the point of celebrating dethronement rallies in the town's streets, but the 'King' has survived. Long may he reign over them.

Clyro Court, a nineteenth century Jacobean style house, is two miles across the river and is most definitely in Wales. However, because it has connections with my walk around Herefordshire, I will give it space in my story. The court is now a hotel but it was built in 1839 by Thomas Mynors Baskerville, descended from a branch of the Baskervilles of Eardisley. A friend and frequent visitor of the family was Sir Arthur Conan Doyle, and he is said to have written *The Hound of the Baskervilles* while staying here. The story is based on the Vaughan legend of 'The Black Dog of Kington', but he was asked to set it in Dartmoor to avoid an influx of tourists to Clyro. Curiously, a report in the *Independent* on 25 August 1989 tells of a mysterious animal running amok on farmland near Clyro. Dozens of sheep had their throats ripped out and armed farmers searched the edges of forests and remote moorland around Hay-on-Wye and the border villages to track the killer which appeared to strike at night. The culprit wasn't found, and there have been many similar reports in the area over the past fourteen years. One wonders, though, if these stories, which are still being reported, are connected in some way to the occasional sightings of large black cats roaming the moors of south west England.

I could not leave Hay without a visit to the Three Tuns public house, a famed hostelry run by Lucy Powell for over eighty years. The building is the second oldest surviving in the town, the first being the castle. Inside the one room pub as the embers twinkled in the grate, Lucy's bright eyes peered over the tiny bar like a country mouse. She is fond of telling the story of the day the great train robbers called in for a drink shortly after their daring heist in 1963. According to what she believed, they were looking for a hideout among the Hay hills. I'm not sure whether they actually said that, or why they weren't successful in finding accommodation in the town, but several days later, some of them were seen again further down the river in Abergavenny. Tragically, Lucy's pub was destroyed by fire not long after my visit and lay boarded up and derelict until its reopening as a gastro-pub in 2008. Lucy survived the fire but did not return to the pub. To me, that is two tragedies in one, but at least the old building has been brought back to life, albeit with a new interior and serving a different purpose.

> *'Hay will be found a good starting point for several pleasant rambles: by following the course of the Dulas brook, for instance, we may visit Cusop, with its little mountain church shaded by venerable yew trees, whence, passing through a narrow dingle, a good walker may range across the hills and penetrate the Olchon glen; or may follow the mountain road to Llanthony, where he will be glad to find homely but comfortable quarters within the precints of the ruined priory.'*

Leaving Hay on Wye early the next morning, I chose the stiff climb to the top of breezy Cusop Hill where familiar views neither disappointed nor diluted previous exhilarations. Then on to Cefn Hill where, in the valley below, are the remains of a ruined Grandmontine priory, dedicated to St Mary and built by another de Lacy church builder, Walter, in 1225. It was one of only three priories established for the order in England. The community of Grandmont was founded by St Stephen of Muret in the twelfth century in the Langue d'Oc region of France. Little is known about them because keeping written records was forbidden, but it is believed that the monks led a very austere life embracing poverty. While St Stephen was alive, the order maintained its disciplines. After his death, however, breakdown in the structure within the order led to a turbulent history of conflict, internal politics, reform movements, and eventual decline.

A little further down the valley is an isolated inn. The Bull at Craswall is an old drovers' inn at the foot of the Black Hill and has remained virtually unchanged for two hundred years. Parking is very restricted on the adjacent narrow lane, but there is ample space, as travellers from centuries gone by have discovered, on adjoining land to graze a horse! I followed an old drovers' road beyond the Bull, a secluded track that hugs the base of the the hill. Although long since abandoned and replaced by a parallel lane lower down the valley, the track is still well defined with holly and hawthorn hedges on either side and occasionally hazel and taller ash and birch. The great green wall of the Black Hill loomed above me and although difficult to detect in the undergrowth, a narrow path climbed steeply from the south east onto its exposed ridge. Beyond is the Olchon Valley and the equally cliff like slopes of Hay Bluff. Around these hillsides, the author Bruce Chatwin set his classic tale of the tragedies of hill farm life in the early part of the twentieth century. *On the Black Hill* was later made into a film and tells the story of twins, Lewis and Benjamin Jones, who lived on the isolated farm which Chatwin named 'The Vision' after hearing a local story. It went like this: In 1737, Alice Morgan, a sickly girl, saw the Virgin Mary hovering over the rhubarb patch, and ran back into the house where she lived, apparently cured. Her father celebrated the miracle by changing the name of the house, Ty-Cradoc, to The Vision and carved his daughter's initials AM and a cross on the lintel above the porch. Chatwin must have known, too, the severity of the slopes on the Black Hill because he transferred the story to the more manageable Welsh side of the mountain but kept the original Hill name for effect. The locations in his book are fictitious, but tantalisingly, on the south western flanks of Hay Bluff near Capel-y-ffin is a property called The Vision Farm. Herefordians will be quick to recognize that Lewis and Benjamin spent much of their time on the English side of the Hill with only the simpleton Jim the Rock from a neighbouring farm for company and occasionally the impish Rosie Fifield, who introduced Lewis to sex when she was just ten years old! Abandoned by Rosie when she married the Lord of the Manor's invalid son, and Jim who preferred a ferret for company and then went off to war, the twins etched out a basic life at The Vision for forty two years where they slept side by side in their mother's bed.

Rounding the eastern slopes, I got my first view of the Olchon valley. Below on the valley floor and nestling beside the Olchon brook is a place that time forgot. Olchon Court is a unique medieval farmhouse dating from the early fourteenth century. It was built by Walter Brut, a leading Lollard and close friend of Nicholas Hereford and Sir

John Oldcastle who spent time here while on the run. Even today, it would be difficult to find a safer hideout. Communication with or from the outside world can't be easy, hemmed in as it is by the long northern flanks of the Black Mountains and the huge spur of the Black Hill. In a remote fifteenth century farm beneath Red Daren Hill, I discovered The Goat Company, a family business making mohair products from Angora goats and the brainchild of Robi Mandley and her partner Robert Cooper. They have a herd of eighty five Angoras and manage the entire production programme from the grass to the garment. The driving force behind the business is Robi herself, who after shearing the goats arranges for the hair to be sent away to be spun and cleaned. When I arrived at their farm, I was met by Robert who, aided by a walking stick, hobbled across the yard to greet me, in obvious discomfort.

'Robi's chasing some of our cows that have got out of their field. As you can see, I'm somewhat indisposed.'

I asked him first if he wanted to postpone a planned tour of the goat house until his partner returned.

'It was Brutus,' he started to explain, *'he got me right behind the knees. My fault, really,'* he painfully admitted.

Just as I began to wonder who or what Brutus was, he pointed me towards a large barn where a small group of young female goats peered at me from the gloom within. Almost at once, they were joined by the biggest goat I've ever seen, the size of a pony, boasting a pair of viciously twisting horns.

'That's 'im. All of 95 kilos. His girls are on heat at the moment and he's jealous of anything and anybody going near them. He went for me while I was loading up the hay buckets and my back was turned. Thought I was competition, see. Hit me so hard, I was in the air for a few seconds.'

Robi joined us appearing tired and hungry, as she had evidently foregone lunch while on the chase, but was nevertheless still keen to show me around. My memory of Angora was of fluffy pink jumpers worn by some of the girls of my childhood and which made people itch, so I asked her to clear up the misunderstanding of what Angora actually is.

'That fluffy itchy stuff was rabbit not goat,' she was very glad to tell me.

'Goat hair is soft but strong, doesn't itch, has excellent insulation properties and can be turned into hard wearing, high quality garments.' she emphasized proudly.

'We produce our own yarns here and turn them into luxurious knitwear, blankets, lace scarves, and socks of many colours, all from our prize winning animals.'

Near one of the pens, a row of large bags full of graded goat hair awaited dispatch to the spinners. She took me into a small shed which she and Robert had converted into a showroom. Along either side of the tiny room were shelves stacked with the most colourful of garments, in stunning patterns and hues. The centre of the room was reserved for carousels of socks of bright greens, reds, blues and mauves. At the back of the store, was an annex stocked high with natural coloured garments awaiting the dyeing process.

'I do the dyeing myself,' she said, pointing to several small deeply stained vats. *'When we first came here, I did this work in the kitchen. We ate standing up with plates in our hands because anything with a flat surface was piled high with socks. I don't knit, though. I have eight tried and trusted knitters who do that for me in their homes, most from the south Herefordshire area, but I employ one in Sheffield. My blankets are woven in west Wales and the lace scarves in Nottingham. Ours is a nationwide cottage industry'*

Robi and Robert had previously run their business at Lampeter in west Wales but found the journeys to the shows in the Midlands and the London area where they sold the finished articles long and arduous. Even from this wild place beneath the Black Mountains, they can save up to four hours in travelling time.

'I spend a lot of time at the craft shows, mostly at large country houses. One of my regular exhibits is at Hatfield House in Hertfordshire.'

As I was about to leave, Robi pointed to some skin rugs hanging on a frame. *'After eighteen months or so, the bucks stop bucking, as it were, and have served their purpose,'* she grinned a little hard heartedly *'so we put them to other use.*

Climbing away from the Angora farm towards the mountain road, I thought of the brutal Brutus and his inevitable comeuppance, and wondered if limping Robert might be looking forward to his ultimate revenge.

This part of Herefordshire is an area of outstanding natural beauty. Enclosed on one side by the high green wall of the Black Mountains and on the other by the ridges of the Golden Valley, the fields hereabouts have been left to grass for grazing and silage. The Olchon Brook falls from Red Daren Hill and descends beneath the green wall to join up later with the River Monnow near Clodock. For most if that stretch, it is a small babbling brook where Dippers and Grey Wagtails perch on boulders awaiting careless insects. Not all the dwellings dotted along the valley floor are inhabited. When I walked by Yellow House Farm it looked empty and abandoned, the yard overgrown, the walls bending outwards no longer capable of holding up the roof of stone tiles. It was a sad picture and eerily quiet. There was little birdsong here. The lark, curlew and plover have been driven away as the increasing numbers in badgers, foxes and mink have devastated their nests. However, the sheep were numerous and vociferous in defence of their domain. Their bleats grew in intensity as they warned their neighbours in adjoining fields of my approach. This was a world in isolation with only a solitary narrow road heading south towards distant Abergavenny. I can think of few places in the whole of Herefordshire that have given me as much pleasure on this journey.

The evening skies above Hatterall Hill were darkening menacingly as I reached the lane to Longtown. I decided I still had time to visit the oddly named tiny church of St Bueno & St Peter at Llanveynoe founded by Bueno, a seventh century Welsh saint. The connection with St Peter wasn't clear to me, but Lanveynoe isn't far from Peterchurch in the Golden Valley, where a legend insists he passed that way. The present building is thirteenth century but the antiquity of the site is emphasized by a crucifixion stone, said to be ninth century, set into the south wall, and the oldest Christian sculpture in Herefordshire. There is an old Welsh story about Bueno, who lived for a time at Clynnog, on the Lleyn peninsular in North Wales. Each Sunday, he would cross the Menai Straights to preach at Llanddwyn, walking on the surface of the sea carrying his book of sermons. One Sunday, as he was returning, he dropped his precious writings into the water and couldn't recover them. When he reached dry land he was relieved to discover his book on a stone out of reach of the tide, and a curlew standing guard over it. In thanksgiving, the holy man knelt and prayed that henceforth the pious bird would be protected, and ever since it has apparently been almost impossible to find where a curlew lays its eggs.

Ivy Pritchard runs a B&B at her pretty farmhouse home which was converted from a barn and cow house by the film actor Robert Newton when he came to live here in the 1950s. She and her husband have been farming in the Olchon Valley for forty two years and since the BSE outbreak in 2002 when they lost their cattle, have concentrated on rearing sheep on the slopes of the Black Mountains. One of their sons has a farm nearby, too. They are semi retired now and reflecting on life in this remote corner of England, Ivy told me,

'Hill farming is a hard life. You don't get the subsidies you see, not like the lowland farmers. The lanes in winter used to be difficult even for the tractor after snow, although we've been lucky in recent years with the climate changes.'

After an excellent breakfast, I sat in her delightful garden in the early morning sunshine and looked across to Longtown Castle keep peeping above the trees on the other side of the valley. For a moment I could not imagine a more peaceful place anywhere else in the world.

As its name implies, Longtown is a linear village. Its ancient name,

Inner Wall and Keep, Longtown Castle

Ewyas Lacy, later became Longa Villa, hence Longtown. The castle was yet another built by Walter de Lacy sometime before 1185 and the enormous earthen motte is an impressive structure, rising thirty five feet. The original tower was timber but was replaced by this robust round stone one in the thirteenth century. Its fifteen feet thick walls were carefully constructed on sloping foundations to minimize the possibility of collapse – a very effective technique as the tower remains to this day relatively intact. Although in England castle keeps were generally built square, round keeps were common in Wales, so it is not surprising to find one here along the border. By the fifteenth century the castle was in ruins but a section of the embankment near to the keep was later used as a gallows. The last 'suspended sentence' occurred in 1811 when Thomas Watkins was convicted of murdering John Gwillim and hanged at Hereford. His body was brought back to Longtown and, as was customary in those times, hung again close to the crime scene as a deterrent.

Longtown is a small community with a big heart and bags of spirit. The post office, pub, and village hall are constant hives of activity and are vibrant reminders of how communities were in days gone by. Bob and Becky took over the Crown Inn in February having moved in from Wolverhampton. Bob took early retirement from the prison service and decided to move here after hearing that the pub where they used to visit regularly on holiday in the valley came up for sale. Now their two daughters have joined them to share their busy life in the countryside. Running a country pub is an exciting prospect, but as Bob explained it has had its difficulties.

'We used to visit this area every year and on each occasion the people were very friendly and made us welcome. As soon as we took over the pub though, they wanted me to stay open all day and all night and didn't like it when I said I would be keeping to the appropriate licensing laws. This is a farming community, and as you know, farmers keep irregular hours so we try to accommodate them with an extra hour here and there and they seem now to have accepted that, but it was a struggle at first.'

In the end, the struggle may have become too much for Bob and Becky because the last I heard they had sold the pub and returned to the West Midlands.

That year (2004) Longtown won the Herefordshire Village of the Year award and the celebrations at their annual fete took on added impetus. Village shows have a character all of their own and bring to the fore talent which one suspects may never appear on any Olympic schedules. But who could doubt the resolve of the competitors for the 'best presented bale of meadow hay' or 'men's sponge baking'. Personally, I would rather witness wellie wanging than beach volley ball any day.

John Farr died in 1992, aged 78. He had lived all his life in a remote house near Longtown where his great-grandmother was born. He had been a carpenter, coffin-maker, and undertaker to the folk of this part of the Golden Valley. Until his death, John Farr spent almost every day in the workshop in the garden of the house, built by his father, a wheelwright, at the turn of the century. Young John had begun working there at the age of fourteen, and throughout his life he claimed he could make anything in wood using his father's old tools which were kept in exactly the same place so that he could find them in the dark. He once bought an electric planing machine but decided it was too much bother and never used an electric tool again. A bachelor with few needs and a rare contentment, John made only one concession to changing times: raising his charges to £1 an hour. He was always bewildered by impermanence, and how the Golden Valley Railway, which ran up to Hay until 1957, could be closed after a mere half a century. Referring to the railway tracks, he once said *'They put it all down and then one day they took it all up. It wouldn't hurt to leave them there, would it, in case someone else could use them?'* He claimed he had never made anything that had broken or fallen apart before it had become worn from use or too old. *'If you don't do a good job, it'll come back and hit you in the face.'*
'Enemies?' He once said. *'I've buried 'em all.'* The villagers say that, in truth, John Farr had none.

Less than a mile from Longtown the Olchon brook has joined the Escley brook to become the Monnow river. In the shadow of Hatterall Hill, the sleepy village of Clodock is dominated by its ancient church.

Its origins go back fifteen hundred years and the dedication to St Clydog is a clue to its antiquity. Legend has it that Clydog, the young son of the King of Ewyas, and who was betrothed to a young lady of noble birth, was murdered while out hunting hereabouts by a jealous comrade. Clydog's body was placed on a cart and driven towards the river where there was a ford. On reaching the river bank, the yoke broke and the oxen refused to be driven any further. It was therefore resolved to build a church on the spot. Apparently, the builders tried at first to erect the church some way from the river, but each morning the builders arrived to find that their previous days work had collapsed. In the end, it was decided to build on the original spot where the oxen had stopped, and henceforth all went well.

The sturdy church tower, though not on a par with the likes of Bosbury or Weobley, reflects the need for protection in the turbulent border regions of the eleventh and twelfth centuries. Inside, however, the nave is remarkable for its complete set of seventeenth and eighteenth century furnishings including box pews, a three-decker pulpit, and a musician's gallery. Here, too, are early fifteenth century faded wall paintings. Most remarkable of all is a memorial stone set in the south east corner of the nave to the wife of a man called Guinnda and dates back to around 750-850 AD. The churchyard is a crowded place. Tombstones line up side by side in tight rows resembling living corpses waiting for their final judgment. Next to the church, The Cornewall Arms, a low-ceilinged white-washed building, has non of the trappings of a modern pub. The front door, I am told, is invitingly open all hours, and inside, the layout is that of a small country dwelling. Armchairs, loungers, and occasional hardbacks face each other where social intercourse is unavoidable. The basic neon strip lighting is turned on sparingly as and when the landlady, Mrs Prosser, considers it necessary. She has run the pub this way for forty years or more.

'In this extreme south-western corner of Herefordshire, where the dark waters of the Honddu, breaking from the circumjacent ranges of the Black Mountains, mingle their flood with that brisk little river the Monnow, lies a district which, in grandeur of scenery and variety of interest, is second to none in the county. The great shoulders of Hatter-

> *rall Hill, rising in bold and lofty cliffs from the Monnow vale, dominate the view; and, by their marked contrast with the serrated peak of the Skirryd and the dark browed Sugar Loaf Mountain, form a scene unrivalled in spacious dignity anywhere on this side of the border.'*

At the southern end of the Black Mountain range, an ancient Welsh manor, Allt-Yr-Ynys (pronounced Acht-ur-unis), nestles beside the Monnow. Much of the present building is the sixteenth century ancestral home of the most influential family to successive English monarchs, the Cecils, of whom William Cecil, Elizabeth I's chief minister and his successor Robert Cecil are renowned. The Cecils settled here as early as the eleventh century and initially became engrossed in aiding local Welsh supremacy. However, from this small constant mist shrouded manor house by a Welsh border river, descendants have succeeded in achieving high office in the English royal house and Parliament, and becoming Marquises of the realm. Their eventual successes in the English court brought the family great wealth enabling then to take up residence much further east at Hatfield House in Hertfordshire which became the head house for centuries after. Their influence continues to this day with the present head of the family,

ALTERYNYS.

Robert Gascoigne Cecil, Marquis of Salisbury, and a member of the House of Lords. But in the way of things, the old ancestral home is now a country Hotel.

I turned north east again, gaining height whilst passing the remains of another of Walter de Lacy's many castellated hideouts, this at Walterstone, a name which derives from Walter's tun or manor, then followed one of the Monnow's myriad feeder brooks. Quite suddenly, and very unexpectedly, I stumbled across a tiny ancient church at the edge of a wood. A metal barrier across the porch and a sign warning of danger told me entrance was ill advised. In the churchyard were the remains of a thirteenth century preaching cross and monuments to the Scudamores of Kentchurch. The scene prompted thoughts of a rural Marie Celeste mystery. Here was obviously evidence of a departed community, but who were they, and where had they gone? I was standing in the parish of Llancillo and I was later to discover that this little church may have origins going back to the 7th century and it is thought there was once a hermits cell here. However, the building in front of me was mostly seventeenth century but has a thirteenth century font. It is listed as being St Peter's, as are many churches in and around the Golden Valley, but it has also been known as St Tysilio's. There is no village here but at the foot of the hill is an old farm house, known as Llancillo Court, next to a small tree topped motte. As I was in de Lacy territory, it is likely that the motte was Walter's doing, so we seem to have the remnants of an ancient community. According to some reports, this tiny church is also on one of Alfred Watkins's ley lines, making this isolated spot worthy of its place in a classic mystery story.

> *'From certain hints received, we decide to make a detour in order to examine the little church at Rowelstone. A secluded and grass grown lane gradually ascends and becomes as steep as they make them, even in these hilly parts, until we descend suddenly upon the little hamlet, and the church we are in search of'.*

The parish church of St Peters at Rowelstone is another of Herefordshire's hidden gems. It was built around 1130 and is a simple Norman construction of nave and chancel. The chancel arch and south doorway are decorated in the Herefordshire School style. Although less spectacularly so than those at Kilpeck, the tympanum in the doorway arch and the capitals at the top of the shafts are of fine quality. On each side of the chancel are rare four and a half foot long, hinged candle brackets which can be swung back against the wall when not in use. There have been many arguments as to their age, some think they are perhaps six hundred years old. No matter, we must be thankful that these unusual pieces of church furniture have remained in situ for so long, protected no doubt by the village's isolation. Astonishingly, this gorgeous little church has another rare surprise. At the time of his visit, Timmins saw on display a first edition Welsh bible, printed in 1558. In 1968, the bible was severely damaged in a disastrous fire at the vicarage, where it was being kept for safety. At the present time, this valuable treasure is being held at the Records Office in Hereford, where it awaits restoration. I am told there are many Welsh bibles in existence, but a first edition of 1558 seems to me, if not unique, at least extremely valuable, particularly to this small community. Herefordshire has many fine churches, each with its unique treasures, yet I have not visited one quite as special.

From Rowlestone, another steep secluded and grass grown lane drops into Ewyas Harold, a fairly large village of about nine hundred people equidistant between Hereford and Abergavenny. Records indicate the village is named after the son of Earl Ralph of Hereford, Harold de Sudeley, but some past historians have claimed that the 'Harold' refers to Godwinson, who succeeded Edward the Confessor as King. Confusion arises as Harold Godwinson, then Earl of Wessex, is reported to have spent time here during his battles with the Welsh after they had sacked Hereford in 1053, and built a castle to protect the entrance to the Golden Valley. Ewyas was considered a strategic spot, even by the Normans coming afterwards. Harold's timber castle was later rebuilt and fortified by the early Norman castle builder, William Fitz Osborn. Further fortifications were carried out on the castle in 1403 on the orders of Henry IV as a precaution against possible attack from Glyndwr. After the Welsh Prince's defeat, Ewyas castle was never again of any importance and was left to fall into ruin. By the time of the Civil War in 1645, it had completely collapsed and today only the steep earthwork remains. The church of St Michael and All Angels is thirteenth century but an earlier church stood on this site in 1100 as part of a Benedictine Priory. In his *History of Ewias Harold*, Canon Bannister wrote of the considerable language difficulties experienced in medieval times. In the Priory, the monks spoke Latin. Up in the castle, the residents spoke Norman-French, while in the village some spoke English, some French, and others Welsh!

In her book *Herefordshire - The Enchanted Land* Mary Andere tells the intriguing story of how after the battle of Hastings, King Harold Godwinson was found alive, though badly wounded, by Edith, his mistress. With the help of some monks, Edith exchanged his clothing for that of a dead warrior and took him to safety where she nursed him back to good health. Harold, either unable or not wishing to take up arms again, decided to dedicate the rest of his life to God in thanksgiving for his deliverance, and built himself a cell in the Golden Valley where he spent much of his time in prayer before finally moving to a monastery in Chester. Edith had identified the 'other Harold' to Duke William who buried him with full honours on the shore

proclaiming the dead King forever defender against future invaders. This romantic revelation has never been promoted as a possibility, but I for one wish it were true.

After a short stop for refreshment, it was time to push forward over Ewyas Common, here green with chest high wavering bracken, there yellow with gorse bloom. A rough rambling track descended steeply to the old village of Dore, the tower of its ancient priory church guiding my way. The modern name for the village is Abbey Dore and as the change implies, there's no getting away from the overwhelming influence of the ruin in its midst. The great Cistercian monastery of Dore Abbey was founded in 1147 and is said to be based on the design of the parent abbey at Morimond in north eastern France. The choice of a site near a river has created doubts about the origins of the name 'Dore', which probably derives from 'D'or', the French word for gold. The question is, did the Normans take that from 'Dwr', the Welsh word for water. Whatever the truth, it is the French who gave us the delightful name for the area where the abbey stands, 'Golden Valley'.

At the dissolution, the abbey was granted to John Scudamore of Holme Lacy, but surprisingly he did nothing with it and left it to decay. Of the original buildings, the chancel and transepts alone survived and in 1632 another John Scudamore, the first Viscount, set out to repair what was left and rededicated it as the parish church. Amongst the many alterations Scudamore made was the addition of a magnificent oak screen, made by master craftsman John Abel. He also erected a new tower to replace the collapsed central steeple using stones from the ruined nave. It is an awe inspiring place with its high vaulted ceilings, reminding us of a once mighty building which was three times the length it is now. The present church forms just the south eastern end of the former abbey. Together with other monastic buildings, the Dore Abbey complex must have been a considerable spectacle. It was certainly of great importance to the nobility and gentry of these parts who instructed that their remains should be buried here. For the most part, the monks lived a peaceful existence in these tranquil surroundings, avoiding even the worst attentions of Owain Glyndwr, until the inevitable suppression and dissolution of 1539.

The tiny village of Bacton is two miles from Abbey Dore by road but I chose a longer route by a delightful stretch of the river that gave the abbey its name. At Bacton is the pretty thirteenth century church of St Faith, whose ivy clad tower can be seen on the hillside. It is named after a little known third century martyr who was tortured on a gridiron before being beheaded. On the north wall opposite the entrance displayed in a glass case is a tapestry believed to have been hand made by Blanche Parry, governess to the young Queen Elizabeth 1 and lady in waiting to the monarch for the rest of her life. It was once used as an alter cloth but the woodland scenes embroidery suggests a previous use, possible as one of the Queen's dresses. Blanche was the daughter of Henry Parry, sheriff of Herefordshire. The Parrys were cousins of the Cecils, and through them became familiar at court. Like her mistress, Blanche remained unmarried and in the Queen's service until her death at eighty two, an exceptional age for the times. As becoming her station in life, Blanche's body is buried in St Margaret's church next to Westminster Abbey, and her splendid monument in the sanctuary at Bacton is said to contain her internal organs. Although not on display, another great treasure belonging to this little church is a rare, pre-reformation, chalice and paten of silver plate reputed to have been made in the late fifteenth century. Bacton's remoteness may have saved them from the Puritans' zealous excesses as chalice and paten are now safely tucked away in Hereford Cathedral.

> *'Let us now pass out through the quiet churchyard, where the warm sun of the spring noontide is flecked by the shade of many an overarching tree. Following the vale of the little Dore stream, we find, hard by its course, a mill leat passing to the mill at New Court. This is but a sorry relic of certain works of irrigation carried out on an ambitious scale by Rowland Vaughan, a worthy scion of the ancient house of the Vaughans of Bredwardine.'*

A shady stroll for me, too, through Llan Arw Wood brings me to New Court. There is a story that one day Rowland Vaughan, who farmed at New Court, was on his way to see a local miller when he came across a narrow strip of unusually verdant pasture which he traced to the banks of a nearby brook. There he discovered a mole hill through which the mole had excavated a channel allowing water from the brook to trickle into the parched meadow. Vaughan's fertile imagination grasped the enormous potential of what he had allegedly seen and he set about devising a system of trenches and sluices to catch the water running off the Golden Valley hills. Linking it to the river Dore allowed him to irrigate his land at appropriate times. By drowning the meadows in early spring, he drove away the winter frosts, providing fresh succulent grasses for his livestock. Further drenching in the summer months yielded an additional crop of hay. The main canal which became known as the Trench Royal was three miles long and wide enough to carry a small boat. At the same time, Vaughan resolved to tackle what he perceived as one of the great ills of his time, namely rural unemployment. In the Golden Valley at that time there were around three hundred unemployed souls, so by utilizing some of the mills fed by his irrigation system, he introduced a commonwealth of skills, a co-operative colony, with everyone contributing to its wellbeing . Whether his utopian project ever came to fruition remains a mystery. The sixteenth century waterways and old

Mysty, moody, magnificent Dore Abbey

hay meadows, which have now become a haven for birds and insects as well as rare plants and grasses, have recently been saved from being ploughed up when the Country Restoration Trust, supported by HRH Prince Charles, stepped in to purchase the land. Abandoned and neglected for nearly four hundred years, Vaughan's achievements are now being re-assessed.

As I walked along the narrow valley floor beside the river with the sun on my back, deep in thought about what may have been achieved here, I again felt blessed, by my good fortune, to know and love a part of England of which few people had ever heard and most will never see, and at that very moment promised myself that I would return to this valley as often as my time on earth would allow.

> *'An hour's stroll across the meadows takes the wayfarer to the twin parishes of Turnaston and Vowchurch. Tradition says that some few centuries ago two pious maiden ladies resolved to build a church which should be available for both parishes; but, disagreeing on the question of a site for the edifice, they fell to words, the elder lady exclaiming, "I Vow I will build my church, before you turn a stone of yours!" And there stand the twin churches to this day, a bow-shot distance asunder.'*

At Vowchurch, the pretty church of St Bartholomews is of special interest to admirers of the work of the Sarnesfield carpenter, John Abel. The timber roof structure of collar and tie beams is supported on unique oak posts, separated from the walls and black with age. Abel's theory was that this method avoided excessive weight being put on the walls of the church and therefore preventing them from collapsing. A similar idea was used in the reconstruction of the church at Brampton Bryan, also dedicated to St Bartholomew, in 1675, and there has been speculation that that too was Abel's work. Mine hosts for the night were Joyce and Melvin Powell at The Old Vicarage, once the home of Skeffington Dodgson, the brother of Charles Dodgson, better known as Lewis Carroll. There is no record that as Lewis Carroll, Charles ever set foot in Vowchurch, but his younger brother was vicar here from 1895 until 1910. Their father was an archdeacon, and it was his wish that Charles, Skeffington, and another brother, Wilfred, should join the priesthood. Charles was indeed ordained a deacon, but he did not proceed with his vocation, taking up a post at Christchurch College, Oxford, as a lecturer in mathematics. It was at that time that he started writing children's stories. *Alice's Adventures in Wonderland* was first published in December 1865, followed by *Through the Looking Glass* in 1871. After his father's death, Charles, being the eldest of his many siblings, assumed responsibility for the Dodgson family, including a growing number of nephews and nieces, and he spent much of the income from the sale of his books on them.

The next day, I walked along the banks of the fledgling river Dore into Peterchurch, the 'capital' of the Golden Valley, and instantly recognizable by the tall spire of another St Peter's church. Amidst such beautiful surroundings the village fails, visually, to impress, but the church is another Herefordshire gem. The building is unusually made up of four sections, nave, *two* chancels and an apsidal sanctuary, all with curved decorative arches. The extra chancel suggests maybe there was an earlier central tower. The altar top is Saxon and said to have been hewn from a stone slab from Arthur's Stone, a chambered tomb, on nearby Dorstone Hill. Built into the south wall of the nave is a stone tablet portraying a fish with a chain around its neck. The legend is that the fish was caught by St Peter in the Golden Well, the traditional source of the Dore, further up the valley, at Dorestone. His unexplained presence in the Valley is given some credence, I suppose, by the number of churches bearing his name.

The church font is a Norman tub type with rope and zig-zag decorations, and the south door shafts are carved with chevrons. Although St Peter's is very Norman, there are traces in the walls of an earlier Saxon church. The west tower was built in 1320 but, and here is the big let down, the spire is a modern fibre glass replacement of the original which had to be taken down in the 1940s. In the graveyard is the last resting place of the tragic Private Robert Jones who fought and survived the battle of Rorke's Drift in January 1879. With just four companions, Private Jones defended the mission hospital in the final Zulu attack. Despite suffering spear wounds and being struck by a bullet, he helped evacuate six patients through holes in the walls during a desperate retreat from the blazing building before it collapsed. He received the Victoria Cross for his bravery. At the end of his army service, Jones settled in Peterchurch and worked as a farm labourer, but in 1868 he became unwell and on 6 September, he tragically killed himself with his employer's gun after claiming he wished to go crow shooting. The coroner heard evidence that he suffered from nightmares about his frightening experiences in South Africa. Jones's sad demise was made all the more poignant when he was carried into the churchyard over the wall, rather than through the gate (suicides were barred from entry), and was buried facing the opposite way to those around him.

> *'Between Peterchurch and our next destination at Dorstone, the hill upon which stands the castle of Snodhill is a prominent object, projecting into the valley and commanding the road towards Hay. It is a fortress built in various periods, and in the reign of Stephen it was counted among the 1,200 castles in the land.*

The visible stone remains at Snodhill date back to the early thirteenth century, but it is certain that there was a timber castle here shortly after the Conquest. The sixteenth century traveller, John Leland, recorded it as being ruinous in 1540, yet Elizabeth I gifted what was here to her favourite, the Earl of Leicester, who sold the site within four months from which we might infer that the gift was more to enable the Earl to raise funds than to enjoy it as a possession. Dorstone is at the western end of the Golden Valley, and is a village of olde worlde charm with a quiet homely collection of cottages gathered around a tiny green. The church is said to have been built, to expiate his crime, by Richard de Brito, another one of the four knights who murdered Thomas Becket at Canterbury. The Pandy Inn is a favourite stop for tourists enjoying a pleasant six mile drive from Hay, but the impression is that without the pub no-one would come here at all, which no doubt would please the few who live here in otherwise splendid isolation. Looking back down the valley from my viewpoint at Dorstone, the emergence of the season's growth of yellow rape on the hillsides was already creating a 'golden' landscape, and I wondered what the artist david Cox or his protoge Joseph Murray Ince would have made of it.

'Returning to Dorstone, we there rejoin the Liliputian train, and thus in leisurely wise, retrace our steps to our starting point at Pontrilas, whence we shall proceed upon further voyages of discovery in other directions.'

The branch line from Pontrilas to Hay-on-Wye opened in January 1854 to serve the villages of the Golden Valley, and like that of the line from Fort William to Mallaig in west Scotland, must have been one of the prettiest in the UK. In its day, the railway was a typical sleepy local service running along the valley floor until its withdrawal on 15 December 1941. Had it survived, it would surely have helped develop a prosperity the valley deserves but does not have.

After spending one more night at The Old Vicarge at Vowchurch, I set off the next morning with a heavy heart for what was to be the last stage of my long journey. At the top of Brampton Hill, I took a long look back across the hills and fields of south Herefordshire towards the blue Welsh mountains and wondered whether I would ever see them again, and decided then and there that I would. Below me, a tree shrouded mystery is perhaps a further encouragement to draw me back. In July 2000, a survey took place on an ancient motte in the grounds of Monnington Court (a different Monnington Court to that on the banks of the Wye) to try to find the last resting place of Owain Glyndwr. Nothing was found, but because the Scudamore family of Kentchurch, descendants of Glyndwr, have always held the belief, handed down through generations, that his remains really do lie at Monnington here in the Golden Valley, the search will no doubt continue. Ahead of me now, the city of Hereford lay sprawled across the landscape, but I had one more stop before the final mile or two through the busy suburbs.

'Near at hand the tower of the beautiful modern Roman Catholic cathedral of Belmont is seen, placed on a fine ascent close to the river.'

At the time of Timmins's view of it in 1891, Belmont Abbey was still new, having been constructed as late as 1859, and must have been a magnificent sight on the hillside free of tree growth. During the Reformation monastic life in England and Wales was all but destroyed and those who wished to devote their lives in such a way went into exile and eventually formed English monasteries in Europe. The Abbey at Belmont on the outskirts of Hereford was one such English and Welsh congregation which had maintained their Roman Catholic beliefs and adherence to the Rule of St Benedict. For the first fifty years, Belmont was indeed a catholic cathedral but in 1920 it was declared an independent priory, then later raised to the rank of abbey by papal consent. The construction of the abbey church at Belmont was originally to have been on a grander scale but lack of money prevented this happening. Compared to the commitment of so much wealth by medieval builders of great churches, the resulting stunted nave is a sad reflection of modern 'down sizing'. All holy houses should have their relics, and Belmont is blessed with two. A fragment of the skull of St Thomas Cantilupe was donated by Downside Abbey in Somerset, after his remains had been traced to the Benedictine Priory of Hildersheim in Germany. Another relic, that of the True Cross was given to Belmont in 1880 by Ghent Cathedral. A relic of the Cross was originally brought to England from the Holy Land by the crusading Richard I in the thirteenth century and secreted away to Ghent at the time of the Reformation.

The silence of the abbey cloister was my last chance of peace before I trundled into Hereford's noisy outskirts. Nothing need be said about this final walk into the city through the depressing suburb of Hunderton. I have been lucky to have had the time for these many months of walking up hill and down dale and discovering a small part of land-locked England that few people will ever see. I was fortunate, indeed, to have visited that little second book shop in Ross on Wye and there found Henry Thornhill Timmins' account of his wanderings. I've been very lucky, too, with the weather which, judging by the destructive floods of 2007, if we are to believe the threats of global warming, seems to have been the last of normal pattern for the foreseeable future, I was far from depressed though, I had too many unforgettable memories to cheer me to the finishing line.

Henry Timmins has been good company these three years or so.

He wrote in 1892 of two more adventures in Pembrokeshire and Shropshire, and I confess to harbouring thoughts of following him again down more lonely lanes. For the time being, though, my weary old body needs rest.

> *'Here, at length, we come to an end of our wanderings amidst the romantic and beautiful scenery, for which this rural English county is so justly admired; where it is been out good fortune to experience an old world courtesy from the dwellers in these haunts of ancient peace, be it cottage or time-worn grange, that causes pleasant memories to linger of many a kindly welcome to the wayfarer rambling, sketch book in hand, amid the nooks and corners of Herefordshire.'*

EPILOGUE

I was thirty-five years old before I attempted my first serious walk. After moving from Manchester to Bristol in 1978 to start a new life with my young family, I had became bogged down with the pressures of business and fatherhood and eventually succumbed to bouts of migraines and depression. My doctor said I should get out more and suggested I try long walks in the countryside. So that's what I did. My free time filled with open landscapes and five barred gates. The cure for my mental ills and headaches was immediate. Before long I had become addicted to my new way of relaxing and in 2002 thoughts turned to a desire long held since my honeymoon in Hereford in 1974 to return there. I had no plans to begin with other than to take a leisurely look around the Herefordshire countryside until, in a chance visit to a second hand book shop in Ross on Wye, I discovered *Nooks and Corners of Herefordshire* and I was instantly grabbed by the idea of following in the writer's footsteps. At first, I could manage only the occasional weekend away from home to do some modest rambles but eventually, a fortunate upturn in my business dealings allowed me to travel between Bristol and Hereford twice each week. Herefordshire is a large county to walk around but the initial plan was simple: identify Timmins' landmark sketches and seek them out. The project would be time-consuming but I knew, even then, it would be satisfying and only hoped at that stage it would be enjoyable too. At Wormelow, Rosemary Rigby allowed me to see the fascinating shrine she had set up in her back garden, her tribute to the war time heroine Violette Szabo and I was moved to tears. By the time I had reached Kentchurch Court and spent a terrifying night in Owain Glyndwr's haunted room, the idea for my book was born. Completion took nearly four unforgettable years. I covered 2,500 miles on foot in all seasons and went through three pairs of walking boots. I did not to have any serious physical setbacks during my long journey, but the effort was not entirely without a lasting effect. My knees had suffered terribly after all and fifteen mile walks are now out of the question. However, no matter how much pain and discomfort I have to bear as a result, I will never regret taking the task on.

As for Henry Thornhill Timmins, *Nooks and Corners of Herefordshire* was evidently successful as two further books followed. In 1895 he wrote *Nooks and Corners of Pembrokeshire* and in 1899 *Nooks and Corners of Shropshire* but in spite of his many trips abroad, these were the only books he wrote. Without doubt, Timmins loved his walks in the English countryside but the lure of foreign travel was strong and a journey to Italy in 1908 was to be his last. He died in Rome on March 11 of that year.

Richard Dobson